Table of Contents

Going Solo
While Raising Children with Disabilities

Laura E. Marshak, Ph.D.

Woodbine House

© 2015 Laura E. Marshak
First edition

All rights reserved. Published in the United States of America by Woodbine House, Inc., 6510 Bells Mill Road, Bethesda, MD 20817. 800-843-7323. www.woodbinehouse.com.

Library of Congress Cataloging-in-Publication Data

Marshak, Laura E.
  Going solo while raising children with disabilities / Laura E. Marshak. – First edition.
    pages cm
  Includes bibliographical references and index.
  ISBN 978-1-60613-180-0 (pbk.)
  1. Parents of children with disabilities. 2. Single parents. 3. Parenting. I. Title.
  HQ759.913.M267 2015
  649'.151--dc23

                                                                      2015007741

Manufactured in the United States of America

10 9 8 7 6 5 4 3 2 1

To my BFF Shelley Stark:

This book is dedicated with love and remembrance.

Some friends make all of life better.

You did that for me.

Introduction

SURPRISINGLY, THIS IS the first book expressly written for parents who are "going solo" while raising children with a variety of disabilities. Going solo is defined as awareness that you do not have the traditional partner by your side. Solo parents differ in their circumstances but often have a similar thought: "It's all on me! And my child needs so much from me."

This book is about the art of life for those who are largely on their own. This includes parents of children with disabilities who have not married or formed a partnership, are separated or divorced, have conceived children on their own, have chosen children through adoption or foster care, or are widowed. It is also a book for parents who are either in the military or are married to a spouse in the military who is often away on deployments. Certainly, there are some people in marriages who feel just like solo parents, and there will be value in this book for them as well. While this is not intended to be a parenting book, readers will likely see that their kids do better as they thrive themselves. And there are many wise and creative parenting ideas shared along the way.

Being "single on Noah's Ark" is a phrase used by Leonard Cargan to capture the feeling many solo parents carry; when they look around, it seems as if everyone is a part of a couple—especially when children are involved. According to the US Census Bureau report

(2009), there are approximately 13.7 million single parents in the United States, and they are raising 22 million children.

Children with disabilities are even more likely than other children to be living in single-parent homes. In 2000, Dr. Philip Cohen and a colleague at the University of North Carolina did a study that found that fewer than half of children with disabilities live with their biological families with married parents. These researchers also found that a full 25 percent of all children with disabilities live with single mothers, and an additional 5 percent live with solo fathers. Being a solo parent used to be the exception and something to be avoided at all costs. I believe this book will contribute to an understanding that lives can be lived well, with children, in a broader variety of ways. However, succeeding as a solo parent may require more resourcefulness, creativity, and resilience than when you are parenting with an easily accessible partner.

My goal was to write a book that would be valuable to the large number of solos who face the complexities of life (mostly) on their own. Like many other psychologists and professors, I have spent years telling people what I think; this time I wanted to immerse myself in learning rather than talking. My personal philosophy is that we need to learn from everyone we meet. Actually, I should not claim this as my own, since Albert Einstein said this better and far earlier when he wrote, "Everybody is a genius. But if you judge a fish by its ability to climb a tree, it will live its whole life believing that it is stupid." Even earlier than Einstein, it was written in the Talmud (the central text in Judaism): "Who is wise? One who learns from everyone they meet." This philosophy became the foundation of this book.

I sought out as many solo parents raising children with disabilities as I could in order to learn from each and every one of them. I did not seek out people who claimed to have any expertise in handling life. In fact, many surprised themselves with how much they had to offer because they were used to being fish judged on their tree-climbing abilities. With help from several people, I spent two years posting requests for participation from solos through websites and organizations.

One of my most fruitful strategies was to post ads on Craigslist in various cities seeking solo parents of kids with disabilities who would be willing to contribute. This brought me in touch with some wonderful people whose paths I might never have crossed any other way. I was privileged to engage in intimate discussions in corners of amusement parks, near the ball pit at Burger King, in supermarket cafes, and across a good number of states. When I couldn't sit down in person, I arranged Skype interviews that typically lasted one to two hours. I also was fortunate enough to be invited to an air force base to learn from a dozen parents there. In this manner, I was made privy to people's very personal life stories about going solo while raising children with disabilities.

As you progress through this book, you will encounter thirty-one life stories that are marked with an open book icon. After having transcribed each person's interview, I condensed them and selected parts that I thought would be most helpful to readers. I changed names for anonymity and some words simply for readability, but I did not disturb the essence of these valuable personal narratives. My personal philosophy framed my decision to include every one of them.

Each personal narrative is followed by some of my own thoughts on the parent's "genius moments." I also highlighted strategies and philosophies that I believe contributed to their ability to cope well so that others could learn from them. Many people think of coping as a process that comes naturally. One of my goals was to deconstruct this process so others could learn some of these strategies.

In order to learn from as many solos as possible, I also wrote and posted a survey for those who would be willing to anonymously share their experiences in writing. One hundred and twenty-two people responded and provided a wealth of insight by sharing their thoughts, feelings, experiences, and advice. Readers will find their thoughts throughout each chapter of the book.

The solo parents who participated in the interviews and surveys varied in terms of race, sexual orientation, age, and religious and spiritual beliefs. They differed in terms of finances, levels of education, and whether or not they believed in a higher power. They included mothers, fathers, and solo grandparents from across the nation in civilian or military settings.

My next step in writing this book was to combine the insights I gleaned from my interviews and surveys with what I have learned as a psychologist helping people make complicated lives work better. My specialty has been parents of children with a wide range of physical, neurodevelopmental, and psychiatric disabilities. I have also worked with many other people facing all kinds of issues, including depression, anxiety, short fuses, perfectionism, resentment, family feuds, loneliness, grief, and a whole host of emotional difficulties.

I have incorporated some of my professional advice and practical strategies into many of the chapters. In addition, I have shared the ideas of other authors that I found to be valuable and thought provoking. I am eclectic by nature, and those who influenced me range from Albert Ellis and his provocative comments on "the dire need for love" to Viktor Frankl and his thoughts on exercising emotional freedom while in a concentration camp.

Lastly, I drew on some of the work I have done in the area of adjustment to disability. As a professor of rehabilitation, I have spent years studying and writing books about how individuals and families adjust to disability. I have infused a lot of what I learned into this book as well. Although the book focuses on unique aspects of the solo parent experience, it also encompasses many parts of life that are relevant to other parents of children with disabilities. This includes emotional responses to diagnosis, problems with extended family members who might not be sensitive to disability issues, grappling with a universe that feels unfair, or learning to delight in a child who is very different from the one you expected to arrive in your life.

The contents of this book are neither sugarcoated nor totally glum. Instead, they are realistic, honest, and intimate. You will have an opportunity to read the stories that people have generously shared about their lives and how they live them. I am grateful for their openness and desire to help others through this process. Naturally, every solo parent's strategies will not suit every reader, so "take what you like and leave the rest." I recommend that you sort through and find the ideas that resonate with you.

The art of living well is about being resilient rather than striving to attain the impossibility of being problem-free. I like Terri Apter's definition of resilience:

> "Resilience does not mean that you no longer feel pain and disappointment. It does not mean that you are not affected by your past. It means that you are not dominated by these difficulties" (Apter, 2013, p. 194).

The goal of enjoying your life while raising children with disabilities, solo, may seem unrealistic to some people. It may feel too hard to even imagine being able to cope, much less live a good life. For some, there is great heartache and fear about a child's future and physical or emotional vulnerability. In addition, daily life can be a test of endurance. (I recently spoke to a mother who said that due to her child's repetitive questioning, she was considering offering her to the CIA to replace other forms of interrogation.) In addition, the pervasive societal view is that having a child with a disability is a "tragedy or a "burden." In reality, there may be *moments* that are tragic or burdensome, but that is also true for life in general.

Although parents often initially respond to a child's disability from a distressed perspective, the majority change their view over time. Some of these positive changes are due to the fact that humans are wired for adaptation over time. The process of connecting and learning from other parents is a large catalyst for positive changes. Parents of children with disabilities demonstrate that living more positively is feasible and that life should not be tragic. This change in mind-set generally becomes a habitual change in how childhood disability is viewed.

An idea from the bestseller *The Power of Habit* is relevant to this discussion about change:

> "For habits to permanently change, people must believe change is feasible. The same process that makes AA so effective— the power of a group to teach individuals how to believe— happens whenever people come together to help one another change" (Duhigg, 2014, p.89).

Although the author, Charles Duhigg, was referring to the power of the group in Alcoholics Anonymous, his point applies to the habit changes needed to live well with childhood disability. Raising a child with a disability can be an isolating experience whether or not you have a partner. Several solo parents I interviewed were not connected with any others; this was especially true for fathers. Others did not feel they had the time or interest to connect at support groups and other places they were likely to meet. So my desire has been to connect readers with a wealth of other solo parents to help them better understand how they cope with their situations. When you read some of their stories, it is easy to initially think, "How in the world could anyone deal with that?" And then you read further and see how someone made it feasible. Each person in this book had his or her own ways to cope, and my desire is for them to be a catalyst for your own resilience.

Bobby, a solo father, expressed his desire to be a "piece of the puzzle" for other people's lives. Pieces of the puzzle can be found in all of the chapters even if you don't immediately identify with the titles. For example, I wouldn't want mothers to miss out on what the fathers share, nor would I want people who are divorced to miss the unique stories in the bereavement chapter. Civilians will benefit a great deal from the military chapter as well. Despite some differences in parents' circumstances, I believe there is a great deal for all readers to learn from all of the chapters. Therefore, readers will find, following this introduction, a brief description of each of the solo stories in the book. But before we get to that, let's preview each chapter.

Chapter One focuses on the relatively more emotionally charged issues that are often set in motion when a child is diagnosed and expectations of life are roughly shaken up. The chapter discusses how parents can feel blindsided by major struggles with issues such as grief, guilt, trauma, and a sense that life has gone unfairly and irrevocably wrong. Readers will find input from others who no longer feel stuck in these feelings.

Chapter Two centers on coping on a daily basis with the additional stressors and problems that are part of the picture when you are raising a child with disabilities on your own. It focuses on being able to gain freedom from the thoughts and feelings that often put you in an emotional box—always too angry, anxious, fearful, or stressed. It is full of practical strategies from solo parents as well as professionals.

Chapter Three focuses on solos who are divorced and facing varied circumstances. Perspectives on effectively living life divorced are shared by solos, including a mother of a very medically fragile daughter, people who are co-parenting with either cooperative or hostile ex-spouses, a solo who reentered a demanding career, and a parent who is struggling to make ends meet because work is impossible.

Chapter Four discusses strategies for finding support and begins with ways to deal with problems with extended family members. It also includes some remarkable comments by solo parents who chose to reconnect with their families after estrangements. Friendships and support groups are also addressed in an equally candid and helpful way. Information on getting professional help is included along with some suggestions on supports for perhaps the toughest problem—working when faced with exceedingly difficult child care needs.

Chapter Five is devoted to fathers, but will be of great value to all readers. Each of the four fathers who are profiled has a great deal to offer that goes far beyond advice for just one gender. Thanks to the information that solo dads have shared, readers will hear about parenting nonverbal children, recovering from mental health and substance abuse problems, and taking the high road even when you are extremely angry with an ex-spouse.

Chapter Six contains essential information about living with bereavement. I think it is relevant to all of us. None of us will escape losing someone we love in life or being involved with others who are suffering such loss. Two fathers speak at length about the aftermath of losing their wives suddenly and their paths to handling the heartbreak while meeting the emotional and parenting needs of their children. The chapter also includes some information from professionals that might help readers understand bereavement in general and a very important discussion of helping people with developmental disabilities with the grieving process.

Chapter Seven looks at the unique experiences that come with adopting children with disabilities. The solo parents who shared their stories differ greatly from one another, as each has walked a very different path. Nobody's life stayed static.

Chapter Eight includes the stories of a few women who decided to conceive children on their own. They did not intend (or expect) to end up in a marriage but deeply wanted children. This chapter also has content relevant to other solos, such as coping with perfectionism and the inevitable guilt of not being able to always live up to your own parenting standards due to demands such as earning a living.

Chapter Nine offers a candid and in-depth look at dating while going solo with kids with disabilities. It is worth a read even if you are skeptical about the prospects of finding romantic love someday. Solos were eager to weigh in on this topic, so it is full of advice from others. The chapter also discusses how three solo parents ended up either engaged or remarried, without compromising their children's needs.

Chapter Ten explores the complexities of living as a solo parent with older children who have more ongoing dependence than either they or their parents expected they would. This chapter includes a discussion of parenting children with severe psychiatric illness and those who are medically fragile, and includes the story of an adult with cerebral palsy whose main obstacle stems from disability-related external barriers.

Chapter Eleven is one of my favorite chapters and shares the stories of parents in military families who had to cope with extreme situations while their spouses were deployed. Their thoughts should be of great value to civilian solo parents as well. Input from military parents can also be found in Chapters 5 and 9.

Chapter Twelve focuses on resilience and on what has been called post-traumatic growth. It includes the stories of solos who envisioned and successfully created new life stories for themselves and their children.

Chapter Thirteen brings the book to a close by sharing some of my thoughts on what I have learned from the diverse solo parents who participated in the creation of this book and so generously shared their lives with readers.

ᕲᕲ

Parent Contributors

ᕲᕲ

FOLLOWING ARE BRIEF introductions to the thirty-one solo parents who shared parts of their life stories for this book. They are listed in the order that they first appear in the book.

Whitney was juggling a high-powered career and had given up hope of having a baby after several failed IVF treatments. Then, she unexpectedly got pregnant and felt incredibly blessed. This feeling changed to devastation (for a short while) when she found out her daughter had Down syndrome. (Chapters 1 and 8)

Amanda conceived on her own and underwent a botched prenatal testing procedure that almost resulted in the loss of her son while in utero. It did result in amniotic band syndrome, which caused malformations in her son's lips, palate, and fingers. (Chapters 1 and 8)

Katie is the divorced mother of three girls with autism and accompanying medical conditions, and one of the fiercest advocates and creative spirits I have met. (Chapter 2)

Jasmine, a divorced mother of two children with autism, was an army wife with an alcoholic husband. Now she lives with satisfaction on what she calls "misfit island." (Chapters 2 and 3)

Betsy, a divorced mother of two children (one with ADHD), was surprised that her ex went on a cruise with another woman just months after divorce filings. She set her mind on cooperative co-parenting despite raw feelings. (Chapter 3)

Maggie is divorced and in her fifties. Her daughter, adopted in infancy, has fetal alcohol syndrome and a hearing impairment, and was recently diagnosed with autism. Upon graduation, her daughter chose to move far away with her father, whom she had rarely seen over the years. (Chapter 3)

Kelly had a steep reentry into the work world while she was newly divorced and raising three children, including one on the autism spectrum. Although it has been many years since her divorce, hostilities continue with her ex. (Chapter 3)

Sarah left her marriage when her daughter with significant physical disabilities was five. Her story includes a successful remarriage. (Chapters 3 and 9)

Sadie made a decision to divorce after realizing that her husband's anger was not going to change. She lives with her son, who has autism and difficulty controlling his aggressive outbursts. (Chapter 3)

Sam has sole custody of a daughter with autism and a son with mild Asperger syndrome. He made a decision to divorce due to his wife's continued drug addiction and fear over the children's safety. (Chapter 5)

Bobby, a divorced father of two, wears many hats, including being a mental health advocate, magician, and advocate for his children, including a teenage son with significant learning disabilities. His story involves deep personal changes. (Chapter 5)

Bruce, a career military man, had little involvement with his son from his first marriage. He learned of his son's autism indirectly and assumed custody after learning his ex-wife was going to place him with the state. (Chapter 5)

Mark has stayed very involved in the lives of his daughter with Down syndrome and his son with autism despite going through an extremely rough divorce. His ex-wife and children's ex-speech therapist are now married. (Chapter 5)

Joseph lost his wife suddenly. Along with heartbreak, he had tremendous logistical problems raising his grieving son and daughter, who have developmental and medical disabilities. (Chapter 6)

Paul had been happily married for many years when his wife suddenly died, leaving him to parent his son with an autism spectrum disorder. The second part of his story includes dating and moving toward marriage. (Chapters 6 and 9)

Lisa adopted a little girl who was born more than two months prematurely to a mother who struggled with a heroin addiction. Her daughter's first three months of life were spent in the NICU. Lisa was shocked by the uphill struggles that followed in almost all parts of life. (Chapter 7)

Frances adopted her adolescent daughter, who was diagnosed with attention-deficit disorder and oppositional defiant disorder, with her (soon-to-be) ex-wife. She had an avalanche of personal losses that resulted in a serious depression, but her daughter continued to mature and heal from her earlier life experiences while living with her. (Chapter 7)

Lucinda was in her thirties when she adopted her son who has Down syndrome. She was content with the idea that it would be just the two of them in life but has since remarried. (Chapters 7 and 9)

Melanie was not sure if she wanted a husband, but she did know she wanted to be a mother. She conceived on her own and became the mother of twin sons, born at thirty-two weeks with multiple disabilities. (Chapter 9)

Corrine is an active air force mother of several children, including one who is on the autism spectrum. After her divorce, she creatively dated her current husband long distance during temporary duty assignments and deployments. (Chapter 9)

Tasha, the mother of an adult daughter with a serious mental illness, was widowed when her daughter was a toddler and abandoned at a time of need by her second husband. Through it all, she has cared for her father with HIV and helped her daughter through darkness. (Chapters 10 and 12)

Donna and her adult daughter, Jen, lived two thousand miles apart while Jen was in graduate school. Now they are living in a very small house that can't yet be made accessible despite the mobility needs stemming from Jen's cerebral palsy. (Chapter 10)

Charlotte described herself as raising five children, "with the youngest being my husband." Now divorced, she is living with an adult son with cerebral palsy who requires 24-7 care. (Chapter 10)

Alyssa and her husband moved to Japan as part of his military service. Then her second child was born with a life-threatening illness that includes multiple organ failure and epilepsy and that required immediate specialized treatment in the United States. She left her husband and daughter behind to care for her son on another continent. (Chapter 11)

Mary had a baby who weighed in at one pound and eleven ounces and now has multiple disabilities. Although Mary is married, her husband is often gone for long deployments. (Chapter 11)

Rashaun is married to a husband who is typically not home due to his military career. This mother of four children, including one with autism, created a structure that benefitted her kids and enabled her to complete two master's degrees—while going solo. (Chapter 11)

Tanya and her husband, who is currently deployed to Korea, have a young son and a daughter, Lucy, who has a rare genetic condition. Presently, the disease is considered life-shortening and progressively impairs the ability to walk, talk, and swallow. (Chapter 11)

Trixie is married to a husband who often deploys as a chaplain. She has three children, and the youngest is a teenager with both Down syndrome and autism. (Chapter 11)

Bea is the solo parent to four young grandchildren with autism spectrum disorders. Their mother died from breast cancer and their father was not capable of parenting them due to his ongoing battle with drug addiction. (Chapter 12)

Julia is a divorced mother of twin boys, one of whom has autism. She uses her military background and creativity to parent exceptionally well. (Chapter 12)

Olivia has prevailed after living a life filled with crises and struggles including the suicide of a husband, an acting-out child with bipolar disorder, and an abusive relationship. Her life is now full of meaning and enjoyment. (Chapter 12)

⟲

Chapter 1

⟲

Sorting Out
the Big Picture

THIS CHAPTER FOCUSES on the paths parents take to deal with
some common concerns that are large enough to pack a huge emotional wallop. Some of these are troubling existential issues that surface very early on:

> "What did I do to deserve this? Why did that woman who
> was drinking and doing drugs have a perfectly healthy child
> while I took such care to be healthy and my child was born
> with a disability? Why does she have an easier life, and I have
> a harder life? Why are all of these people happily married and
> I'm single? Why is my life filled with so much frustration, but
> theirs isn't?"

Like many, this solo parent felt that the cosmos violated the rule
that "good things happen to good people, and bad things happen to
bad people." Consciously, few people really believe this phenomenon,
but on a subconscious level many have held onto this belief since
childhood. Beatrice Wright, one of the first authoritative writers on
adjustment to disability, referred to this belief system as the "just
world theory" and stated that it is part of the initial distress parents
feel when their child is diagnosed. She adds that this accounts for
why the surprise of a child's disability is so earthshaking as well as

why parents so often feel guilty and think they must have caused the child's disability.

Parents also need to come to terms with the frustrating reality that many other people do have simpler lives and can pursue personal goals with far fewer constraints. Here is how one parent expressed this sentiment:

> "It has been very difficult at times to come to terms with the personal sacrifices I have made over the years to successfully raise my child with disabilities. I suppose you could say I have suffered in silence about this, as I never wanted my son to feel as if he was a burden. This is definitely the hardest part of raising a child with disabilities on your own. Sometimes it has been hard to watch as my friends and family, even my ex, move forward with their careers, their social lives, and grow in ways that have been a challenge for me."

The two parents quoted above struggled with issues that could have led to protracted depression, anger, and resentment. Like many others, however, they found personal resolutions that had meaning to them. As Beatrice Wright wrote, most people experience changes in beliefs and values as a result of struggling with these issues, and they are often changed in positive ways.

We will return to these two parents toward the end of this chapter for a more in-depth understanding of their pathways to adjustment. As you may already know, all good lives are not necessarily easy lives.

For a seed to achieve its greatest expression, it must come completely undone. The shell cracks, its insides come out, and everything changes. To someone who doesn't understand growth, it would look like complete destruction.
—Cynthia Occelli

Grief, Mourning, and Sometimes Trauma

Not all parents experience grief and mourning when learning of their child's disability. For example, Mark (in Chapter 5) described the birth of his daughter with Down syndrome as the "happiest day" of his life. He meant it. He acknowledges that he had a head start in adjustment because he already knew many kids with Down syndrome from previous volunteer work.

Professionals used to mistakenly assume that if someone did not mourn over having a child with a disability (or having a disability themselves) they were in denial. The implication was that this would delay the acceptance process. Research has shown that this is not true, and there are a variety of responses to childhood disability.

Some parents feel sorrow but won't admit it because they know others will be quick to pity them. And some simply want to keep feelings of grief private, even from other parents of children with disabilities. So don't let the nonmourners make you feel there is something wrong with your reaction. If you do experience grief and mourning, you are probably in the majority among many other loving parents, and like them, you will eventually stop crying so much. All too often, parents feel that if they are mourning a child's disability or feeling self-pity, it means they don't love their son or daughter. This is far from the truth.

Mourning is healthy for those who experience grief and is an intrinsic part of life, since we encounter it repeatedly from birth to death. Although the following discussion pertains to adjusting to a child's disability or illness, much of it is also relevant to the grief triggered by divorce, bereavement, loss of employment, or loss of the life you had known previously.

The Loss of the Imagined "Perfect" Child

"For a special needs parent, I believe that there is a lot of anger and grief bubbling up under the surface. It is important to grieve the loss of the child you planned for, and embrace the child you have."

Grief may have begun with the first glimpse of your baby, upon hearing a diagnosis, or with the chill of recognizing that something was "not right." All of a sudden, you knew that your son's talent for sorting toys by size and color was not a sign of budding genius but one of those scary things that make you suspect autism. Grief can also begin when your dream of the child you adopted turns out to be very different from the actual child you brought home.

Mourning is defined as the response to feelings of grief. At its core, it is a healing process, although it doesn't always feel that way. Lisa (in Chapter 7) describes how she cried every night for a year. Her tears were partly because her daughter had so many disabilities that were not disclosed at the time of adoption. She also cried because life had changed *so* much in such a short time. She described her strategies for balancing her need to mourn, her love for her daughter, and her daughter's need to not have a sad mother. Not everyone is as comfortable as Lisa was with such grief. Some are scared that if they acknowledge grief, the floodgates that contain their sorrow will open and never close. Acute grieving does end, although as will be discussed further, it tends to be cyclical. Tears and time both heal.

What if you mourn the loss of the perfect child of your fantasies? Does this mean you don't love the one you do have? Many people struggle with this question. Over the years, I have heard from hundreds of parents of children with disabilities and I am convinced there is simply no relationship between grief and how much a parent loves (or will eventually love) his or her child. This is very true of Whitney, in the story below.

Turning the Corner

The Backstory: Whitney is in her forties and is a highly successful career woman. She had given up the hope of having a baby after having no success with infertility treatments. Later, she got pregnant by surprise and felt incredibly blessed. This feeling immediately changed to devastation when she realized that her daughter was born with Down syndrome.

"I missed a lot the first year of her life because I was so sad. There was huge trauma. You're so conflicted when this happens to you because you still love the baby, but it's like the baby died or something."—Whitney

Part of her story follows:

I really believed 100 percent that it wouldn't happen to me because I was protected by God. I went to church every Sunday. So I think that's why my daughter's diagnosis was so hard for me. I've been blessed in every other way, so I believed I would be blessed with a perfect baby. I just thought about this again a few weeks ago. Sometimes I think this might have happened because I prayed for the wrong thing. I was so focused on childbirth not being painful. Instead, I should have been praying, "God let me have a healthy baby."

During the first year, I just couldn't get what happened at birth out of my head. I kept seeing it and hearing the words people said; those scenes played over and over again in my mind. I still think about this but not as much. I do still remember being on the gurney, unable to move and fearing something was wrong because they wouldn't give me my baby. My daughter's father (my ex-boyfriend) heard the nurses ask, "How old is the mother?" "Forty-three" was the answer, and he knew something was wrong. He knew first. I still remember him telling me there was something wrong with the baby.

When I got to my hospital room, my mom was there. I kept saying, "I'm sorry." When I think about it now, it was almost like it wasn't me. It was as if I was having an out-of-body experience or something. I guess it was numbing. Maybe that's why I didn't feel anything for this baby. I remember thinking I didn't want anyone to take her picture because I was embarrassed. On that first day, I remember feeling like I didn't love my baby. I didn't think she was cute, and I didn't connect with her. When I think about it now, I feel like such a horrible person.

I remember some things about the moment my feelings changed. It was late, and I was in my room and heard all these people running down the hall of the hospital with a crash cart. I thought that was God giving me a sign. It meant: "Hey! Do you want this baby or not?" I snapped awake and said, "Yes, let me go get her if there's something wrong." It scared me, and I went out and down the hallway and said, "I want this baby," and ever since then I have been totally in love with her.

But, I need to mention that there still was conflict. You love your baby, but you don't want him or her to have Down syndrome. A lot of the time I think that no one would ever choose this for their child. But sometimes, I'm glad she has Down syndrome because she'll always be with me. After all, I'm a single person. Feeling this way may be selfish, but I will always have her with me. It won't be eighteen and out.

We will return to Whitney in more depth, along with her coping strategies, in Chapter 9.

Trauma

This mother wondered why the scene surrounding her daughter's birth kept replaying in her mind—over and over again. Most likely these were signs of psychological trauma. The shock of her daughter's Down syndrome coupled with childbirth was overwhelming and too much for her to fully process quickly and rationally.

I am grateful that Whitney was so candid about her initial lack of loving feelings for her baby. Although this was hard for her to talk about, she said she was motivated to help other parents and added that she wished that somebody would have helped her understand that she was not a bad person for feeling how she did. Many parents find that a disturbing lack of loving feelings lasts far longer than they did for Whitney. Love is not always automatic. I have known some very loving parents who told me that they sometimes wondered how their lives would have been if their medically fragile children had not survived.

Trauma is not unusual in parents of children born with dis-abilities and illnesses, although most articles focus on babies born prematurely. Dr. Perri Klass addressed this topic in a recent *New York Times* article that included an interview with Dr. Richard J. Shaw, a psychiatry professor at Stanford. Dr. Shaw's comments included the following: "It's my belief that a parent who's traumatized is al-ways expecting the other shoe to drop, and will always be scanning the horizon." He added that posttraumatic stress disorder (PTSD) is likely to affect up to 40 percent of mothers of premature infants.

As Whitney's story illustrates, it is common for parents to be unable to stop thinking about what happened throughout the day. If that were not enough, nightmares often follow. Many professionals believe that repeatedly thinking about a traumatic event is the mind's way of coming to terms with an overwhelming event. A normal re-sponse to trauma includes feeling tightly wound and frightened, and having thoughts and images repeatedly running through your mind. With trauma, all sense of security is ripped away and you wait for the "unthinkable" to occur again. These reactions persist for weeks, but they gradually lift.

In contrast, with PTSD you feel "stuck," and there is a worsen-ing that is characterized by three main types of symptoms:

- reexperiencing the traumatic event,
- avoiding reminders of the trauma, and
- feeling increased anxiety and emotional arousal.

Reexperiencing feels like involuntary flashbacks, avoiding re-minders of the trauma may disrupt your ability to function, and your body is often in a state of alarm. Readers who feel that their responses to trauma are problematic in some of these ways are encouraged to seek help from a counselor or psychologist.

One reason some parents are hypervigilant and overprotec-tive is because they are dealing with unresolved trauma. If the un-thinkable can happen once, why wouldn't it happen again? I also think that the patterns of behavior that parents use to cope during a time of trauma and ensuing personal crisis can often get frozen in place. For example, I know a parent who speaks of being traumatized as she helplessly watched her son have seizure after seizure. Twenty years later (and with no treatment), she is overprotective and controlling, even though her son is well into middle age and has been seizure-free for years.

Processing Loss

> "I know that parents of disabled children often go through five steps of mourning. I have been through all of these unintentionally preparing for my son's death. I've realized that one day, one of his surgeries or illnesses might take his life, and that is always crossing my mind. What eases it is seeing him so darn happy."

It may be jarring to read of someone preparing for their child's death, but some people recognize their personal need for anticipatory grieving. This solo parent described a process of anticipatory grief that feels involuntary to some parents—and helpful in its own way. A colleague, Lisa Greene (coauthor of *Parenting Children with Health Issues*), once spoke with me about coping with the news that her second child had been diagnosed with cystic fibrosis. She had already received this diagnosis with her first baby. Her anticipatory grief led her to seek out another mother who had lost both her children to cystic fibrosis. Lisa explained that she needed to see the worst-case scenario and to see that other parents survived it. In daily life, she is far from fatalistic about her children. Those interested in this conversation can visit her website and see our video discussion (http://www.happyheartfamilies.com).

The mother who spoke earlier of a five-step model was referring to the work of Elisabeth Kübler-Ross about the stages of grief. The steps are commonly identified as denial, anger, bargaining, depression, and acceptance. Originally developed to describe how terminally ill people responded to their own approaching deaths, this model is now often used to understand how mourning in general often unfolds and progresses. It was meant to be explanatory rather than a guide to how people are supposed to mourn. One of the many valuable contributions of Kübler-Ross's model is that it provides a way to make sense out of the incredible anger many feel when grieving (and may displace on to others).

> *Anger is really disappointed hope.*
> —Erica Jong

Anger is complicated. Some people transform sadness into anger because it feels empowering. As much as anger can be understood as part of the mourning process, it is also just a realistic response to reality. As one solo parent said, "How can we expect kids to accept our kids when the public stares and adults are so ignorant?" I also heard from several solos who struggled with anger because their child's disability stemmed from the actions of negligent physicians. Clearly, those feelings are more than a "stage" to work through, although parents need to find a way over time to live with less emotional turmoil.

Ambiguous Loss and Frozen Grief

The concepts of ambiguous loss and frozen grief may help readers make additional sense of some of their feelings. Pauline Boss wrote about losses that seem unclear and "defy closure" and dubbed these "ambiguous losses." This concept fits the experiences of many parents of children with disabilities because life is forever changed. There are parts we are grateful for as well as unresolvable losses, such as loss of peace of mind about the future—or the fact that daily life will never be what you pictured.

The term "frozen grief" describes the toxic and potentially combustible residue from feelings of grief that were compartmentalized and not processed. Some solo parents find themselves so busy that they feel they can't possibly deal with feelings about a child's disability. So, they keep marching ahead. I am not suggesting this is not an adaptive strategy for some people. We deal with things as we can. But if you find yourself puzzled by your own frequent emotional outbursts, consider the possibility that you have simply shoved your mournful feelings into a freezer. If so, defrosting some feelings may be helpful.

I knew a mother of three young children whose son was diagnosed with an autism spectrum disorder just as she decided to end her marriage. Divorcing was a frightening transition that she had delayed for as long as she thought was possible. She had to shoulder the family finances by herself, so she worked long hours to support her family.

Often, she found herself overly angry at her son for having meltdowns at school as well as other autism-related behaviors. She *knew* he had autism. In fact, she had read many books about autism and readily attended IEP meetings. But, she continued to expect him to behave like typical children *no matter what.* She was ashamed of her anger at him, which sometimes broke through, and of her unsettling lack of empathy for his struggles. One day, she spoke about feelings of deep grief appearing out of the blue. After experiencing great sorrow for a while, she turned a corner toward being the mother she wanted to be.

Looking back, this mother understood that her feelings were due to not having mourned when her son was diagnosed despite feelings of grief. She felt that there was no way she could have been made vulnerable by sorrow while embarking on her initial transition to being divorced. When her life stabilized, she opened herself up and experienced her grief. This was of great benefit to both her and her son.

Cyclical Grief

Even if you have not compartmentalized your feelings, you may find yourself suddenly reexperiencing feelings of grief and saying something to yourself like "I thought I had worked through this!" This may disturb you because we often think about mourning as a series of stages we can progress straight through. But mourning is cyclical, not linear, so it is natural for grief to recur. This brings us to the term *chronic sorrow,* which is a bad name for a very useful concept. Chronic sorrow pertains to the idea that grief and mourning are never entirely left behind. But the term obscures the fact that daily life often includes joy, contentment, gratitude, and, occasionally, grief.

Parents rarely stay stuck in perpetual sorrow on a daily basis. But it returns now and then, especially when there are milestones that are emotionally evocative or symbolic. For example, parents may have renewed grief when a friend's child leaves for college, gets married, or has a child. For parents of children with disabilities, there are some predictable triggers for resurfaced grief. These include being given additional diagnoses, disturbing medical findings, or disappointing evaluation results.

Although you may be surprised by your grief, you will most likely find that it is not nearly as long-lasting or intense as feared. Sarah (in Chapter 3) described her resurfacing of grief:

> "It is not as if I didn't know that she would need to be in a wheelchair one day. I knew it. But it hit me again when she got older and could no longer be in a cute little stroller. When children are in a stroller, they look more normal, and when you're walking the street nobody can really tell. But I was facing the realization that she would need to be in a wheelchair, and it sank in that she is severely disabled and is not going to be functioning on her own."

Guilt

> "My job was to carry them for nine months, keep them safe, and allow them to grow. I didn't and I couldn't. I'll always carry that belief that I failed them."

Guilt is perhaps the most common emotion parents feel when they have a child with a disability. I tend to think it is nearly universal. In more than twenty years working with parents, I can recall only a few who did not have at least a few fleeting troublesome thoughts that they were somehow to blame for their child's disability. I have listened to parents blame themselves for anything and everything. This relates back to the "just world theory" discussed earlier. For centuries, disability has been associated with divine punishment for past misdeeds (in all major religions). As much as we may consciously reject that notion as ridiculous, so many people do think back, find something they regret, and wonder if they have been punished. I have even heard this from agnostics and atheists.

When people don't see their child's disability as divine punishment, they often blame themselves for having "bad genes" or for not being careful enough during conception and pregnancy. Other reasons are as varied as people themselves. For example, some parents fear that disability was caused by fertilization that took place in a cold Petri dish, not wanting to be pregnant, working too hard, or waiting "too long" to get pregnant. Mothers who have had abortions often view a child's disability as their God's retribution. Self-blame knows no cultural boundaries. In India, I met parents who blamed themselves for not having lain still enough during an eclipse or for having eaten too much papaya. So if you struggle with guilt, it doesn't mean that you are to blame—just that you are a member of a worldwide club.

Many parents learn to dismiss these thoughts. That includes a solo mother I know who will never be 100 percent certain that her son's disability was unrelated to her actions: "Was it the chemicals that I worked with? Was it the drugs I took in my youth?—I can't waste my time worrying about it."

As if there were not enough sources of self-generated guilt, others can also stir up the guilt for you:

> "Even with recent publicity regarding autism/Asperger's, people
> don't recognize it when they see it. It's always seen as bad
> parenting. I spend some time every day questioning past and
> present decisions and wondering 'what if.' It becomes very easy
> to believe it is my fault, even though I know it's not."

The next comment from a solo parent includes some great advice she received from a professional about how not to feel guilty about having a child with behavioral problems:

> "When my son needed behavioral services, it really hit a place
> in me that said I was a bad parent because we needed these
> services. The first time the behavior specialist came to our

house, I just said to her, 'This makes me feel like a bad parent.' She was able to talk with me and tell me, 'Yes, it's hard, but a bad parent would ignore or refuse to seek behavioral services.'"

Coping with Societal Attitudes

A parent's emotional reactions to a child's disability often go far beyond grief, trauma, and guilt. Often, a great deal of distress comes from recognizing that societal attitudes are a major source of disability. Let's turn now to excerpts from the life story of one solo mother who dealt with this issue as well as her own anger over the cause of her son's disability. She has a lot of insights and coping strategies to offer.

Empowering Her Son

The Backstory: Amanda chose to have a baby on her own. Due to her age, she agreed with her doctor's recommendation to have CVS (chorionic villus sampling), a form of prenatal testing. She described a terribly botched procedure, which almost resulted in the loss of her son while in utero. When her son was born, he had amniotic band syndrome, which caused malformations in his lips, palate, and fingers.

> *"I have to admit, the first couple of months when he was a newborn baby, I would cover up his stroller when I took him for a walk. This was mostly because I didn't want to deal with other people's crap. Other people can be highly judgmental and hurtful, and you don't want to hear their remarks."—Amanda*

Part of her story follows:
> *The moment my son was born, the room fell silent. It was the loudest silence you've ever heard. The nurse spoke to me as if I'd done something horribly wrong. She started by*

*saying, "There are two things wrong with your baby." After
telling me about the bilateral cleft lip and palate, she was no
longer straightforward with me. I was lying there, having just
had a c-section, and this nurse was playing Twenty Questions. Although she did not tell me at the time, the fingers of
his hands were fused and were very short. I finally demanded that she show him to me. Like a typical baby, he was all
scrunched up. But, I swear he was smiling at me like he was
saying, 'It's okay, Mom, everything is going to be fine."*

*Everybody wants the perfect Gerber baby. And then
your baby is born and is different, and it's heartbreaking. I
had so many questions. Is he going to be able to write? Is he
going to be able to speak properly? I knew a cleft lip and palate could be repaired. But I worried so much about his hands.
Was he going to be able to do the things other children can?*

*It does take some time coming to terms with it. Every
time your child can't do something that he should be able to
do, you blame yourself. Even today. He showed me his hands
because he had accidently cut himself, and I said to myself,
"God, if only I hadn't had the CVS."*

*It was also hard because we were always taking our
baby to doctors and getting ready for surgeries. By fifteen
months, he had had three surgeries. It was also hard to think
about taking him to places like Gymboree. I could imagine
the mothers thinking, "Oh, I have a perfect baby and you
don't." You don't want to expose yourself to those judgmental
jerks. And you kind of dread when your child finds out he is
different. Is he going to hide his difference? Are people going
to laugh at him? Are they going to criticize him?*

*When he was little, it was worse. When he was two and
a half, we moved to a new neighborhood. He was playing
outside, and a new neighbor said she would like to bring her
little girl over to play. They started playing, and all of a sudden, the mother noticed my son's differences. She asked me,
"Is he mentally retarded?" This woman is a pharmacist! I've
never forgiven her for this remark.*

Of course, this was not an isolated incident. When my son was around seven, we were at the park one day, and a little girl screamed out to her friend, "Come and look at this boy's hands. They are so weird!" Let me say that little girls are far meaner than little boys. My son is very social because I have always encouraged him to go ahead and talk to people. When little boys in the park have asked about his hands, they accept his answer that he was just born that way. Then they go skate. But girls don't. They want to know a whole story. I said to him, "Just tell them you were bitten by a lion," and we laugh!

I am thankful that he's a smart boy and he's in honors classes. My son says, "You know, Mom, I really don't care about my hands. It's not that big of a deal." It probably bugs me more than it bugs him because he's used it. I always raised my son to be proud of who he is. He doesn't hide his hands in his pockets. He reaches his hands out to shake people's hands and says, "My fingers are different." He tells them right away. He's very proud of them.

Now that he's older, he has made friends with this group of kids who are all a little nerdy and smart. They've found one another.

Genius Moments:

Amanda was a genius at raising a child who did not feel shame about his physical differences. She responded to her own worries about the stigma he would encounter by being very proactive about addressing her largest fears. Her strategies included:

- *Teaching her son not to be embarrassed.* She said, "I always told my son, 'Don't let other people form your opinion of yourself for you.' She encouraged him not to try to hide his differences. She armed him with humor and taught him how to engage others rather than to try to fly under the radar.

- *Keeping the big picture in mind.* Amanda put it well when she described how everything seemed so important when her son was small: "The monkey bars are a great example of how things change over time. When your child is little, it's all about the monkey bars, and you want your child to be able to go across the monkey bars like the other children. It was so important. I used to hold my son up to help him go across the monkey bars because his fingers were misshapen and he couldn't go across by himself. Now, I always say, 'Life is not about the monkey bars.' What you think is so important the day when your child is born ends up being irrelevant."

▪ *Not letting others make decisions for her.* She says, "Educate yourself to become an expert. And advocate, advocate, advocate. You always have to be in charge and take control. People love to label you as an angry, mean parent. If advocating for your child means being called a bitch, then go ahead and do it. Don't be afraid to say 'no' and don't be afraid to ask for what you want. Don't ever be afraid to question anyone about anything."

Acceptance and Finding Meaning

When parents are told to accept their child's disability, they may feel as though they're being told to become resigned. My favorite definition of acceptance is quite different. Beatrice Wright defines acceptance of disability as simply refusing to be *devalued* or seen as "less than" others.

Amanda's son is a wonderful example of someone who refuses to be devalued. His mother worked hard not to let "the perfection palooza" cause feelings of inferiority. In *Shut Up about Your Perfect Kid*, Gina Gallagher and Patricia Konjoian encourage parents to reject the notion that we must be perfect people with perfect children. They write:

"Because whether we like it or not (and we don't), we live in a perfection-preoccupied society. A society that admires people who live in perfect houses, are married to perfect spouses, have perfect bodies, and of course, above all, have perfect children. For many of us parents, this perfection-palooza starts early on in our parenting careers. Usually from the moment our kids are born—when we look for creative ways to make our children stand out and be admired by others."

They encourage parents of atypical children to rebel against this, talk openly about their children, and embrace who they are.

How do you feel good about your life when someone wants to pity you? Finding someone who seems to have it worse off than you is a major way people feel better about their lives. This same coping strategy has also been documented as one that can work for parents of children with disabilities and illnesses. Researchers call it *downward comparison*. There are different ways parents learn to deal with pity.

One solo parent of a child with severe cerebral palsy shared her excellent strategy for dealing with strangers' pity and their questions:

"People look at me and my daughter and often say, 'Oh, I am so sorry.' And I end up reassuring them that it's okay. I don't think there is any way around that. I can tell they want to talk about my child, but I don't talk about her disability to perfect strangers, even when they are so curious. I don't feel the need to share details of my life with everyone I meet. Having been in sales, I learned how to talk to all kinds of people. Quite frankly, it's really easy to get people to talk about themselves—then *you* don't have to share. People like to share, and I'm not particularly interested in sharing myself. I don't have to throw my whole life out there. I only share if it feels appropriate to me."

A mainstay for handling pity is to come to terms with the value of your life and who your child is. Parents of children with disabilities often experience a process of redefining what is valuable in life. Often, we have trouble untangling what makes a life good because there is so much emphasis on happiness and being problem-free as the ultimate states in life. I often think about the work of Viktor Frankl, a Viennese psychiatrist who survived the concentration camps during the Holocaust but whose wife and all but one member of his extended family were killed. He is the author of

Man's Search for Meaning, a book that has worldwide acclaim. Viktor Frankl wrote, "It is the very pursuit of happiness that thwarts happiness." He believes instead that a good life is a life where meaning is found. He believes we often find meaning when we are facing adversity and sacrificing for others. The meaningful life is often transformative and brings its own happiness.

Let's revisit the parents whose comments about their struggles opened this chapter. Their reflections on their lives are wonderful illustrations of the rewards of a meaningful life and personal transformations along the way.

Remember the comments from the mother who questioned why she had a child with a disability while others didn't? Here's what else she had to say about her life:

> "Thoughts about unfairness come up, and they're irrational thoughts that aren't healthy. Celebrate, don't compare. Celebrate the good health of the child whose mother was drinking and using drugs. I celebrate my own life well. My daughter may not be walking or talking at the same rate as other children her age, but I can see her progress. Every time she does something she wasn't doing before, we make a big deal out of it. We clap and we sing and hug and say "Yay!" a lot.
>
> "This concept might be easier to understand if I explain how I can apply it to myself. If I compare myself to every woman I see in every magazine who's my age, I'm going to feel pretty frumpy. My hair is frizzy, I've got Oreos bulging over the waistline of my size 12 jeans, and I have never been to Paris. Based on that, I'm quite a failure. But I disregard the magazine images in order to celebrate my own life. Getting the kitchen floor mopped is something to celebrate. And today I was able to fit into my favorite size 12 jeans (even if they were a little snug). I had a pretty nice day worth celebrating. I'm the one who gets to experience love when I'm dog-piled by these amazing children. I'm the one who gets to feel my daughter's soft hand on my cheek.

"I wouldn't trade one moment of this life with my children for any other life where they did not exist. I want to be the one who gets to love them, and I accept the price of all of the frustration, anger, and stress for the opportunity to live this life with them. They can be stinkers sometimes, no doubt, but for me, they are everything. I can't cheapen that by comparing it to some alternate reality that isn't mine.

"I never thought I would find myself pregnant and have a medical professional suggest that I consider not bringing my child into the world. I never expected that from the medical profession! It called up a defensiveness in me that I didn't know I had. My daughter is a human being, and I love her unconditionally. I chose to be her parent. Before she was born, I knew she would be different, and my heart loved her unconditionally.

"No matter what comes our way, I know I love my children. I can drop every other thing in the world, and I can get through a stinky diaper or someone staring at us a little too long or a tantrum in the grocery store or a flying red rubber boot. These children are my world, and I want no reality where they are not."

Let's also revisit the woman who spoke at the beginning of the chapter about her initial difficulty accepting her personal sacrifices. She has redefined success in life after a struggle with having to relinquish what she *used* to want for herself:

"I have had to put many things on hold, but I have always tried to remember that my son is counting on me to do what is best for him. I remind myself that he is only young for a short time. The more time, dedication, and love I put into raising him as a child, the more successful and independent he is likely to be as an adult living with Asperger syndrome. I always reminded myself that there will be a time for me to focus on growing my career, starting a new relationship, or taking that hard-earned tropical vacation.

"Other parents have often told me, 'I wish I could dedicate the time you do to raising my child with disabilities.' My answer has always been, 'You can.' It's a matter of priorities, and you have to make a conscious decision to put your child first and focus on helping him become the most functional, happy, healthy, and productive adult he has the potential to be. There was a time when professionals were telling me my son needed to be placed on multiple medications and institutionalized. I followed my gut, hired an attorney, fought, and sought out the best professional opinions available, and I have never regretted one ounce of my time or energy doing so.

"Today at fifteen, my son with Asperger syndrome is in all mainstream, grade-level classes with minimal special education supports. He has a 3.3 GPA, has received a four-year college scholarship, is a starting football player, placed in a state wrestling tournament, and maintains a healthy social life. He still has many, many challenges (especially social ones), but he has already reached a level of functionality and success that many along the way told me would never be possible! So, as I sit here at thirty-six, single, struggling to reinvent my career goals, and feeling as if I am so behind my peers in so many ways, I take solace in the idea that it was all worth something monumentally important!

"There are so many ways to define success in life. Although I may not be successful in the eyes of mainstream America or even in my own selfish definitions of success, I cannot think of a more noble, worthwhile, and significant way to gauge your success in life than to prepare a child, disabled or otherwise, to live a happy, healthy, and rewarding life. That is what helps me get through the difficult times, and I wish that for every single parent raising a child with disabilities alone."

Celebrating Your Child

It is extremely important to celebrate who your child is, especially since others may not necessarily see his or her strengths.

Dr. Robert Naseef's (2009) writing on acceptance draws on his experiences with a son who has autism:

> "I learned deeply through my experience, what Kahlil Gibran meant in *The Prophet* when he wrote that joy and sorrow are inextricably woven together, for sorrow opens our hearts to the experience of joy in everyday life. Accepting that [my son's] condition would be enduring was imponderable. Nonetheless, I learned the developmental approach of celebrating what he could do. This made a huge difference for our relationship. He became a happy child, and I learned to enjoy him and accept him as he was" (p.72).

In closing, I need to share the response of one solo father when I asked him what he loved most about his young adult son who is on the spectrum. His face lit up, and without hesitation he said:

> "He has a wonderful way of looking at things and I admire, in many ways, the simplicity and thoughtfulness of his viewpoint. He's always been my hero, and he's taught me so much. I remember one time he said to me, 'You know, if your elbows didn't bend, you'd never be able to scratch your head.' And then he paused for thought and added, 'But you can scratch somebody else's head.' That is terrific and brilliant!"

And I totally agree.

cho

Chapter 2

cho

Coping Day to Day

WHILE WRITING THIS book, I asked hundreds of solo parents to tell me what situations they found particularly stressful or difficult. In response, one solo parent shared the following comment with me:

"One of my most difficult problems is getting transportation to my youngest child's multiple appointments. My ex took both vehicles and left me with no transportation and two kids. The bus ride is more than fifty-five miles each way. We need to do this to get to appointments four times a month."

I don't know anything else about this woman, but I hope this situation does not continuously rob her of peace of mind each time she has to make that trip.

This brings us to the focus of this chapter: the art of protecting the quality of daily life when living with difficult circumstances. The chapter begins with a collection of general coping strategies for handling problems that can affect the daily life of solo parents. Next I address practical strategies for coping with specific powerful emotions such as stress, fear, anger, and worry. These strategies, used together, can help you exercise a stronger sense of freedom over how you respond to difficult daily events. This is the antidote to feeling controlled by others or by life itself.

I have included excerpts from the life stories of some solo parents who demonstrate good coping strategies under very hard circumstances. In addition, you will find general strategies that many other solo parents rely on. These strategies offer tools to help you respond to, rather than react to, life. So, take what you like. As with any new habit, it may take a little time to get the hang of some of them. Hopefully these suggestions will give you ways to be able to feel and respond differently *when you want to.*

Emotional Freedom: Managing Your Emotions So They Don't Manage You

Between stimulus and response there is a space. In that space is our power to choose our response. In our response lies our growth and our freedom.
—Viktor Frankl

Viktor Frankl's words about emotional freedom are compelling. As mentioned in the previous chapter, they were written after he spent three years in concentration camps and lost much of his family.

Let's start with a strategy for dealing with tough emotions offered up by a parent whose spouse is often away on long military deployments:

"Personally, I demolish cheap lawn furniture if there's no other way. :) Dollar store plates make a nice resounding crash. Sometimes, you have to let it loose, because all the anger and anxiety will eat you up."

Smashing cheap objects has its merits and is certainly one strategy for coping with strong emotions. It may not be ideal, but it can be a useful last resort for letting off some steam when nothing else seems to work. But now it is time to go on to strategies that can be used on a daily basis and are a little more versatile. (Then you can save smashing plates for those very special occasions.)

The Calming Breath

There is a reason that almost anything you read about stress management includes diaphragmatic breathing. That is because it is a highly effective technique that calms down the nervous system when you are under stress. It is quick and easy and takes just a few minutes. Even better is the fact that this technique is entirely portable. You can take this tool everywhere, including to your next IEP or treatment team meeting, to family dinners, or when dropping the kids off at your ex's house. It is a good technique for responding to anger, stress, fear, and sadness, and for simply increasing daily contentment over time.

Diaphragmatic breathing (also known as abdominal breathing) uses the diaphragm, a muscle located in the chest cavity, to regulate the contraction of the lungs and abdomen. This way of breathing expands your abdomen, instead of just your chest, and gets more oxygen into the bloodstream. This helps slow down your body's "flight or fight" stress response. There are many variations, but here are the basic steps:

1. Get into a comfortable position, either sitting or lying down. Lying down is easier when you are first learning. (It is helpful to place your hand lightly on your belly so that you can tell if you are breathing into your abdomen rather than your chest.)
2. Take a long, slow breath in through your nose. A leisurely count of 1...2...3...4... works well. Think about filling your abdomen with air much like you would fill a balloon. It is better to keep your chest as still as possible (to avoid shallow breathing).
3. You may wish to hold your breath for another count of 4 and then exhale through pursed lips to another slow count of 1..2..3..4...Try to empty out as much air as possible.
4. Repeat this sequence 3 to 5 times.

Margaret Wehrenberg, the author of the *10 Best-Ever Anxiety Management Techniques,* suggests an easy way to remember the rhythmic process of breathing: "Smell the roses...blow out the candles." This helps to emphasize that your breathing should be slow and intentional. Other people come up with variations that work for them. Some people like to repeat a word or phrase as they breathe. The words may be as simple as: "Breathe in relaxation…breathe out tension." Or, "Breathe God in…Breathe Fear out." Choose anything you like or simply enjoy the sound of your own breaths.

There are some nifty apps for smart phones that make this breathing routine simple. I use one that begins with a beautiful meditation bell. I am conditioned to just begin to relax when I hear it. The app also sends a reminder to breathe and slow down during the day. I made a commitment to myself to respond to this cue when it appears at random once a day. It takes two minutes, slows down the world, and is only a tiny fraction (1/1000) of the day. New apps are coming out every day, and you only need to do a quick Internet search to find highly rated ones. Many are free, and most are under three dollars. Some set a timer and tell you exactly when to inhale and exhale. Some explain different breathing techniques in a step-by-step approach. Others rely on visuals and music to help guide your relaxation.

Whether or not you choose the latest technology or the workings of your own mind, it is important to relax. Some people find that adding a peaceful mental image can transport them away from their stress. Personally, an image of a peaceful pond with a breeze rippling the surface works for me.

Freedom to Choose Your Focus

> "We can endure the hard times but forget how to enjoy the simple things, like noticing the leaves on the trees."

Whether or not this solo parent realized it, she was speaking of the art of mindfulness. Mindfulness is the process of being attentive to the present moment, with all your senses and without making judgments. This may sound like a lot of bother, but it is very important for two main reasons:

- Life is only made of moments. It is possible to miss life while waiting for it to be smooth. (We might as well also wait for a unicorn to appear.)
- Staying in the present also makes life manageable.

Sam, the solo father whose story appears in Chapter 5, recommends the following strategy:

> "I always tell people at work, remember to look through the
> windshield and never the rearview mirror. Let's not dwell on
> what happened last week and let's focus on this week."

Mindful Approach to Emotions

Awareness of your feelings, *without judgment,* means accepting all of your feelings. As one solo wrote, "When it comes to feelings of grief, I need to feel it and then walk through it in order to move past the grief." Many people try to quiet or numb their feelings for fear they will simply be so overwhelming.

Several of the solo parents who contributed to this book spoke of stuffing their feelings, often along with food. One said, "I gained fifty pounds in the first year, and it's like, oh my God who am I?" Even when eating large quantities of food, there is only an illusion that we can (or need to) keep feelings out of our awareness. Learning to use feelings to our benefit, while also managing them, works much better. We don't want to wall them off, as if they were not permitted to exist. It is important to welcome any and all emotions that "visit" you—the issue is a matter of how long you welcome them to stay. As discussed in the previous chapter, parents who strive to entirely shut the door to any feelings of loss or grief often end up with the door tightly shut to other emotions and access to their genuine selves.

One solo parent shared this useful approach to accepting her feelings:

> "I have to be careful to still be real—still acknowledge them—
> but not focus on them because I don't want my life to be
> full of all of those negative emotions. I want joy, peace, love,
> blessings, happiness, and fun times with my kids. So I don't
> want to focus on the negative. My yoga teacher told me to
> imagine the negative thoughts as balloons—see them—even
> look closely at them, and experience them if I want—and

thank them for being there, and then cut the string and let them go. That was very helpful."

What we focus on grows (for our benefit or to our detriment). This solo parent understood this intuitively:

> "For the negative emotions, I schedule my life so I have time to decompress. During the years I struggled most, on my way to work or home from work, I would stop at a park and look into the trees or across the water for fifteen or twenty minutes and then head home. I spent my day looking forward to the moments with nature. I also spent lunch breaks at such places. I fed the ducks stale bread. I would go to the bread store with my slew of little kids, and I'd get tremendous deals. It's a great feeling when crows and ducks swarm down and take crumbs from your hand. You think of nothing but how majestic birds are when a flock is hovering over your head swooping down— that and 'I wish I had a hat on.'"

Once we get better at learning to shift our focus, even if it is tedious at first, it provides a way to gain some additional control over how we feel. It is easy to get stuck on the wrong thing. By *wrong*, I mean ruminating over the most recent hurtful comment someone made, or something we fear and have no control over. This is all very different from the type of focus that produces problem solving or acceptance.

Following is what one solo parent has learned about not getting too stuck in her sadness:

> "For acute sadness, focus on the feeling for a predetermined amount of time. For example, give yourself ten minutes (or half an hour, or whatever amount of time you feel is appropriate) to think about how and why you feel sad. Crying may help you feel better and reduce levels of stress hormones. When you've reached your time limit, stop and focus on something else. Think of something that makes you happy

or something that can distract you from your sadness. For example, jot down your grocery list, check your e-mail, or do something else unrelated to what has made you sad. Repeat as needed. Eventually, the bouts of acute sadness will become less frequent. Doing something that helps someone else can also help you cope with sadness."

I know another solo parent who controls her focus by minimizing the amount of time she dwells on upsetting things. She is a very responsible and conscientious mother with a very contentious ex and is engaged in an ugly divorce battle. She has decided to only retrieve her mail three times a week from her mailbox so there are several days a week when she does not have to have her buttons pushed. This strategy does not keep her from being on top of what she needs to know. It exercises her freedom to limit unnecessary aggravation from an ex who wants to interrupt her peace of mind.

Changing Your Perspective

The freedom to choose *how* to look at situations is at the heart of a technique called *cognitive coping* or *reframing*. It is a mainstay in psychology because it has been shown repeatedly that how we interpret a situation determines how we will respond emotionally. Much of this plays out in terms of our self-talk. One solo parent quoted Shakespeare in her explanation of cognitive coping: "Nothing is good or bad, but thinking makes it so." Of course there are some exceptions, but very often this is true. This parent understood the power of our thoughts and their ability to influence our outlook on the world.

Ann Turnbull, along with several others, wrote a book called *Cognitive Coping, Families, and Disability* that includes examples provided by parents of how they use reframing. An excerpt offered by a mother of a child with cerebral palsy follows. She states that the way we think about a situation can be the greatest form of empowerment:

"...What stands out for me the most was the first occurrence of the notion that maybe suffering was not necessary. What that thought allowed me to do was to begin to observe what was actually going on in the world rather than my head. While this was not an instantaneous change of behaviors or beliefs, I began to cultivate the view that disability was a natural part of life, that there was nothing inherently wrong with having a disability."

Solo parents I surveyed offered many examples of reframing their thinking about situations:

- "When I start to feel bad because my kids don't see their father very often, I remind myself that he is not a good influence on them—so why miss a bad influence? When I think this way, his absence is no longer sad."
- "My divorce was a blessing, since I'd been in a very abusive relationship."
- "Our daughter's disabilities make her incredible, not a burden or something to be ashamed of."
- "Life isn't always easy, but it's always a learning, growing experience and always filled with love and pride."
- "Being divorced, I don't have to worry about managing another person's feelings, issues, concerns, etc. I am able to make decisions on my own and can devote myself to my children as opposed to sharing them with a partner."

Gratitude

In a TED Talk entitled "Want to Be Happy? Be Grateful," David Steindl-Rast offered these insights on the relationship between gratitude and happiness:

> "Is it really the happy people that are grateful? We all know quite a number of people who have what it takes to be happy, but they are not happy. Because they want something else or they want more of the same. And we all know people who have misfortune…and they are deeply happy. They radiate happiness. Why? Because they are grateful. So it is not happiness that makes us grateful, it's gratefulness that makes us happy."

One way to change your mental frame on a daily basis is through the practice of gratitude. It's easy to get seriously bogged down by all the things that don't seem right. However, by shifting your focus to the things in your life that are going well, you can start to retrain your brain to look for the positive aspects of life.

Recent research shows that a daily practice of gratitude can improve your overall well-being. Taking time to give thanks for the good things in life actually has an impact on your body. It decreases stress, reduces chronic pain, and helps you to manage stress-related illnesses. It also has psychological benefits such as reducing anger, jealousy, or other negative feelings and helps you to have more compassion and connection. One study conducted at the University of Miami found that people who recorded why they were grateful in a daily journal were more likely to be optimistic and content with their lives than people who wrote about problems or neutral experiences. The same individuals also reported more energy, better sleep, and improved relationships with others.

It is of great benefit to cultivate this practice in your life, even if you just start small. You can get a journal and put it next to your bed. Upon waking or right before you go to sleep, take just five minutes a day to record the things for which you are most grateful. Don't get caught up in making the "perfect entry"—just try to keep it simple and consistent. Even just a bulleted list of the highlights from your day can go a long way in improving your overall health and wellness.

Another strategy is to create a "gratitude box" in which you deposit statements about things in your life you are thankful for. I know someone who collected her gratitudes throughout the year. On New Years' Eve, she opened her box, and said she had a transformative experience by reading every single one of them.

Changing Expectations

Life is not what it's supposed to be. It's what it is. The way you cope with it is what makes a difference.
—*Virginia Satir*

This quote from a world-famous family therapist underscores the fact that many of us become disturbed because we believe that life should be easier. There have been studies that conclude that reading other people's posts on Facebook lowers mood. We assume that everyone around us is happy and that is how life is supposed to be these days. The cultural expectation causes trouble.

Sometimes I think about how different it was for pioneers crossing the plains, who did not even expect their families to all arrive alive and well. Accepting our lives as they are is more about knowing that things may be different from how we want them to be, but that doesn't make our lives "worse." It's not that we must lower our standards and expect to live disappointing lives. Instead, we can accept that life is different and perhaps harder than we imagined it would be. I sometimes think about daily life in third world countries, rather than my little corner of the world, when I get stuck in the "easier life" mind-set. When we expect less, we are disappointed less. This can create more space to revel in life's little or big surprises.

- "I have learned to have *no* expectations for anything: holidays, birthdays, Mother's Day, plans, etc. I just go with the flow and what was meant to be is meant to be."
- "My ex is disabled with severe depression and anxiety and is recovering from a traumatic brain injury from electroconvulsive therapy. So, he can't handle it when the kids have incidents. And I can't expect it of him. I wish that he wasn't like this and that he could be more than a 'babysitter' for when I am at work. *But* I am thankful he is able to do that much and has basically a 'big kid' relationship with my kids. He nearly died before he received treatment, so I am thankful that they have a person to call Dad, even though he isn't much of a father. When I get frustrated, I have to do deep breathing and remember that he is truly doing the best he can."

The solo parent in the section below transformed her expectations and her house to align with the realities of daily life. Her interview, which I recorded next to a lively play area, was hard to hear, so

I tell this particular story largely in my own words. Since she made an indelible impression on me, this was easy.

The Queen of Transformations

The Backstory: Katie is the divorced mother of three girls with autism and a host of medical conditions that need careful attention. She set her mind to making their lives better.

"We'd be wading in the kitchen."—Katie

I think about Katie as the queen of transformations since she could easily have had a martyr's storyline. She has so many kids with problems, so little help from her two exes, and even less time and money. But, martyrdom is not what happened. Katie was determined about what she wanted for her three little girls. Each was diagnosed on the autism spectrum, and collectively their additional disorders are celiac disease, reflex neurovascular dystrophy, asthma, diabetes, and seizures.

Katie has always been loving and fierce in her approach to her daughters' needs. One of her daughters, who had the most severe sensory dysfunction, would withdraw at her touch. Knowing what her daughter needed to get better, Katie was not deterred. While holding her daughter, Katie would say, "You are going to scream and I am going to cry. But I am still going to rock you, and love you, and give you all the deep pressure, touching, and brushing you need to get better."

Katie told me that all three of her children were crazy for the sensation of being underwater. So, even with the bathroom door locked at night and alarms on their beds, they "liked to climb like monkeys, rip the doorframe, and flood the bathroom to swim naked."

Eighteen months and $36,000 in damage later, Katie had the tub ripped out and embarked on a wonderful art project. The ceiling tiles for the house had been scavenged

*from dumpsters and were mismatched. So, on a blizzard-like
day when the kids were climbing the walls from boredom,
Katie suggested they paint the ceiling tiles. Now the ceiling is
a patchwork of color, and there are tiles for Valentine's Day,
Saint Patrick's Day, and the Steelers—you name it.*

*Katie changed her expectations of her children and
her own life. Katie's original plan for a graduate degree did
not happen, but as she fought for the best services for her
children, she became an even stronger, more informed, and
more creative advocate. Katie has no extra money or free
time due to homeschooling and facilitating the services her
daughters need. But she sees her focus on her children's
needs as her choice, and she did not speak of resentment at
all. She knows her children have bloomed, and she helps parents and schools statewide on compliance with the spirit and
letter of the law.*

Making Ourselves Laugh

As part of choosing their focus, some people consciously choose
to concentrate on what's funny. Laughter can coexist well with sadness and be a tool for healing. One solo parent expressed this well:

> "I believe that the hardest and most difficult thing is heading
> back home after having my kids for visits. This includes those
> long hugs and tears when I don't wish to say good-bye. I have
> had to become stronger. Part of this is learning how to laugh
> again with them. I believe laughter has kept us together. Not
> ignoring the pain and hurt, but recognizing that it is okay to
> laugh in the midst of pain."

Another mother echoes her sentiments about the healing power
of laughter:

> "One thing that has been actually therapeutic has been
> laughter! I have become addicted to the TV show *The Big
> Bang Theory*. The character Sheldon is so much like my son,

and it has actually helped me to see how my son feels and interacts daily. And it's also hilarious! My son and I actually watch the show together. It totally cracks me up."

Dr. William Glasser, a famous psychologist who developed Reality Therapy, explains that fun is one of the five basic human needs. Glasser reminds us that even animals play and that people must include it in their lives. The two mothers quoted above understand intuitively what Dr. Glasser wrote about formally.

Having Fun on Misfit Island

The Backstory: Jasmine is a divorced mother of two children with autism. She married at age eighteen and was an army wife. She managed to make her marriage last five years, but only to keep her extended family from having the satisfaction of saying "I told you so." Her husband was an alcoholic.

> *"My favorite saying in the whole world is 'to truly laugh, you must be able to take your own pain and play with it.' That's Charlie Chaplin."*—Jasmine

Following are excerpts from her life story.

> *When my kids were first diagnosed with autism, I went to support groups and was as optimistic as can be. I declared, "Let the healing begin!" I even took donuts. The meeting opened up, and the first couple started talking. They said, "We go to church and are Christians, we pay taxes, we don't smoke, we don't drink, we don't do drugs, we pay our bills. Why would God do this?" I busted out laughing. I didn't mean to. I attempted to apologize. I said, "I don't personally think the big man is up there with a clipboard thinking, "Oh, beautiful couple that doesn't swear—kid with autism." And they booted me out. I took my donuts, got a bus, and shared my donuts with the people on the bus. From that point on, it's like you know, I gotta do what fits us.*

Either you laugh or you cry. Find something to laugh about. That's what we do at our house. I call my household the island of misfit toys. It's myself and my two children. My eighteen-year-old son is severely autistic. When he was seven years old, one of the resource coordinators said he was the most autistic kid in our county. I said, "Give me the damn plaque and bumper sticker; that's what I want!" My daughter is on the autism spectrum as well, but higher functioning. It's the simple things we laugh about, even in the middle of chaos. There's humor, you know?

You learn a lot from your parents. You learn what to do, but more importantly, you learn what not to do. I'm the youngest of seven. My mom thought she was going through menopause, but she was actually pregnant with me. I call myself lucky number 7. As a kid, I don't remember a morning where (at breakfast or getting ready for school) my mom wasn't telling us how miserable she was and how poor we were and how she couldn't believe she had all these kids. Mom couldn't compartmentalize.

Nobody could figure out why, during first grade, I was going to see a neurologist for migraines. I just remember either always being scared or always being sad. There was a pretty significant amount of abuse in the house. Now I understand—back then, where was a woman going to go with seven kids? My mother was always unhappy, I don't remember my mom laughing, so it just became simple; if you're laughing, you're happy. That's where it started. I like sarcasm and humor; it's fun. I guess I didn't want to be my mother. Now, after years, it's just natural."

Genius Moments:

Jasmine chooses her point of view, and she favors irony and fun. This is her version of reframing. She makes her struggles funny rather than sad. She also doesn't want to be hampered by holding on to negative feelings or licking any wounds. Readers interested in this very unconventional free thinker will find more of her life story in Chapter 3 and small excerpts in Chapter 4.

Some of her strategies and philosophies include:

- *Finding the words to make herself laugh.* Once you name your home "the island of misfit toys," you are free from trying to seriously compete with the Joneses for the All-American Dream life. And her choice of words tickles her.
- *Choosing to swing the pendulum toward happiness.* So many people model their parents and attribute their own glumness to how they were raised. Jasmine pulled out a positive lesson from her past without giving it a second thought.

Taming Stress
Recharging Batteries

Managing daily stress requires us to recharge our batteries. I recognize it is too simple to just say "take time for yourself." Some parents feel there is no way to do this without compromising something they need to do for their children and without feeling guilty or anxious. Others may jump at the chance, but encounter obstacles such as lack of respite. There are ways to convince yourself to make time for yourself, though, as these solo parents explain:

- "I refuse to feel guilty about finding time for myself. If my children did as much as I do, I would hope they'd know 'when to say when,' and that they would give themselves a break on occasion."
- "We are at our best for ourselves, our children, our endeavors, our community, and our world when we give ourselves breaks and allow restoration of our mind, body, spirits, and whatever else we are made of. Take the break."
- "It helps us remember that there is much more to us than being a parent and caregiver, and if your child is on course to gain independence as a young adult, making time for yourself over the years will help you adjust when they leave the nest!"
- "We forget sometimes that children, even with disabilities, need their own time away from Mom or Dad just as much as we need time for ourselves!"

The problem of *how* to get out of the house without your children is harder for some people than others. Like many other problems, this one is not easy to solve. You may have a medically fragile child or one with difficult-to-manage behaviors, or you may be unwilling to deal with the risks that come with having others be alone with your child. Finding a solution requires brainstorming possibilities. With brainstorming, we think outside of the box and understand that "quantity breeds quality" in terms of ideas. If we generate many ideas (open-mindedly), there is likely to be at least one that works well among them. Some solo parents have found respite in creative ways. One solo mother, without nearby family, shared her advice after finding a caregiver for a now nineteen-year-old son. She provided seven potential resources:

1. School staff members: "My son's school has a policy that any staff member who does not work with a particular student at the school may be that student's caregiver outside of school."

2. House of worship: "If you are a member of a church, a fellow church member might be a good caregiver. If you aren't a member of a church, a church near you might still be a good source of caregivers."

3. Former professional helpers: "Someone who was once your child's teacher, therapist, or TSS [therapeutic staff support] might be willing to be a caregiver."

4. Respite services: "If you have respite funding, respite service providers offer trained staff; if you have no funding, you could contact a respite service provider and ask whether any of their staff would be willing to mind your child for a few hours and be paid directly by you."

5. College students: "Especially those studying special education, nursing, etc., can be great caregivers. You can contact the college's employment office, place an ad in the student newspaper, or post ads on campus bulletin boards."

6. Peers: "A neurologically typical person near your child's age might be willing to come to your house for a play date with your child, keeping him occupied while

giving you a little time to yourself while you're at home. For example, a Boy Scout or Girl Scout, a member of a church's youth group, or a high school student looking for a community service project might make a good companion for your child."

7. Another parent: "In addition, and especially if you can't risk trusting someone you don't know really well, you can consider swapping off with another parent whom you do trust."

While getting out by yourself can be a great way to reduce stress, there are other ways to get recharged. One parent shared her experience:

"I have a friend who 'gets it' because she has children with disabilities too. Last summer I went over, and she had a whole bowl of cut watermelon. We sat on her back deck and watched while our sons chased each other around her fenced yard. My son kept digging up toys out of the corners of her yard, and the other mother and I took turns reminding the boys to be safe, and it was so nice. I was shocked that we finished off that whole bowl of watermelon. Not being the only adult on watch and having someone to talk to, it was such a sweet, sweet, unanticipated, relaxing afternoon."

Even closer to home are quickie rechargers. As one parent said, "Sometimes, we can't afford to take long breaks or find caregivers outside of the home. Instead, we can focus on quick and easy ways to recharge at home."

Here are some examples of short recharges used by solo parents:

- "My secret is a bag of Epsom salts in the bathroom cupboard. It's not much, but I treat myself to these scented salts every now and then. Before bedtime (and after my youngest is asleep), I'll light some candles, put on some music or a good movie, and fill a plastic tub with hot water and bath salts. My oldest and I just sit there and relax for a while. My son loves it, and the whole house smells nice for a few days after that."

- "I always keep Oreos or chocolate stashed somewhere in the house. It's truly emotional eating sometimes, but I like to be my own friend sometimes, so buying those things and tucking them away is one of my ways of treating myself to something."

Exercise is the key to taming stress for others:

"To manage stress I work out. At 4:30 in the morning, I'm on the treadmill or at the gym. If I don't get my workout in before work, I'm not the same person. I need that mentally for myself. On the weekends, I like to go biking throughout the trails and I'll go out for three hours. The physical part releases it all for me. My brother and my father ask if they can go with me sometimes, and I say, 'No, don't come; it's my Zen time.'"

Dealing with Overload

Part of stress is sheer overload. Some is unavoidable, but, as we all know, the reward for doing a lot well is being asked to do more. While it is great to be able to help others, every time we say "yes," it is saying "no" to something else, since no matter how we want to stretch it, there really is limited time in a day or a life. Margaret Wehrenberg, a specialist on anxiety, recommends adopting the practice of never agreeing right away to someone's request for your time. Instead, she advises using the phrase "Let me check my schedule and get back to you."

Coping with Common Negative Emotions

Now that we have examined some general strategies that solo parents can use to cope with their emotions, it's time to take a look at some negative emotions that can seem especially intense when you are raising a child with disabilities on your own, either temporarily or over the long term.

Anger: For Better or for Worse

When we are sad or depressed, we can become unmotivated. But feeling angry is different. Anger can be energizing, and we can use that energy and channel it into productive uses. We have to be careful not to get stuck in anger, but if we use it thoughtfully, it can be a great source of energy for making change. One solo parent said this particularly well:

> "Use anger to give you energy to do what needs to be done to resolve the situation that's making you angry. You can also use the energy to do something useful, like cleaning the house or pulling weeds."

Professionals also recommend using anger constructively to address a need or goal. Feeling the emotion, rather than suppressing it, enables this to occur. Harnessing anger also can give us a way to stand up for ourselves.

Without a doubt, anger can also do great harm, and cues for anger are everywhere. Parents of children with neurobehavioral disorders, among others, need strong skills in managing anger simply due to the frequency and intensity of cues that could provoke too much anger.

Sam (in Chapter 5) shares the following thoughts about managing anger toward his children:

> "I have a bad temper. I'm the easiest-going guy in the world until you get me angry. With my daughter, it's the same way. I get angry in ways that embarrass me, and I'm not happy with the way I do it. But then I try to step back and say to myself, 'You got angry at her? Look at her. She's totally confused by the whole world. You're going to be angry at her?'"

Sam's strategy with his son, who is mildly on the autism spectrum, is different because he has excellent comprehension and good verbal skills. Although Sam doesn't always stay calm, he has found ways to keep their relationship healthy:

"I get angry at my son; we have a very passionate relationship. We can have these big blow-ups, and then we can let it all go. As he's getting older, he's getting better at telling me when to calm down."

And there is power in a good, heartfelt apology when attempts to control anger just don't work.

Another solo parent shared some wise words on the importance of being a role model for her children when handling anger:

- "I believe that Martin Luther King Jr. was right when he spoke about how to rid our world of violence, and I work every day to not react to my child's violence in a way that goes against what I believe. It's so difficult sometimes, and I am not perfect. But I believe that we will get through the rough stuff, and my children will learn to use their words and ideas to express their emotions, not fists or teeth or throwing things. My child's actions may test my patience and my faith at times, but only I choose what I believe and whether I will have the integrity to stick it out."
- "When my anger gets the best of me, I always tell my kids, 'Mom is going to take a time out.' I normally do this outside; I get some fresh air, which helps to clear my mind."
- "I have to remember not to take out my hurt and anger over my ex on my daughter."

Calming Yourself Down

Learning to calm down starts with understanding what goes into the emotional mix. There are often three main ingredients:

1. physical tension from stress;
2. self-talk that feeds anger (e.g., "How dare she...She always does this to me...I can't stand this..."); and
3. an over-learned habitual routine that needs to be interrupted.

By *over-learned routine,* I mean a sequence that we often go through. For example, we feed our anger with incendiary self-talk and stay (pit)doggedly engaged in the conflict. This is usually accompanied by breath holding that increases physical tension. The routine culminates in saying (or shouting) the same old things. We forget that we can exit from this routine at any point (rather than playing the whole sequence through). So, tug yourself away from the routine. This doesn't mean you need to bury your anger, but it helps if you get yourself off automatic pilot.

You can try the following to calm your anger:

- Release physical tension: run, walk, or put on music and dance.
- Do diaphragmatic breathing for a few minutes.
- Interrupt your own escalation with absolutely anything. I used to walk out to the backyard, take a break, and check the flowers. I also learned to put a cool wash-cloth on my face—it is the intention to "stop action" that works.

The safety advice given to people who catch on fire is stop, drop, and roll. John Rifkin describes an easy-to-remember, useful technique for people who are about to "catch on fire" with disproportionate anger:

- STOP reacting to the small stuff.
- DROP your irritation and anger.
- ROLL on with your life.

This doesn't mean you can't return to the issue with some calmness and clarity, if need be. I am not simply suggesting we all just calm down and do nothing about maddening situations. Bringing anger down a few notches will help you take any needed actions. I am thinking about the wisdom of having a well-burning fire to motivate action but not an out-of-control inferno. Try not to tell yourself things that inflame you further.

Additional good advice for coping with anger was offered by many solo parents:

- "I bought a punching bag for all of us to use when we get angry or frustrated. It's a great stress reliever, and the kids have fun. So we are all smiling by the time we are done."

- "Patience is the key word. Give yourself a time-out. Lock yourself in your room if possible."
- "The anger is the worst for me. I have to let it out, or it just consumes my inner thoughts. But realizing I am not in control of what other people choose to do or not to do is one way to help me manage my anger. Knowing I can only do so much is also comforting."
- "If you become angry during a conversation, you can say something like, 'I need to give this some thought. I'll get back to you tomorrow' and leave. Take a walk until you calm down. Once you've calmed down, think about what you want to do next (doing nothing is sometimes an appropriate option). If you're not sure what to do next, get advice. You might need to talk to a knowledgeable and neutral third party."
- "There are days when my son is having a rough day and I realize that if it gets any worse, he's going to take me down with him. He may be punching or slamming doors, and I need some time for a reality check. I have another friend who has four children, all adopted, all with disabilities, and she's a wonderful mentor. She's always there to say, 'Bring your son by; my boys can all run faster than he can.'"

Several solo parents recommended adopting mantras to keep calm. A mantra is a phrase that comforts and soothes us. Parents often use them with children, and there is no reason why we can't use them with ourselves. Two examples follow:

- "My favorite mantra is 'This too shall pass.'"
- I sing Dory's song from *Finding Nemo*: 'Just keep swimming!' What else can I do? My family is several states away."

Taking Action

There are times to vent and times to take action. Sometimes venting enables us to take action well. For example, Sadie (in Chapter 3) recommends venting by writing a letter that lets it all out, and then not actually sending the letter. She views it as cathartic and helpful in terms of eventual clarity. Extended ranting indicates that it is time to empower yourself and to do something about a situation.

Assertiveness is the foundation for advocacy and differs from being aggressive. Being assertive is more effective than being passive-aggressive, which refers to making indirect hostile comments rather than directly expressing your opinion or making a request.

One seasoned parent offered some great advice on assertiveness and advocacy in an article posted by Vicky McKinney on the website for the North American Council on Adoptable Children:

> "I would simply like to relay the best advice I have ever been given. Years ago, a wonderful elderly advocate with a disabled child told me, 'Dear, don't ever let anyone tell you no when you are working so hard to find help for your little girl. You just walk away with a smile on your face, but consider them a dead body. Step over the dead bodies and go on.' I've been following her advice ever since."

Some great lessons in advocacy can be found throughout this book. Lisa (Chapter 7) is absolutely worth checking out.

Handling Loneliness

For all parents, raising a child with disabilities can be isolating. But there are additional sources of loneliness for solo parents. A common one is the loss of an intimate partner. And for some, it is the partner who has never been found. Solos who contributed to this book shared some great ideas for coping with loneliness:

- "To cope with loneliness, it helps to be prepared. Sometime when you're not feeling lonely, draw up a list of friends and friendly relatives, and jot down their phone numbers. If your list includes people who live in another time zone, all the better! When you feel lonely, phone someone on your list. If you don't reach him or her, leave a message saying that you just called to say hello, and leave your number in case they'd like to call you back. Then hang up, and call someone else on your list. When you reach a friend who has time to talk, talk! If it's feasible, make arrangements to get together immediately, or as soon as possible. Can't think of anyone to put on your call list? How about a member of your local support group?"

- "I have created a new support network to make up for not having my husband. It was not easy because I lost some friends and all of my in-laws through the divorce. I go through this list when I need someone to talk to."

- "I use an e-mail support group. Just a quick note asking for prayer or saying that I am having a rough time can be very helpful because it reminds me that even though I feel very alone at times (not in a sorrowful way, just factually!), these other parents are in the trenches with me. And I am not alone."

- "I do feel isolated, and I have dealt with a degree of situational depression. Connecting to online support groups (in an area where we don't have the type of support groups I would want to access) has really helped me. The groups help me self-advocate, find real-time information, and just work through my emotions at a safe distance. I may not be able to leave my house for days at a time, but being able to connect with a real person who is going through something very similar (or more difficult) has helped me feel connected without ever having to actually go anywhere. (No need to find childcare when I can be right here in my own living room, and no one preaching at me at a seminar where I'm being talked at, not to.)"

Containing Worry

Robert Leahy, the author of *The Worry Cure*, sheds light on the process of worrying. Drawing from research, he makes several very important points about who worries and why. First, people are less anxious while worrying. So, the habit of worrying is oddly reinforcing, although not necessarily a good thing. Having peace of mind is far better. Secondly, people who have difficulty tolerating uncertainty are much more likely to be worriers. Worrying gives the illusion of control. And, third, many worriers prefer to worry rather than feel their emotions or process meaningful events. So being mindful of your emotions, tolerating uncertainty, and finding other ways to fight anxiety are all approaches that can diminish chronic worrying.

Worry Productively

Leahy also advocates differentiating between productive and unproductive worry. Unproductive worry includes running imaginary "what if" scenarios in your mind over and over again. This unproductive kind of worry does not lead to any concrete actions. Productive worry, on the other hand, identifies specific problems and problem-solving strategies. Productive worry leads to action.

Here is one solo parent's advice about productive worry:

"Get more information about the thing that you fear. Think of things you can do to help prevent the feared thing from happening. For example, get background checks done on potential caregivers to weed out people who might abuse your child. Find people who can help you deal with the thing you fear. For example, get an advocate, paralegal, or lawyer to accompany you to IEP meetings to help ensure that your child's rights are honored and that he gets the services he needs."

Separating productive from unproductive worry is consistent with the Serenity Prayer, which was originally written by Reinhold Neibuhr, and was later adopted by AA:

God grant me the serenity to accept the things I cannot change;
courage to change the things I can;
and wisdom to know the difference.

Worry Consciously

Psychologist Margaret Wehrenberg also provides good advice about worry. She advises, "Worry well and only once." She promotes the idea that we should explore our worry as fully as possible and then identify what we can change and what we can't. Many of her very helpful strategies relate to the idea of *containing* worry. In other words, we won't eliminate realistic worry—but we can rein it in so it does not pervade so much of life. She recommends several related strategies. She says if you notice yourself starting to worry again, think, "Stop! I already worried." This is similar to Leahy's idea of deciding that reworrying is not productive since you have already productively worried something through.

Wehrenberg also suggests scheduling a time to worry. For example, you could set a timer for fifteen minutes and sit down and write out your worries. Once the timer goes off, your worry time is up. If you want to make it even more ritualistic, you can pour yourself a cup of tea, put on some music, and do your worrying at the same time every day.

Containing your worry in time and space can be very helpful. Many find it useful to relax and visualize themselves dropping their worries into a container. The process takes about five minutes, and helps you clear your mind and relax your body:

- Sit in a comfortable spot and use a calming breath for a few moments (i.e., inhale through your nose slowly and slowly exhale through your lips).
- Imagine there is a large container right in front of you. The container is open but has a lid that can be firmly closed later.
- Ask yourself, "What is pressing on my peace of mind?" "What is nagging me?"
- Notice each worrisome thought, problem, or thought that arises. Name each one and then deliberately set it into the container.
- When no more worries present themselves to your consciousness, imagine yourself firmly putting the lid on the container. Then mentally put the container away with the knowledge that you can get access to those thoughts, if desired, at a later date.

I often use an abbreviated version of this longer visualization. Mentally you imagine a file cabinet, pull open a drawer, and put your worries in. Close the drawer until you need to open it.

Use a Worry Box

A worry box draws on the principle "out of sight…out of mind." This is especially useful for those "what ifs" in life that we have no control over. I don't know about you, but I don't want my worries scattered all over the place in my mind. Making a worry box is simple. You can construct it the same way a kid would make a box for valentines—i.e., decorate a shoebox and cut a slit in the lid. You simply write a worry on a slip of paper and deposit it in the box. There is probably no need to take them out again, so you may want to tape your box closed. Some choose to make their box a God Box and deposit their worries and fears. They embrace the idea of turning their worries over to "a higher power." This embodies the common phrase "Let go and let God."

You can even drop your worries into a virtual worry box by using an app for your phone! The most common one is just called "The Worry Box," and it's free. If you are interested in participating in a community whose members share their worries, there is a project piloted by the University of California at Santa Cruz called "The Worry Box Project," where a new worry is uploaded each week. Inspired by collective expressions of grief like the "Wailing Wall," this project is intended to provide a safe space for mothers to express their shared experience of anxiety and motherhood. Similarly, there is a more general website at www.worryboxproject.net, which has great visuals and options to view your submitted worries.

Be Wary of the Internet

Lastly, let me add that watching what you read on the Internet can help insulate you from worries and fears. As one solo said, "I got the negative from the Internet and the positive from the doctor." This is not to say there is not a lot of good that can be gotten from the web. But check in with yourself and see if your usage is causing you additional anxiety. I have known parents who repeatedly became distressed when reading bad news from other parents on blogs or on Caring Bridge pages.

Living Well with Fear

There are three particularly useful and easy-to-use strategies for dealing with recurrent fear.

First, **stay in the present.** So many fears occur because we have our heads in a fearsome future. Then we end up responding emotionally as if that scary thing is actually happening. I am partial to the saying "Keep your head and your feet in the same place." One solo endorsed this point of view: "I have no fear, as I just take life one minute at a time."

A second approach suggested by some is to **expose yourself to thinking about what you fear the most.** Some think of this as desensitizing yourself to the worst-case scenario. Sometimes, if we are too scared to think about something, it becomes the elephant in our mind that we can't ignore. One solo parent advises, "For fears, listen to them but *not too much.*"

The third approach is **hope.** Lisa Greene, the mother of two children with cystic fibrosis, parent educator, and family life specialist, wrote a compelling article about the need to keep "scary statistics" from robbing life of joy. She focuses on cystic fibrosis, but her words are also helpful for parents dealing with other disorders:

> "With many medical conditions, there is a strong correlation between good self-care and longevity. Parents can use statistics to inspire hope and spark an 'I can beat this' attitude. Parents who give off positive, 'we can beat this' vibes generally raise kids with the same determined spirit. We have met many CF parents and their children who demonstrate this indomitable and inspiring attitude."

According to Greene, wise parents handle statistics and medical predictions by:

- "Emphasizing that significant medical progress is being made in almost all areas, and that health and longevity are increasing for almost all illnesses."

- "Realizing that for all individuals, the future is unknown. Many lives are shortened by unexpected illness and traumatic events."
- "Encouraging their children to believe that they have every chance of being one of those children who fall on the high side of the bell curve because you take such good care of yourself."
- "Understanding that the quality of a life is measured not by its length, but by the amount of love, accomplishment, and giving that fills it."
- "Understanding that worrying about the future and dwelling on yesterday's challenges rob hope and joy from today and tomorrow. The resulting hopelessness, negativity, and worry can shorten lives and certainly diminish the quality of life."

In addition to sharing wisdom about the role of hope in coping, Lisa Greene's article shows the power of reframing and the impact of what we choose to focus upon.

Many solo parents who contributed to the book highlighted the important role hope played in their lives:

- "I tell myself that it's not going to last. Tomorrow is another day and things may be different. You should always keep your hopes up and keep your faith that there's a reason that it is happening. And you cannot question it."
- "My philosophy is to try to get as much information as possible and never give up hope; be realistic, but hopeful."
- "Hang tough, work hard, and hope everything works out."

Sometimes More Is Needed

This chapter focused on daily coping and offered a range of strategies that help a great many people with daily life and difficult adjustments. These include breathing techniques to calm the nervous system and ways to shift your focus rather than remain stuck on the most distressing thoughts and feelings. It included ways to rein in anger, boost mood, and deal with fear and stress. But, there are times when self-help is not enough and professional help is needed. Chapter 4 contains a discussion of how to determine if this would be helpful or actually essential.

℘

Chapter 3

℘

Divorced Parents Making It Work

IF EVER THE phrase "one size does *not* fit all" applies, it is in this chapter about divorce. There are all kinds of relationships and complexities after divorce, and the ideas shared in this chapter reflect the thoughts of divorced parents facing varied circumstances. These include solo parents who have healthy co-parenting partnerships and those whose exes are hostile or entirely absent. Some of solos struggle with great financial problems due to difficulty working while parenting children with intensified needs and limited support. Others are financially comfortable but have faced other daunting challenges. They all share one thing in common, however: they have all experienced major transitions. If you read each one of their stories, you will likely find some strategies that resonate with you.

In addition to sharing personal stories and strategies, this chapter will address some common divorce-related issues. These include relationship aspects of co-parenting, communication when there is hostility or intimidation, sources of support, terms of divorce agreements, divorce-related sadness, and gender-based custody issues. Note that stories, ideas, and strategies from divorced fathers and mothers are not just confined to this chapter; they can be found throughout the book. Chapter 5, which is devoted to fathers, has a discussion on the educational rights of noncustodial parents that will be useful to some readers.

One commonality that runs through the stories is that the solo parents who chose to initiate the divorce do not appear to regret that particular decision. Many certainly had regrets about the demise of their marriages, and some had crushing pain. They tried hard to make their marriages work and were often frightened by the prospect of going solo—but did so because they knew they needed to move on.

In this chapter you will meet:

- Betsy, whose co-parenting exceeded all expectations despite very raw feelings
- Maggie, who divorced after twenty-four years, and has a daughter who just left to live with her previously absent father
- Kelly, who is juggling a career, her own life, three children (including one on the autism spectrum), and a hostile ex
- Sarah, now remarried, who decided it was better to raise her medically fragile daughter who has multiple physical disabilities alone
- Sadie, who is coping with a young child, aggressive outbursts, and very little involvement from her ex
- Mark, a father of two young adults with developmental disabilities whose wife became a couple with their speech therapist
- Jasmine, who is co-parenting under one roof with her ex for financial reasons

We will begin with Betsy, whose story leads us into a discussion of co-parenting relationships.

It's All about the Goal

The Backstory: When Betsy filed for divorce, she had no idea that her ex would be on a cruise with another woman just four months after the papers were filed. A desire to protect their children from the aftermath of divorce became her guiding principle.

> *"I actually think it was the healthiest thing for our child with a disability because he finally had time with his father."*
> —Betsy

A part of her personal story follows:

Our middle son had really extreme ADHD, was a head banger, and had tantrums from a really early age. For the past four or five years, he's been a beautiful kid, and you would have no idea that he has ADHD except that he's still really fidgety. For so long, this wasn't the case. He saw a psychiatrist from the age of two, and the doctor actually thought he had rage disorder linked to the ADHD. I read so many books and tried everything in terms of treatment. We tried all the possible medicines, but they all failed and caused more aggressive behavior. It was scary, and I have scars from him lashing out. It was so sad. I remember one time he said, "Mom, I'm in class and my fists are just clenching." He couldn't help it.

My husband spent a lot of time attending to our oldest son and all his sports, and I was left at home with a new baby and this one who was out of control. I think along the way we chose separate paths, so we let ourselves drift apart. I filed for divorce and did not foresee that four months after the papers were served he would be on a cruise with the woman that he is now engaged to. She was a safe haven for him, and he didn't have to see what was going on at home. I didn't want to be with someone who wasn't in love with me. I didn't want anything from him—not even child support. I was just done. I don't regret it; it made me work harder and create a business.

I wanted to make sure the focus was on the children because you hear so many horror stories about how divorce affects them. You have to be so adult during a divorce, but it wasn't easy and we were still fighting. But, we tried to make it as easy as possible for the kids. It took a lot for me not to be negative, and I was always aware of my actions. You have to turn the other cheek and be the bigger person because the kids didn't ask for this. They were not brought into the world to be exposed to this dynamic.

In the settlement, I got the house, and we split the time with the children 50/50. Now, half of the time, he has to be a

*parent instead of running from the issues. The kids go on va-
cation with their father, and they spend a lot of special times
with him. I don't think that our middle son with the disability
would be the kid that he is today had we not gotten divorced.
He wouldn't have had that time with his dad. My younger
two also benefited from the divorce because they had time
with a father they wouldn't have had before.*

*The first year was stressful for my ex doing the laundry,
getting things done, and getting dinner on the table. But a
light bulb went off at some point and he realized, "Wow,
these are some cool kids." I wish more parents could see that
staying together for the sake of your children might not be the
best decision for them.*

Genius Moments:

Betsy is a very goal-oriented woman who decided that her
number-one goal was protecting the children from emotional
harm. She was fortunate enough to have a cooperative ex, but her
strategies are useful even when the other parent is not cooperative.
Betsy displayed genius at following through on her decision to be
"adult" in her interactions (for the sake of her children) *no matter
what.* She also was a genius at not letting her negative experiences
with her ex overshadow his value as a father. Some of Betsy's strategies include:

- *Trusting her ex's potential competence in parenting.* Betsy
  demonstrated open-mindedness and optimism about her
  ex's ability to develop more competence in parenting, even
  though he had not fully stepped up in the past. She explained her beliefs: "You have to trust your ex. I think it's
  easy for females to believe that men aren't as competent. We
  get into the habit of being the head of that household, mul-
  titasking, and getting things done. But, they have to learn
  how to do more than open a jar of Ragu. My ex-husband had
  never prepared a meal but is now enjoying making chili and
  ribs. He had to learn."

- *Promoting her ex's parenting success.* She used her best communication skills to help him learn to be a more skillful parent. This reminds me of a quote by Amy Sutherland about the communication lessons she learned from watching exotic animal trainers: "After all, you don't get a sea lion to balance a ball on the end of its nose by nagging." Along these same lines, Betsy was thoughtful about how she approached helping her ex learn the skills he needed. In her words: "I think we had success because he would never feel threatened by opening up to me about things, and because I'd say, 'Well, you need to do x, y, and z' and not belittle his childrearing. It was just different tactics on how to handle this difficult child."

- *Conceding with intention.* When you read the word *concede*, bear in mind that this woman is a dynamo and anything but passive. "I would have to say that it's going to take one parent to be the bigger person. I don't want to say that I am a pushover, but I do concede a lot just to make the kids happy. For example, I never stuck to a rigid schedule [regarding who has the kids], simply to 'hold my ground.' I think you need to step back and really look at why you hold your ground on particular issues. Are you doing it for all the right reasons? Is it about you and your ex-spouse, or is it about the child? People should put their children first because that's why we had them."

- *Removing unnecessary obstacles to the acceptance of a stepparent.* Betsy explained, "My oldest son came to me after my husband got engaged, and he said, 'You know I'm never going to accept her.' And I said, 'Listen, I appreciate the honor and respect that you're giving me, but if this is what will make your father happy, you should be happy for your father. She's a good person. He'll be disappointed if you don't open your arms to her.' It's hard to do that, and you step back and it's like 'ugh.' But I eased the burden off him to allow him to think it's okay to hang out with her. Internally you might feel tormented, but it's the right thing to do for your child."

Co-Parenting Relationships

The co-parenting approach used by Betsy and her ex-husband embodies many of the principles emphasized in *Co-parenting 101*, by Deesha Philyaw and Michael Thomas. This former married couple advises parents to consistently prioritize their children's welfare above their own feelings about their ex. They put it simply: "Love your child more than you hate your spouse." More specifically, they exhort parents to commit to protect their children from any unavoidable harm in the process. They add that a parent can make this commitment even if emotionally raw and even if his or her ex does not. Some couples, such as Betsy and her ex, handle this together by separating their personal relationship from their parenting partnership. Philyaw and Thomas (2013) provide a great way to think about this whole process:

> "At the same time that you're burying this relationship, your post-breakup parenting partnership is being born. Imagine that your 'dead' relationship is a zombie, threatening the newborn infant that is your post-breakup partnership. Protect the partnership just as you would that infant. Keep them separate and apart, so that the parent partnership has a chance to thrive, untainted by any residual bitterness and unresolved hurts from the old relationship" (p. 30).

To facilitate this worthwhile but very difficult process, they recommend making a shift from thinking in terms of "your ex" to "your co-parent."

Protect Your Children's Right to a Good Relationship with Both Parents

Betsy also exemplified another principle highlighted by Philyaw and Thomas, the need to respect a child's relationship with the other parent. They write of the importance of not begrudging your child the right to love a parent unconditionally:

> "Regardless of what happened in your marriage or since the breakup, your child has a right to have a relationship

with both parents if both are fit and willing, without micromanagement or interference from the other parent. Divorce brings a lot of change and uncertainty for children, but having a relationship with both parents is one thing they should be able to count on, enjoy, and not feel conflicted about" (p.101).

Another solo parent shared thoughts consistent with this philosophy:

"Even though we are getting divorced and are separated, and even though my husband is mentally ill, he is still their father. They need to have the opportunity to love and respect him. I am sure this sounds odd. I should interject that we were married for twenty-one years when we separated. It was his choice and one year following ECT (electroconvulsive therapy). The ECT was a blessing and a curse. It saved his life because he was on the fast track to suicide. But it also changed him. We actually grew up together and were best friends since age thirteen, and after the ECT he completely changed and didn't want to be married anymore."

Yet another mother shared her practical strategy for supporting a child's relationship with the other parent, even though she has negative feelings about her ex.

"I generally just focus on my child's thoughts. If she is excited that her dad is coming, I may say something like, 'You're so excited! Just five more days.'"

The concept of reflecting a child's excitement, without commentary, is a simple, useful strategy for those circumstances where you don't know what to say and want to refrain from being negative.

Other ways to protect your child's right to a good relationship with both parents include the following:

- Keep children neutral. Make it clear that they are not to take sides in conflicts.
- Do not use children as "messengers" to the other parent.
- Vent your feelings to adults outside of your children's earshot.
- Do not attempt to alter your child's view of his or her parent.
- Understand that you cannot control how your ex chooses to parent on a daily basis (unless he or she poses a risk to a child's welfare).

Following these suggestions is often really hard in general and even harder when children have disabilities. But the stakes are high because parenting is often intensified, time is more limited, expenses are higher, and there is a relatively greater need for cooperation. Let's turn to the voices of solo parents who have shared their strategies and insights regarding these principles.

"I have always tried to refrain from saying anything negative that I would not wish to be said about me in my absence. Children with disabilities need to know that they are safe and secure in every situation. If parents talk negatively about the other parent, they will miss out on that security when they are on visitation."

"As my son with Asperger syndrome has reached his teenage years, there have been moments when he has vented his negative feelings about his father. I try to acknowledge and validate his feelings and let him know I do understand, but I don't take that opportunity to indulge in my own feelings. It is tempting! I recently started my son with a counselor to give him a place where he could vent his feelings to a neutral party. I explained to him very clearly that although I am always available for him to talk with about any topic, I felt it best he have his own safe place to work out his feelings about his father."

"I have tried my best to support the relationship between my son and his father, but I keep in mind that only so much is expected of me as the custodial parent. The other parent has to do their part. When I feel negatively about his lack of co-parenting, I remember that my son with disabilities, like 'typical' children of divorce, has to process his own feelings about his relationship with his father without my personal influence."

These are the times to use every strategy for self-control available, including some of those for handling anger described in Chapter 2. Following are strategies from other solos who have chosen the path of self-restraint:

- "I didn't speak negatively about him. I knew my son would figure it out on his own. He did—but he has displaced his anger for Dad toward me. So I am being punished for Dad's actions or lack thereof."
- "Don't forget that most communication is done through body language, so what you don't say with your mouth can be said very loudly with your nonverbals."
- "Negative feelings for my ex run *soul deep*. However, I was raised in a two-parent home with lots of conflict and their back-and-forth attempts to 'get at' each other. I would never do that to my babies. So now I ask myself what my parents would do and do the exact opposite! I'm an ol' military wife...I SUCK IT UP AND DRIVE ON!"

Before we move away from Betsy's story, which involves very cooperative co-parenting, I want to mention the concept of the "bird's nest" co-parenting arrangement that I first learned about at a disability conference. Bird's nest custody occurs when children stay in a home base, and each parent rotates in and out of the residence on a predictable schedule. Parents of children with disabilities such as autism spectrum disorders who believe in the necessity of maximizing routine and minimizing change of neighborhoods (and who have the resources) have gravitated toward considering this option. But, it is not without considerable cost and has its own challenges.

Co-parenting after a Long Hard Time

For many divorced parents, hostilities lessen over time and co-parenting becomes more cooperative. Referring to their very active website (www.coparenting101.org), Philyaw and Thomas write that they regularly hear from parents who took years but eventually turned the corner into parenting partnerships and civility after open hostility or cold war. This parallels the experience of Maggie, although her route has been littered with paternal absences and a threatened bench warrant.

Letting Go

The Backstory: Maggie is divorced and in her fifties, and her daughter, adopted in infancy, has fetal alcohol syndrome and a hearing impairment, and was just recently diagnosed with autism. The father had little involvement in his daughter's life, but upon graduating from high school, her daughter moved many states away to live with her father. Maggie was interviewed a few days after.

> *"Leaving me is one thing, but stay in this area so that you can see your child. How can you not do that? I never got that, and still don't understand it."—Maggie*

A part of her personal story follows:

> *We were planning our twenty-fifth wedding anniversary party when a friend of ours called to say that I needed to know what was going on. My ex had gone down to another state to work, and the friend said that he was doing a lot of drinking, hanging out at the bar, and spending time with the bartender, who was fourteen years younger than he was and ten years younger than I was. My ex had given sermons at church and had gone on mission trips, so it was a total shock to me. I thought I had close to a perfect marriage. He was a loving husband. He was a great guy...very moral and church going.*
>
> *When he left, I went through a depression and I could barely get off the couch. I got off long enough to get my*

daughter to school and to feed her. Eventually, I went to my minister and said, "I'm feeling guilty I'm not doing anything with her." And she said, "Well, you can't do anything with her until you take care of yourself." She was right.

For the first six months after he'd left, I didn't hear from him at all. He wouldn't answer phone calls or anything. Abby was in sixth grade at the time. He did this to HER, and she was always mad at ME. I didn't even have an address for him. When we had paperwork that needed to be signed, he would have me send it to a FedEx store. I took a loan out on my life insurance policy just to keep the house payment going.

My ex first saw Abby again when he came back after six months. He picked her up, hugged her, and was bawling his eyes out. He said, "How can you think this isn't hard for me?" I said, "I don't want to hear it. You made this choice. If you want to see her that badly, then you have decisions to make." He went two more years without seeing her.

I remember driving to work every day, praying, "God, take my husband out of my heart...It just hurts so bad." I prayed every single day, and one day, while driving to work, I realized that it really was gone. I could feel it. It took about two and half years and those feelings just left. I used to say that if I ever find somebody, he's going to have large shoes to fill. Now, six years later, I thank God that it happened. Because now the guy that I'm seeing is totally different—which is amazing to me.

About four years after he left (about a year and a half ago), my ex said that he wanted our daughter to go down to visit him for two weeks in the summer and then again for Christmas. At that point, he had not seen Abby for a while and he was also behind in child support. Actually, he's always been, so I've struggled financially that way.

To make a long story short, he and his girlfriend came up for Abby's graduation. We talked about Abby going down to live with him—only because she wanted to. She graduated and went down to see her dad for eleven days this summer, *and she loved it. Of course! He took her to Universal Studios and car races. He's into NASCAR and now she's into NASCAR, and he took her to the Daytona One and the Coca-Cola 400. So she's all excited she got to do all that.*

The reason he wants Abby now is that I talked about her living in a group home after graduation, and he says his daughter is never going to do that. He is surprised that I am willing to let her live with him. I have tried to be cooperative all along. There was a time that I did file to put a bench warrant out for his arrest when the support entirely stopped. Well, Abby's grandma told her what I did and she came home one day and questioned me. She said, "You're having my dad arrested?!"

To come to terms with all of this, I did a lot of praying. And I also knew it was what Abby wanted, and I needed a break. It's a very emotional situation for me, and sometimes I wonder if I made a mistake. Is he going to undo all the things I helped her with?

So now he's finding out what it's like. He called me on Sunday because Abby had been out of her ADHD medicine for two days. Since it is a controlled substance, the doctor couldn't call the pharmacy. For insurance reasons, I had to get it filled here, so I will have to do the refills. I sent two weeks' worth of her supplements and vitamins down there because she's gluten- and casein-free. They all come from a special lab. I sent my ex the list of everything that she takes, but when he makes his initial order, it's going to be about $200. And he's going to get his eyes opened. After six years of me doing this all by myself, he's now going to see it's not as easy as he thinks it is.

He does love Abby. The developmental specialist said that he is finally stepping up and wanting to be a father again. The specialist knew him in the past when he used to go to all the doctor's appointments with her. I still have the faith that there's still something in him of the guy that I married. It's hard for me to remember what I used to see in him, though.

Genius Moments:
Maggie has a wonderful capacity to not have a fixed image of her ex-husband. She tries to revise her view of him depending on current circumstances and understands that people's behavior changes both for better and for worse over the years. She neither clings to her view of who he was during the earlier years of the marriage nor at the lowest points when he removed himself from her and her daughter's lives.

Some of her notable strategies are consistent with the co-parenting principles discussed earlier:

- *Protecting her daughter's relationship with her father.* Maggie said it well: "I always gave him the benefit of the doubt that he would do what he said he was going to do. Of course, 99 percent of the time, he didn't follow through. But he's still Abby's dad, and I didn't want to, nor did I ever try to, turn her against him."
- *Keeping her relationship separate, so she can co-parent.* The conversations she has with her ex-husband are all about parenting their daughter. Her story illustrates that this may be possible despite great hurt and anger. She and her ex successfully negotiated conditions for her daughter's move including the "requirement" that she attend church on a regular basis, participate in the choir, and not spend too much time in front of the television. She also respected her ex's desire to not move their daughter into a group home and to consider whether learning to drive is possible for her.

Coping

The next three solo parents that we meet share their stories and strategies for living life well while coping with very difficult circumstances.

A Positive Approach Even When It Really Hurts
The Backstory: Kelly became a stay-at-home mother while her three children were young. This was particularly important

to her because one was on the spectrum. But, divorce changed this and required her to deal with a steep reentry into the workforce while also meeting her children's needs. Although it has been many years since her divorce, hostilities between her and her ex-husband have not abated.

> *"It felt like they put a knife in my heart. I received a phone call from my son's school, where he sees the guidance counselor and the school psychologist. They wanted me to know that my son is getting more depressed and he is indicating that he doesn't have a relationship with his mother because she works a lot. (This came up in a discussion of Mother's Day!). And he wanted me to know that he has a better relationship with his father, who he only sees a few days a month."—Kelly*

A part of her personal story follows:

> *When I heard this from my son's school yesterday, I cried. You struggle as a single working mother to make it all come together the best you can. You try to make all the meetings at school, do your job well, make everyone feel loved, and get up in the morning and make everyone a hot breakfast. When you hear something like that, it just hurts. Today, I was able to change the focus from internalizing it. I said to myself, "I do a lot, and that's not fair to have someone make that call. What do I need to do to change my son's perspective? I have to support us as a family."*
>
> *It was a struggle to get back in the workforce after being out of the career track for about eight years. It was like starting over, but now I had to juggle IEP meetings, calls from school, and coordinating and anticipating needed schedule changes so that I could get him to school. When my son said that about my not spending time with him, I was in a bind. I wanted to explain that I needed to work and was busy, but I was afraid my ex could use that against me.*
>
> *In terms of the bigger picture, I'm in a great place in life. It was a process that occurred over time. I moved away from*

feeling "woe is me." Everyone needs to find their own formula, but, since you asked for my beliefs, I will tell you. First, it started with getting over the loss of what I thought of as my family unit and the picture of growing old with my husband. It also took "getting over" why our marriage didn't work. Second, there was a need to find myself. I asked, "Who am I now? Who am I besides being a mother and an employee?" This questioning led me to feeling better about myself and gaining more confidence. It is easy to lose self-esteem and confidence during divorce. And, third, I needed to take that new confidence and go with it. Part of this included doing for others. Then pieces of my life began to fit together well.

This is not to say that there are not still many problems related to my ex. It is so hard to have someone in your life with so much power over important decisions, despite their limited contact. One example is with health and diet. I have my children on a specialized diet, and I can see the behavioral changes linked to what they eat. So it is hard knowing he never follows the diet, but I remind myself that I can't change what is not in my control. This took me years to learn. Now I just wait until my kids get back from the visit to return to the status quo. My mantra is "there are just some things I can't control and I will do the best that I can do with the time I have with them."

I have been dating a man for several years. I see some couples who are in new marriages, and I think, "Wow, look at how much easier it would be to have that arrangement and share income." But I have decided that I juggle enough, and I want to be there for my kids fully on the weekend that I have them. So, I just see my boyfriend on the weekend that I am not with them. I chose this as a starting point to ease into blending my relationship and my family. I really want to do this well.

Strengthening myself included learning to thrive in a healthy relationship, and for me, that worked better if I did not have to simultaneously focus on my children at first. That

*was initially better for my children too. As a parent, and espe-
cially because one of my children has a higher level of need, I
wanted him to be my focus. But, as I became more confident
in myself, I realized that I could blend both relationships without anyone feeling left out.*

*My former spouse always criticized me and said that I fo-
cused so much on the needs of our kids that he needed to go
elsewhere rather than turning to me. It took me a while to get
over those statements. I know now that someone who cares
about and respects all that I do for my kids will not resent
the love and devotion I show to my children. This person will
want to be with me, and, naturally, I will want to be with him.*

*It is not easy to balance all of this. I do work long hours.
I need to stay positive so I can be happy around my kids and
give them a good life. They may not understand it now, but I
need to take care of myself as well as them. I personally think
that if you feel good about yourself, you can do great things.*

Genius Moments:

I loved the way Kelly began by rebuilding her own sense
of self, which had eroded during a bad marriage and divorce.
We so often focus on strengthening the self-esteem of children but
forget about our own. She was able to bounce back after the painful
phone call from the school counselor because she is clear about who
she is—a loving, capable mother who is working hard.

Some of her additional strategies follow:

- *Appreciating the power of love.* Kelly said, "Love is the most positive force there is. You can't do everything perfectly. My theory
  is that I can show my children a lot of love during the time that
  I have them and hope that it is enough to give them that base
  regardless of what happens when they are with my ex."
- *Remembering the concept of "good enough" parenting.* Kelly
  said, "I have been told by professionals that 'children are really
  resilient.' That resonates with me, and I remind myself that
  they will be okay." I think Kelly was referring to the wisdom

of Donald Winnicott, who has been quoted as saying, "The way to be a *good* mother is to be a *good enough* mother." Of course, this concept pertains to fathers too. Perfectionism doesn't help, and attempts to be perfect often hurt.

- *Hanging out with people who are positive.* Kelly added, "Your environment is really important, so if you are not hanging out with a positive person, you need to think about cutting that relationship loose." Attitudes tend to be contagious.

- *Childproofing her buttons.* Kelly explained, "The kids are going to push my buttons about Dad. After all, they're kids! Of course they'll do that sometimes. I try hard not to react, no matter how much it hurts inside. So when they say, 'Well Dad says...,' I try hard to simply say, 'People do things differently,' and then I stop." Kelly is one of many solos who experience ongoing problems when trying to communicate with their exes. This brings us to the topic of handling intimidating and potentially hostile interactions.

Communicating When It Is Rough

Naturally, there are times when face-to-face contact becomes predictably negative, no matter what. As one solo parent wrote:

> "He sees my child as a product of bad parenting and thinks it is 'my fault' that I 'failed.' My ex has not been present in my son's life. He wanted a child who was all boy. He doesn't relate to my computer geek. He doesn't acknowledge the effects of his absence in my son's life."

Several solos contributed strategies for handling communication with exes who too often belittled or intimidated them or twisted their words. They made sure they had a friend hang out with them when interactions with an ex had to occur. Two parents cited how this benefited them:

- "I try not to be alone with my ex—I try to have a friend come over if I have to have a conversation with him *so that I feel more like myself.*"

- "I feel like I need a witness since I don't trust him. Having someone else in the house makes it more likely that he will be on 'good behavior' when I actually have to see him."

Sometimes there is no alternative to meeting in person. Here are some strategies that solo parents find useful:

- Choose a neutral public location.
- Exercise or destress through relaxation strategies before you meet.
- Be positive and purposeful. Remind yourself the goal is to get a positive outcome (rather than an opportunity to vent).
- Choose to focus on only a few issues (so you can quit while you are ahead).
- Be assertive rather than aggressive.
- Make a commitment to yourself not to raise your voice.

If the discussion becomes negative, end it and agree to try again another time. Julie Ross and Judy Corcoran, the authors of *Joint Custody with a Jerk,* provide excellent advice to solo fathers and mothers who feel anxious or intimidated when pressured by exes into responding right away to their requests. Ross and Corcoran (2011) explain that pressure to respond quickly is a highly manipulative technique that we often associate with salespeople who know that, with time to reflect, we may not buy. They add that it is often used in the same manner by exes and provide some excellent practical advice:

"Whenever you begin to feel pressure, it's appropriate to say things like, 'I'm glad I got to hear your side of it. Now I need to think it through and then make my decision.' Or, 'I know you want an answer right now, but it would be unfair to all of us if I didn't think this through. I'll get back to you in an hour.' Or even, 'If you want an answer now, it's no. If I have time to think about it, it may be yes'" (p. 183).

This strategy works well with children too.

If your ex makes hostile remarks, exercise your freedom to respond as you choose. Most often, "not taking the bait" to respond with hostility is to your advantage. Consider the value of deciding you will simply not raise your voice no matter how much he or she wants to provoke an angry response. This doesn't mean that you are a pushover, but simply that you will retain the ability to stay in control. There are some useful metaphors for staying in control when provoked. Philyaw and Thomas call this process "not swinging at everything that is pitched." They also cite a parent who put it particularly well: "My ex brings the fuel and I refuse to light the match." Chapter 2 has many practical strategies for helping you pause and respond (when ready) rather than react.

What about hostile e-mails? Once again, you can respond on your own timeline and can always do a draft reply and revisit it when you have cooled off. If the email needs a response—because it is a matter pertaining to your children—keep it brief and just address the facts.

The professional literature on co-parenting includes the concept of *parallel parenting*. This term pertains to an arrangement where exes have very limited direct contact (as an act of disengagement) but follow a specific parenting plan. This approach was developed for use with high-conflict couples who needed to minimize contact with each other but were able to commit to a parenting plan and to not letting their conflict affect their children.

Handling Parenting with Minimal Involvement from an Ex

At this point we are turning to the lives of solo parents whose stories illustrate strategies for "going it alone" (without much shared parenting) under tough circumstances.

Choosing What Weights to Lift
The Backstory: Sarah realized when her daughter was almost five that it was better to end the marriage than continue. Her

daughter has multiple disabilities, and the prospect of caring for her alone was daunting, yet she did not shy away from it.

> *"For a long time I was resentful and angry that he wasn't a shared parent with our daughter's care. So, when I moved out, it was okay that it was all on me. Then, I didn't even have to try to depend on somebody or resent somebody for not doing what they're supposed to do."—Sarah*

Excerpts from her story follow:

> *I was in the hospital for a month before my daughter was born at thirty weeks. It was a very traumatic time; she was very sick and had brain injuries and a seizure disorder from the very beginning. There were all kinds of issues, and she came home ten weeks later.*
>
> *My ex-husband was a guy who had been successful his entire life, and everything had come his way easily. When our daughter was born with so many problems, he didn't know what to do. When I made the decision to leave the marriage, it was like this huge weight off my shoulders. I felt like I could breathe again.*
>
> *When you are a single parent and are dealing with a medically fragile child, it can be very scary. I don't ever want to be in a position where I can't manage her. God forbid there's a fire or something. When my daughter started getting heavier, I realized that lifting was an issue. So I went to a gym and started weightlifting. I said to myself, "I just have to do this."*
>
> *One thing that has made it possible for me to handle all this is the tremendous support we have gotten from a family who has been salt of the earth. When she was really sick, I was able to call them at three o'clock in the morning. I asked them to go to the all-night pharmacy and get some pain meds for her. And they're the kind of people who do that. I never considered moving back to where my family lives because there was too much here for my daughter in terms of a support system.*

*I'll tell you the other thing that's kept me going. I re-
member a parent of a son with a disability telling me her husband was going to retire the day their son turned twenty-one
because they were going to stay home and take care of him.
And I was appalled. I've always worked. I have always needed to have that balance. Naomi was not as medically fragile
when she was younger. It's gotten worse as she's grown older.
Things start to accumulate.*

*There are times when it's frustrating and hard. For ex-
ample, last Friday night, she had total insomnia and was literally up all night. I was back and forth putting stories on her
machine to listen to. Then I went and took my little cat nap
for an hour and came back and took care of her when the
story was up. Finally, it was seven o'clock in the morning and
I needed to cancel her bus for the morning because clearly,
she was not going to her day program. I needed to look at my
calendar and see what else to cancel—what could I do? She
went to sleep and slept till one o'clock; then we started the
rest of her day.*

*But, it's not hard to be a great person for Naomi because
she is so loving and so sweet and doesn't complain. She has a
lot of care for other people and communicates that love. For
instance, I'll get text messages saying, "mom careful snow."*

*So anyway, what made it work for me? I had to have a
support system. I always worked so I had balance. I really felt
strongly about that.*

Genius Moments:

- *Stepping up is the only option.* As Sarah said, "You just have
to step up. In addition to weight lifting, I learned (from physical therapists) the mechanics of moving people. In my fifties, I
can still lift her, and she's 105 pounds."
- *Understanding the importance of grandparents' love.* Although
Sarah was fortunate to have great in-laws, she also was sensitive to their needs. In her words: "I understood that my

daughter was my in-laws' heart; I would never separate them
from my daughter." They ended up being instrumental in
driving her daughter to her programs, and they remained very
close to her. She added, "To this day they're still very close to
her. Very frail, but good people."

- *Refusing to be consumed.* One of the reasons she continued
  to work was to limit the extent that she focused solely on her
  daughter's care. In her words: "I'm still a very overprotective
  parent, and I'm probably way more than I should be. But, I
  decided that I could not be consumed by her care. That is one
  of the reasons I decided I must always work."

- *Living without resentment.* It wasn't until we finished this
  interview that I realized that she never touched on any resentment or criticism. My sense was that she did not want to waste
  her time with these feelings, so she simply spent her energy
  productively to meet the challenges at hand.

Sarah's story continues in Chapter 9. Much to her surprise, she ended
up remarried after many years on her own.

Finding Support

The solo parents who offered their advice for this book emphasized the importance of finding support systems. Many did not
have cooperative family close by and shared what worked for them in
terms of finding support:

"I divorced when my son with Asperger syndrome was about
five, and his father left our home state. It was emotionally
overwhelming to deal with the loss of my marriage around
the same time that my son was entering school and needed
an educated, assertive parent as his advocate. I had no time
or energy to 'move on' in the way a new divorcee without a
child with disabilities could by dating, spending more time
with friends, taking vacations, or just taking more time for
myself to relax and redefine myself as a single person. In those
days, asking family for help and support, seeking out advocacy

agencies, and limiting expectations I placed on myself were key to my sanity."

This woman chose to cope with the losses of relocating in order to gain proximity to supportive extended family. She provides food for thought that will be relevant to some readers. Others might wish it were possible, but it's simply not.

"Being single after twelve years has been so much easier with what few friends I retained after my son's accident. After my son's accident, I found out who my real friends were. My family has *not* helped me. My friends saved my life."

The solo parent below described how she formed a deeply supportive partnership with another mother:

"When my daughter was in the NICU, she took care of my son for me. When her mother was very ill, I took care of her son so she could be with her mother. Our parenting ideals, although not identical, are similar enough that I feel safe trusting her with my son. When she had no vehicle, I frequently gave her rides. When my car broke down, she was there for me and helped a lot until I had mine repaired. Without her help, we would have done a lot of walking and using public transportation.

"Sometimes the simplest things are extraordinarily difficult. To just have a friend willing to run to the store for me or sit with my children in our home (where everything is familiar) while I get something done is invaluable."

Sometimes very meaningful support is experienced through on-line connections:

"I am part of an online support group for parents of kids on the spectrum—and just a quick note asking for prayer or saying that I am having a rough time can be very helpful because it reminds me that even though I feel very alone at times (not in a sorrowful way, just factually!), these other parents are in the trenches with me. And I am not alone. There are people who understand and who *get it*. When I tell them I am having a rough day, they know that it's not just the 'normal' stuff—it's stuff that parents of kids without any disabilities couldn't conceive of."

On Her Own and Finding Uncomplicated Pleasures

The Backstory: Sadie made a decision to divorce after realizing that her husband's anger with her and her son (who is on the autism spectrum) was not going to change. This woman is small in stature and soft spoken and has found ways to live well with a child who is very loveable but has great difficulty controlling aggressive outbursts.

> *"The hardest thing to cope with is when my son is being aggressive. I can lock myself in my room, whereas before I could leave the house for ten minutes."*—Sadie

An excerpt from her story follows:

> *The diagnosis of my son's autism was a wedge in the marriage, and I think a lot of what I was seeing in my ex was actually anger. He was grieving the fact that our child wasn't "normal." What makes me saddest is that my son's dad does not accept his diagnoses and never will and doesn't want to be a dad. There was a lot of verbal abuse toward both of us, so I decided to divorce for both my son's and my own sake.*
>
> *Sometimes it's harder on my own. I'm doing everything, but in a way it was like I was expected to do everything anyway. So it's not much different. When my son's behaving, I can leave and take out the garbage or take down the laundry, but not when he's being aggressive. A couple days ago when it got extreme, I called the crisis number for the family-based services, which hasn't been very responsive. But fortunately, one of his therapists was on call, so she could help me through it and calm me down a little bit.*

There are good parts to divorce. It's just so much calmer. I especially enjoy it in the evenings when my son goes to bed. I don't have his dad there asking to get his back scratched or other things. It's just me at night.

The courts don't take into account the fact that my child has special needs. It's difficult to work full-time with all the therapists coming into the home. It is really hard for me to only have alimony for two years and then need to ask for more child support. The autism diagnosis had nothing to do with how the divorce settlement went.

Genius Moments:

Sadie uses several techniques to cope on her own with a parenting situation that is frequently very rough. As she explained: "I sometimes need to hide in my room to calm myself down. It's a challenge, with a child banging on my door, but I usually just find something I like to do. I like to read; I like to listen to music. I like to sing."

Some of Sadie's strategies include:

- *Limiting reflecting on problems.* One of Sadie's strengths is her ability to shift herself into enjoying the everyday activities of life. She explained how she does this at work: "There are a lot of customers at my job, so I can just start by pretending I am happy. And then I do feel happy. It's rewarding to help other people all day long."

- *Appreciating the value of a good therapist.* When asked what advice she would give to others, she replied: "You definitely need to find a therapist. I find that the therapist is helpful because I can tell her details of my life—things that I wouldn't talk to others about, or even with my closest friends. Because I know that I can say whatever I want. I feel safe, and she's someone I can bounce ideas off of. She never tells me what I should do, but she's there to really listen, and focus on me for that hour."

- *Finding ways to deal with her anger.* Sadie talked about the importance of coping with anger at her husband over parenting issues. She added that she turns to writing to express her anger. She explained, "I find it very helpful to write in a journal. I even found an article saying to write a letter, not mail it, but just pour out that anger. I've done that and found it useful."

Financial Support

Sadie is one of several parents I surveyed who had regrets over overlooking some financial considerations unique to raising children with disabilities. Many parents who have been through divorce contributed advice regarding the legal aspects of divorce for consideration of parents still in the process.

Below is their advice about issues they recommend considering while you are working out an agreement:

- "Our divorce agreement includes clauses about providing financial support throughout our son's life, but doesn't stipulate any penalties for noncompliance. I wish I'd had advice about that, and that I'd had more information about how parental support would affect government-provided support after my son's eighteenth birthday."
- "As the custodial parent, I was sure to include that I have final and full authority over our children's medical decisions. I do wish there were a clause requiring my ex to pay child support beyond the age of twenty-one, since it is likely that my children will need to live with me beyond that age."
- "We have joint custody of our son. It is easier for either of us to take him to his appointments or if he needs to go to the ER."
- "My ex left the state when my son was only five and he insisted my son fly alone, as an unaccompanied minor, to visit him in Florida. I was not comfortable with this from the start, as my son has Asperger syndrome and would cry to me over the phone about being in unfamiliar surroundings, have increased episodes of vocal and motor tics, and act out behaviorally. It was traumatic. I wish I would have understood in those early years just how traumatic this experience was for him and fought harder to insist on other arrangements for visitation."

- "I wish I had impressed more upon my lawyer that my son will have lifelong needs and need financial support. As of now, I will have to go back to court when he comes of age."

Coping with the Aftermath of Custody Battles

Up to this point, this chapter has only included the stories of women. That is because of the demographics of the parents who volunteered to participate in this book and because I chose to group many of the fathers' responses into Chapter 5, which includes the stories of three divorced fathers. But below are some quotations on the aftermath of divorce that give the father's side of the story.

- "My ex-wife acts like our daughter is a burden. She does love her but does not have the same patience, pride, and understanding with our daughter as she does with our typical son."
- "I am not able to be as effective as I might be if the children regularly visited with their mom every other week. This would give me the opportunity to refresh and be ready to add more to the kids upon their return. Respite funds have helped me to get some much-needed breaks."

As Mark states so accurately in the father's chapter, there is often an assumption that fathers are the ones to be "blamed" when a marriage falls apart. As discussed in detail in Chapter 5, he is a very devoted father to an adolescent daughter and a young adult son who both have disabilities. He is a very active father who has been diligent about meeting his children's needs. In his words:

"There is still a huge perception that men are the bad guys. The courts look at us as being just that. I wanted everything split down the middle—including custody. After all, I wasn't the one who ended the marriage with an affair. I didn't believe it when my attorney said that the judge would never go for it and that my ex-wife would simply be looked at as the mother of two special-needs kids. My attorney predicted the judge would give her the kids and I would just have the standard visitation. I fought for my kids and spent $40,000 to $50,000 in legal fees over two years.

"My kids are more important to me than anything. But the courts think the motive for fathers wanting more custody is to reduce the amount of child support they have to pay. I wanted co-custody of my children, though. I even had custody evaluations done, and they came back in my favor. But do you know how much it would have cost to go to trial?! In the end, even after I got a new attorney, I only got a little better than the standard visitation. My attorney said, 'Most men in your position would have left. They would have gone, moved on, and gotten married and started a new life. There is something really remarkable that you wanted to stay and put up with this.' People assume that the mother is always the model citizen here."

The details of how Mark copes can be found in the father's chapter and are relevant to fathers and mothers alike.

Similarly, Bobby, the magician in Chapter 5, has fought for a long time to get custody. He sees his children on weekends only. He related his great concern that his children are living without hot water, a fact that he has brought to the attention of child welfare agencies repeatedly. He states that he has been told that as long as the water is heated on the stove, it should suffice.

Both fathers and mothers often go through a mourning process after divorce that is often not understood by others. One solo mother shed light on this process:

> "Other people assume that because the divorce was initiated by me, that I no longer loved my ex-husband. Therefore, they did not 'get' that there is a valid grief process attached to the end of my marriage."

Solo parents who participated in this book shared some useful advice on what helped them cope with their feelings about the break-up of their marriage.

- "I coped with the termination of my long-term relationship by asking myself, 'What is more important—a relationship? Or happiness without a relationship?' I stepped outside of my situation and gave myself the advice that I would have given someone else. I figure that the end of this relationship is a type of death, but it is not worse than a physical death. So, I said to myself, 'If I can get over the death of a family member, I can surely get over the death of this relationship!'"
- "Coping with divorce and breakups has been hard. I have treated all my kids the same, but with regard to my daughter who has a rare genetic condition and mild autism, I just spent a lot more time dealing with her loss and her pain. But she is actually quite empathetic, and also helped me by bringing me tissues and blankets and ice tea. She treated me the way I treat her when she is sad or out of sorts. I know some psychiatric professionals would have strong opinions regarding that, but screw them. My child is great, and we went through issues as a family. We cared for each other and held each other up."

Whatever It Takes

As you know by now, this book is all about individual strategies for making life work. So, I want to add one last story from Jasmine, whom you met in Chapter 1 (*Living on the Island of Misfit Toys*).

Having Fun on Misfit Island, Part 2

The Backstory: Jasmine is a divorced mother of two children with autism. She married at age eighteen and saw herself as an "army wife." She managed to make her marriage last five years, but only to keep her extended family from having the satisfaction of saying "I told you so." Her husband was an alcoholic.

"I was just totally captivated by him, and he was just dynamic. Then six weeks after we were married, the only utterly

dynamic thing was that he could build these elaborate pyra-
mids out of beer cans."—Jasmine

An excerpt from her story follows:

I was seventeen and Ken was a twenty-five-year-old
army guy when we got married. The truth is that he and I
should never have gotten married. It took seven years until we
were finally divorced, but it should have been sooner. I didn't
want to give my family the satisfaction of being right about it.
It was really hard while we were married. There was a lot of
belittling and isolation, and Ken drank a lot. Sometimes when
I came home from work, he would be drunk and asleep. My
son would be just sitting there crying, and there would be a
stack of movies on top of the TV. And that's what their day
consisted of: I would leave for work, and they would get mov-
ie-ed to death. They were miserable.

Once the kids both got diagnosed, I said to myself, "He's
got to go. I already have enough to take care of. I've had
enough." I decided that life was hard enough without Ken
acting like this and looking at them with disappointment in
his eyes. I felt like I wasn't protecting them by keeping him
around, so he had to go.

When I kicked him out (fifteen years ago), it was in-
tended to be a wake-up call to change. He didn't, so waited
those two years and got a divorce for $199. He didn't contest
it. For a while, the three of us moved into my family's home.
The three of us lived in the living room, and it was a constant
battle with my own mother over how I should raise them,
but my babies and I had a roof over our heads. I got a little
job and moved us out of there. I got a little crappy house that
was ugly as sin but I didn't care—it was our crappy house.

You'll be surprised at the twists and turns my story has
taken when I tell you that I broke all contact with Ken for
about five years, and he had no contact with the kids. It's a
long story, and I will skip some details. But I didn't get any
child support for the first nine years until I decided to pursue

it when he was in the army overseas. Then I got his com-
mander involved.

I never stood in the way of Ken being a father. The prob-
lem is that he never took advantage of the opportunity. Then,
after five years without contact, he asked if he could come
see the kids. So I told him that I needed a day to think about
it. But I didn't need a day. In fact, before the conversation
was even over, I said, "Yeah, come on over."

Now Ken is under my roof. He sleeps in another room,
and I get the bills paid. I haven't had a shut-off notice—since
November, I've had each of the bills paid and so much food I
had to buy a chest freezer.

By valuing her autonomy and setting her own boundaries, Jasmine protects her freedom to do what she wants. Jasmine said:

"You should have heard the hell I got from people for
my decision to let my ex see the kids. They'd say things like,
'What if he goes to Iraq and gets killed after they see him
again.' I ended up saying, 'Well, then I'll have my daughter
standing in front of me saying 'thank God I got to see him
one more time' rather than 'I wish I could have.' I didn't talk
to family members for months because they thought I was
wrong. I have a pretty good track record. I didn't want to hear
it. I don't have to explain what I do when it comes to my kids.
Obviously I don't put me first!"

If you missed the first part of Jasmine's story, it is worth back-tracking to pages 35-37 to read her strategies for living well and with humor.

Reclaiming Your Personal Freedom

Divorce upsets the status quo. The opportunity to exercise personal freedom is part of this process. Virginia Satir, an internationally renowned family therapist, has described five personal freedoms that are important to embrace in life and may present themselves clearly as a marriage ends. I highly recommend you pursue these freedoms:

1. the freedom to see and hear what is there instead of what should be, was, or will be;
2. the freedom to say what one feels and thinks, instead of what one should;
3. the freedom to feel what one feels, instead of what one ought;
4. the freedom to ask for what one wants, instead of always waiting for permission;
5. the freedom to take risks on one's behalf, instead of choosing to be only "secure" and not rocking the boat.

Chapter 4

Finding Supports in
All Kinds of Places

IT IS NOT realistically possible to live well while single-handed-
ly raising children with disabilities unless you have several different
kinds of support. Parents need emotional support—that is, "a soft
place to fall"—as well as people who believe in their abilities. They
also need support that provides information and occasional tangible
help. For those of you who may cringe at the idea of needing help or
support, think about balancing it by knowing you will "pay it forward" when you are able.

This chapter casts a large net when discussing topics related to
social support. It begins with a realistic discussion of relationships
with our own parents and siblings. Although some solo parents I
consulted reported feeling incredible support, many found family interactions to be disappointing or problematic in some ways. As one
solo said, "The truth is they want to get it, but they don't and they
won't ever get it." This was a comment made by one mother of a
son with Down syndrome who is well surrounded by family and
friends. Because families are so complicated, our discussion of family
will include managing expectations, preventing resentments, setting
healthy boundaries, and implementing strategies for forgiveness. I
will include the experiences of solos who, after becoming parents
themselves, had the urge to reconcile with their own parents after a
period of emotional distance or estrangement.

Given that we can pick our friends and not our family, a discussion of what solo parents have learned about friendship follows. Strategies for developing supportive rather than frustrating friendships are included. You might think that friendship should not involve strategies, but dynamics change when any children are involved, much less atypical ones.

The chapter also includes insights from solo parents who spoke candidly about the joys and maddening aspects of interacting with other parents who have children with disabilities. This discussion is followed by tips on getting professional help and how to recognize when other forms of support are not sufficient. Finally, specific supports related to employment are included since this is often one of the most difficult problems for solo parents to manage.

Family

Dodie Smith described family as "That dear octopus from whose tentacles we never quite escape, nor, in our inmost hearts, ever quite wish to."

Many solo participants in this book described good relationships with their families. But, if you are not so fortunate, some of the following comments from solos who participated in the book might resonate with you. If you believe misery loves company, you are in luck:

- "My family members like to believe that I have it under control, but they really just don't care to be bothered to understand, offer support, or lend a hand. My family doesn't even acknowledge my children on their birthdays, although they do acknowledge all the other children in the family. They can't even try to make simple accommodations for holidays and family gatherings. They expect my children to be able to comply and function as other children do. We rarely go to any family events because it is just way too stressful for myself and even more so for my children. The risk is just not worth the reward."
- "My family thinks that my son's mental health problems are my fault because I am a terrible mom."

- "Sometimes people think I am using my child as an excuse if I don't participate in something."
- "My family just thinks having a child with a disability is the end of the world. They should have a book written for them on things they shouldn't say."
- "We are often excluded from plans because they don't want to have my disabled daughter coming along. For example, they didn't want us to go with them to Six Flags. They find it frustrating to deal with her constant questions and to remind her to wash her face."
- "My child has a disability that can easily be concealed, and that is exactly what my child's father's side of the family seems adamant to do."

Enough misery. Sometimes, it really does get better over time and through a variety of approaches.

Setting Boundaries

Good boundary setting makes all family relationships easier. They allow us to enjoy close relationships with supportive parents as well as to be able to engage with those who are more difficult. Boundaries can be thought of as limits that are necessary in order to protect your sense of self, peace of mind, or the way you want to raise your children. Boundaries clarify where you are entitled to act in an autonomous manner—without deferring to others. You may think about boundaries as a fence or a marker that makes it clear when you are on someone else's personal territory. You have probably heard the saying "Good fences make good neighbors." This applies to family as well.

It is sometimes easier to mark off your proverbial territory with strangers than with friends and family members, and even harder when you are a solo parent of a child with a disability. Getting married is a widely practiced cultural rite of passage into adulthood; women are "given away" by parents at their wedding. But for never-married solo parents, the culturally established line between being someone's child and an independent adult (with his or her own life) is less clear. And if you are a divorced parent, your own parents may feel as if you have reverted to a less adult status—as if the divorce is a "failure" or demonstrates a need for parental protection.

One solo-by-choice mother I interviewed for this book spoke of having this struggle even though she was well into her forties and a very successful career woman. She also shared the step she took to set a healthy boundary around her role as her daughter's mother:

> "My mom just commented a few weeks ago, 'Why don't you spend some time with your daughter?' That really bothered me! Right now, I am working and moving, and I was still spending time with my daughter. Right then and there, I thought, 'I do have a lot on my plate.' At first, my jaw just kind of fell open and I didn't know what to say. It took me a few minutes to recover and finally say to my mom, 'You know, every other person who knows me gives me a lot of credit for what I'm able to do. But I've never really given myself credit for that until a month ago.' The thing is I'm still very much defined as the daughter instead of my daughter's mother. And I think it is finally sinking in."

This mother engaged in one step of setting a personal boundary—protecting herself by communicating honestly and respectfully about how the other's behavior affected her.

A second reason why boundary setting becomes so important is that when you ask for support, lives become more interdependent. When there is more help, lives become more intertwined and boundaries become less clear:

> "My family is a great support, and they fill in as surrogate parents when I can't be there. At the same time, they also try to parent my children in ways that I don't approve of. I feel that I can't say much because they are helping me, so it can be frustrating."

In order to avoid developing resentment, it is important not to relinquish the role of the parent to your own parents. Let them be amazingly helpful and loving grandparents, but not surrogate parents.

The "fences" that mark off healthy family boundaries are sometimes taken down following a crisis such as divorce or bereavement. During a time of crisis, this may make great sense. However, these changes may persist after a crisis and require more attention to boundaries. This holds true on both side of the boundaries between you and your parents. That is, you may need to shore up your own boundaries but also reflect on whether you encroach on your parents' boundaries by always expecting their help. Similarly, your own parent(s) may be in the habit of offering ongoing unsolicited advice or disregarding rules you have established with your children.

A few pointers for attending to your own boundaries follow:

- Bear in mind that there is no way to totally avoid some hurt feelings when setting boundaries with a parent. All you can do is to be as diplomatic as possible so you do not rub additional salt into the wound of feeling not needed or disrespected.
- If necessary, remind yourself that it is natural and healthy for your relationship with your parents to change from *parent-child* to *adult-adult.*
- But there are usually growing pains in the process.
- Edit your list of "do's and don'ts." Make sure it includes the important rules but is not overly controlling on nonessentials. I have seen some parents who felt compelled to make it clear they were "the boss" through sheer volume of rules.
- Pick your battles and hold firm on important issues. For example, special diets such as gluten-free ones are not negotiable. If your parent disregards these rules, avoid a tirade but make it clear that you simply won't negotiate some matters. If challenged to defend your child-rearing practices, the best response is something like this: "I appreciate your concern, but I am not willing to argue about this with you. I am asking you to respect my right to make decisions for my own child." Of course, this does not always work the first time because children are not the only ones to test limits; it is human nature. So the best course of action is to hold firm, refuse to debate, and keep from losing your cool.

Cultivating Supportive Grandparents

I follow the Serenity Prayer, from Chapter 1, when it comes to people. Before I accept what cannot be changed, I think about what can be changed. Sometimes, your child's grandparents have the potential to be key supports if provided some help along the way. It is not as much about changing them as changing their relationship with you and your children.

Many parents of children with disabilities flounder mightily at first in embracing the reality of their child's diagnosis. As described throughout this book, many have struggled with acceptance, grief, and learning how to best parent an atypical child. Grandparents often have a related struggle, but they do it with less support and under different circumstances. Evonne Miller and her colleagues wrote that grandparents are in a unique position to help, but that this often requires dealing with what has been termed a "double grief." As discussed in Chapter 2, parents often need to grieve the loss of the child they imagined they would have in order to best love the child they do have. Miller and her colleagues suggest that grandparents need to mourn the loss of both the grandchild they imagined they would have as well as the imagined (idealized) image of their own child's future.

Like parents, grandparents are prone to seeing offspring as a bit of a link to immortality by passing on their history, memories, and characteristics. Andrew Solomon, the author of *Far from the Tree*, writes with great insight about the ways parents initially struggle with children who are different due to disability or other characteristics. His comments on these parental struggles pertain to grandparents as well:

> "There is no such thing as reproduction. When two people decide to have a baby, they engage in an act of production, and the widespread use of the word *reproduction* for this activity, with its implication that two people are braiding themselves together, is at best a euphemism to comfort prospective parents before they get in over their heads. In the subconscious fantasies that make conception look so alluring, it is often ourselves that we would like to see live forever, not someone

with a personality of their own. Having anticipated the onward march of our selfish genes, many of us are unprepared for children who present unfamiliar needs. Parenthood abruptly catapults us into a permanent relationship with a stranger, and the more alien the stranger, the stronger the whiff of negativity. We depend on the guarantee in our children's faces that we will not die."

Liora Findler suggests that desires for this type of immortality get disrupted when a grandchild is diagnosed with a disability. Grandparents who need to mourn these losses are faced with relatively less support as well as fewer opportunities to process their feelings. As Findler suggests, they often aren't part of everyday life, which presents many opportunities to work through feelings, as well as pleasant interactions with the actual child. This makes it harder for grandparents to channel their feelings of anger or sadness into productive activities on the child's behalf.

Shira Katz wrote that it is common for grandparents to initially feel helpless in a way that prolongs their grief. According to studies conducted by both Liora Findler and Evonne Miller and her colleagues, once grandparents come to terms with the diagnosis, they are able to adapt and take pride in the perseverance of their families.

If you are struggling with family members who might not understand what you are going through, consider whether they might need more time to process their feelings. They may also need a way to be able to express their feelings. If it is too painful for you to hear about their feelings, encourage them to join a grandparents' group, if one is available in the area, or on the Internet.

Encourage Shared Activities

Another way to build the relationship is to encourage your parents to do special activities with your child. This often makes it easier for grandparents to feel more at ease in connecting and helps meets the need for predictability and routine that is especially important to some children. Distance does not have to be a barrier to building that relationship through activities. For example, one mother of a daughter with Down syndrome described how her own mother plays Scrabble with her daughter online while living many states apart. With Skype, there are so many possibilities, such as reading or singing together.

A useful book that focuses on connecting from a distance is *Stay Close: 40 Clever Ways to Connect with Kids When You're Apart,* by Tenessa Gemelke. By the way, this book is not just useful for grandparents. The ideas in it also apply to others who live apart, including noncustodial parents. The author emphasizes creativity in engaging in joint activities that go beyond Skype or e-mail. These include ideas such as sending children a package with all the ingredients and a recipe to bake something. Baking can be done together using the phone or Skype or the children can simply let you know how it turns out. Gemelke also suggests activities such as writing stories together—taking turns writing a sentence or paragraph at a time.

These small steps can help to build a relationship over time. In addition, they help you have fun together. Skype and phone conversations can lack that element.

Try to See Things Their Way

Although you may feel as if your parents need to make more of an effort to see things your way, you may also find it helps if you try to walk in their shoes. Shira Katz states that parents should not underestimate the magnitude of the adjustment for grandparents and the time it takes. As Evonne Miller and her colleagues note, many grandparents have sacrificed their own hopes of traveling or retirement in order to better support their grandchildren. Many grandparents also experience tensions in their marriages about how to handle the new family dynamics. They are concerned about keeping the peace in all of the extended family and balancing all their roles. Many want to make sure that the extra attention given to the child with a disability does not lead to resentment among other family members. Grandparents sometimes feel as if they have to choose between families, and this is distressing for them, especially if they do not have peers they can share their unique experiences with.

Suggest Resources

You might also want to suggest some additional reading for your parents so they get the information they need. For example, Autism Speaks suggests this book for further reading: *Autism and the Grandparent Connection* by Jennifer Krumins. The organization also has a grandparents' guide that can be found online at www.autism-speaks.org. For grandparents of children with Down syndrome, there is a free booklet called "Your Loved One Is Expecting a Baby with Down Syndrome," available from www.downsyndromepregnancy.org, and the Down Syndrome Association of Central California offers a "Grandparent's Guide" as well. Other organizations devoted to other conditions often have their own materials.

Learning to have Realistic Expectations

Now for the second part of the Serenity prayer: sometimes we need to accept what we cannot change. Expectations and resentments are closely tied in with each other and easily lead to anger, sadness, and all kinds of hurt feelings.

As they wisely say in a variety of twelve-step programs that focus on recovery and personal wellness: great expectations (of others) lead to premeditated resentments. This doesn't mean we should set the bar low for others. It is still important to set boundaries and be reasonably assertive with our requests. But not having great expectations of someone who has repeatedly disappointed us is a way to conserve emotional energy.

I think it is important not to keep expecting someone to be different from how they have been in the past. Then each *predictable* disappointment becomes accompanied by new negative emotions. It reminds me of people who get upset when there is too much traffic on a city road when congestion is absolutely predictable because it happens time and time again.

Managing personal expectations requires us to be realistic about what family members are willing and able to provide us. Like it or not, heeding those limitations helps with peace of mind. I once heard it said that going to the wrong person for help and support is like going to the hardware store for bread.

Personally, I find two additional strategies to be useful in managing resentments in the making. First, I find I am more tolerant of people's imperfections if I remember the times my own behavior has fallen short. Many people find that type of look in the mirror to be a good antidote for feeling self-righteous about someone else's flaws. Second, I find it useful to judge (myself) and others on their intentions. One solo who described a loving relationship with her family shared the following:

"They are very helpful but sometimes their remarks do hurt. For example, my mom would say, 'No one would want you because you were dumped by your husband.' My father would say that my focus is to raise the boys and I should not think about getting married again."

I don't know if she shared her hurt feelings over this boundary violation; I hope that she did. But it was clear that she judged her parents as loving, although thoughtless at times.

Often solo parents are disappointed by their siblings' lack of understanding.

Commenting on her brother, one solo mother wrote:

"I think people just naturally don't think too much about other people's situations. I know I don't sit here and wonder what the people who can't afford heat in Russia do in the winter. So I accept the fact that others just aren't thinking of me. They think life is peachy for me because they see my children playing outside. They don't ponder what it is like to never go on vacation, to work so hard to support the children, and to never get a chance to go somewhere alone.

"In fact, my brother would tell you how lucky I am to have gotten disability [payments] for my daugher for a number of years. He would even say that raising her is no more difficult than any other child. He would say that she might even be easier because I can just set her in front of a television or let her listen to music. He's wrong, of course."

Another solo mother spoke of the fact that her parents and siblings have provided a ton of invaluable help since her child's adoption. She is grateful for all of this, but also noted that they don't understand some of her difficulties. Being helpful and well-intentioned and "not getting it" are not incompatible. As she says,

> "Inevitably, at most family events, they say something that either offends me or pisses me off. They don't know what it's like to sit in an IEP meeting and have fifteen people tell you what your kid can't do! They want to 'get it' but they can't. So I have to be smart about it. I don't say anything, and when I can leave, I go and call a friend who has a child with a disability."

Lowering her expectations for their understanding and venting to a friend has worked for her.

Sibling Rivalry

Just like parents, siblings can be our best supports but are also a source of disappointment and frustration. Sibling rivalry that begins in childhood and extends into adulthood is often the cause of some problems. Margaret Mead, the famous anthropologist, wrote that sisters have the most competitive relationship within the family system during childhood. Sometimes adult sibling rivalry has roots in childhood family dynamics that have nothing to do with you and your sib.

If you are upset by adult sibling rivalry that you have experienced, bear in mind that the dynamics often got set in motion by someone other than you and your competitive sibling. This is important because we often blame our sibling for starting it when it was really set in motion by a parent's separate dynamics with different children. For example, some children are favored due to gender or birth order (the oldest or the "baby") or because they share traits of the particular parent. There may also be lingering bitterness if a younger sibling does not receive as much parental attention as an older one due to the onset of health problems in the parent, or if an older sibling needs to take on more responsibilities due to the death or illness of a parent.

These historical roots may exacerbate situations. In adulthood, the rivalry can take on many forms. For example, one sibling might tell the other how to parent. In other cases, nothing one sibling says is "right" or "acceptable" to the other. Sometimes, there is still tension about their parents preferring one child over the other.

Similarly, having a child with a disability complicates these adult relationships that may already have rivalry and resentment bubbling up. I know of several situations in which siblings were frustrated with their relationships with their parents and wanted their parents to be more attentive to them and their children. In turn, they focused their resentment on their sibling who had a child with a disability. They envied the parent's involvement with their sibling and their children. For example, one solo commented:

> "Some members of my family think my parents favor my child who has Asperger's more than the other family members. So that is a constant battle at almost all family get-togethers."

Envy can go both ways. Some solo parents envy siblings who have an easier life. So what can be done with that feeling? You can't simply convince yourself that this is not true because it often is. I suggest reminding yourself that we can confuse easier with better or more meaningful. You might also sometimes ask yourself if you would trade your *entire* life for someone else's.

As with most relationships, if we change our part of the relationship "dance," our partner often changes his or her steps as well. So, if you change your patterns of behavior, it may help change the adult sibling dynamic. Some possible strategies follow:

- Make sure you are not doing anything to perpetuate a rivalry. It is easy to miss your own role in this type of interaction.
- Don't participate in problematic dynamics. If one of your siblings tries to push your buttons, disengage. Do not participate in jealous behavior or hurtful bantering. Don't blame siblings for the way that your parents acted. Try to let go of your own jealousy or ill feelings. If you notice yourself feeling negative around a sibling, keep it to yourself.

- Try to cultivate something positive with your brother or sister. Not all problems can be talked through, but you can often grow something new in a relationship. Or see if you can just find something you enjoy doing together and spend time doing that. As a psychologist, I have seen adult sibling relationships greatly change even for those in their sixties, seventies, and eighties.
- Don't try to change your siblings. This can only lead to greater frustration and aggravation. When you refrain from criticism, not only are you creating less tension in the family dynamic (by not overstepping boundaries), but you are also modeling noncritical behavior that your sibling can hopefully replicate toward you.
- Find support in other places. As discussed earlier, it often helps to lower expectations of our parents and siblings. When we can get the support we need from other places, we will come to resent our families a little less. We might want our families to be something they never will.
- Cultivate your own family. It can be helpful to put that energy into building your own family, creating the kinds of bonds and connection that you wish you had with your own. A great deal has been written about the impact of having a sibling with disabilities on typically developing children. Don Meyer's work on siblings of children with disabilities is an invaluable source of information, and his books and other materials are easily obtainable.

Forgiveness

Forgiveness is included in this chapter because it is an essential life skill and one used frequently by many solo parents in this book:

"When my son was younger and lower functioning and had significant behavior and emotional outbursts, my family and friends were very distant. Many of them were scared to have my son interact with their children. I recall family gatherings where I wanted to go outside and chit-chat with others but couldn't because no other adult was willing to watch over my son for a short time. It was heartbreaking! As a single parent, I found myself wishing that I had someone, anyone to share the responsibility of my son, even if for a brief moment, so I could relax like everyone else.

"As my son has grown older and my family has seen the amazing young man he is turning out to be, many of them have commended me on my efforts as a single parent and apologized for not always being there to help. I have learned many lessons in forgiving others."

Many of the parents interviewed for this book spoke of forgiveness. Some people forgave naturally as they aged. Jasmine (Chapter 2 and 3) said:

"Mom is going to be eighty next month. I adore that crazy old lady, but you know, I just remember either always being scared or always being sad. There was a pretty significant amount of abuse in the house. Now I understand what it was like for her."

Bobby (Chapter 5) is one of many who eventually chose to forgive his parents for hurts and disappointments:

"I think that forgiveness is another key in the process of being a whole individual. For me, it was about relinquishing bitterness, so I forgave my dad. He still drinks a lot. But I just realized that I can't hold him completely accountable for my upbringing. I think sometimes you need to get to that point *for yourself.* My dad never said that he forgives me or that he loves me. But the forgiveness was for me. There's been a lot of forgiveness there.

"More recently, I am working on forgiveness with my mom. My mom has always been a very conservative Christian; it's all about the church, and she doesn't have time for family. We hadn't talked for about two years, but we did recently. I said, 'Mom, I think we need to sit down, have a talk, and try to make some amends. I'm willing to accept the fact that I haven't been there as a son. And I'm willing to forgive you about certain areas about how I was raised. I think this is a long process, and we need to figure out how to work through this.' Later, I actually had to go to the doctor, and she ended up going with me."

Frances (Chapter 7) speaks of a reengagement with her family. It was prompted by the end of her marriage to another woman whom her parents disliked.

"After my wife left, my mother had triple bypass, so she had to stay with us, I was able to nurture her back to health, and that kind of reunited us. And my daughter is wonderful, very nurturing, very caring. My mother loves being with her because she's respectful, whereas my other nieces and nephews aren't very nice to her. Crystal will do anything for my mother; she'll do anything for me. That part is absolutely wonderful. Both my brothers, my father, my mother, they're back in my life, and my older brother doesn't want anybody to get in-between us again."

Lest you think this was a perfect change of events, it is important to add a little more. She said: "I still don't have relationships with this brother's family because his wife thinks their daughters would catch it from me, being gay and all."

I would assume that this required a lowering of expectations that enabled her to stay well connected with this brother. I suppose it was in keeping with the essence of the serenity prayer.

The Benefits of Forgiveness

After becoming parents ourselves, our relationships with our own parents may change in many ways. Sometimes our relationships deepen with an understanding of parenthood, leading to even greater gratitude, closeness, and forgiveness. But sometimes when you become a nurturing parent, you may become sad or resentful that your parents did not provide you with the same degree of care when you were a child. In essence, growing into parenthood yourself often "stirs the pot" of related feelings.

Although many of us were taught as children that forgiveness is the "right" thing to do, the benefits were not always clear. If you were anything like me, you were told that it was the nice thing to do for the *other* person. And the concept of forgiveness was bound up with religious teachings.

It is now becoming clear that forgiveness is often a choice that can benefit ourselves. The benefits of it and the steps toward forgiveness are being looked at differently these days. For example, Stanford University is researching this through its notable Forgiveness Project.

The practical benefits of forgiveness are not new. As the author C. Joybell wrote:

> "If you want to forget something or someone, never hate it, or never hate him/her. Everything and everyone that you hate is engraved upon your heart; if you want to let go of something, if you want to forget, you cannot hate."

One of the best things I have read about forgiveness is *Forgiveness: Why and How,* written by Paschal Baute. He refers to a great quote by Robert Enright that defines forgiveness as "...giving up resentment to which you are entitled, and offering to the persons who hurt you friendlier attitudes to which they are not entitled."

Advocates of forgiveness practices consider it a technique to enhance your own personal freedom. In other words, when we forgive someone, it frees us from the emotional baggage that tends to control our thoughts and hearts. For some, it is a useful strategy for releasing feelings of anger, hurt, and resentment that end up occupying people's minds.

I used to think that someone had to earn my forgiveness. Yet Baute and others state this is absolutely not the case. In researching the skill of forgiveness, I learned a lot that I did not know about forgiveness and want to pass it on:

- Forgiveness is an act of "letting go" for your own sake.
- Forgiveness does not mean you will forget what someone did to you. Forgiveness does not require forgetting.

- Forgiveness does not mean you are somehow excusing someone's behavior and becoming vulnerable to their hurting you again.
- Forgiveness does not mean you will take the next step of reconciling with someone. It serves a personal purpose, whether or not you ever want to connect with that person again.
- Forgiveness does not mean that the other person somehow "won" or that you are weak.

And the most surprising thing I learned was:
- Forgiveness does not require the person who wronged you to admit his or her wrongful behavior.

Paschal Baute explained this in an interesting manner that may resonate with some readers: "Be aware that forgiveness is, believe it or not, 100% your responsibility, and that you DO NOT really need the other person to admit that they were wrong. Waiting until they admit wrongdoing keeps YOU stuck in the past. Many crucify themselves between two thieves of regret (or resentment) and guilt, then believe that others or 'the world' had owed it to them."

Putting this into action takes practice. I find that if I start to ruminate about something that I chose to forgive, it is useful to say, "I forgave that! I forgave that!"—about five times so I don't get seduced down resentment lane. Then I feel like I am carrying a smaller load. We all have plenty of other things to carry.

A powerful example of applying a combination of forgiveness and effective boundary setting is illustrated in the following story by a mother who is now lovingly connected to her father, who had been very abusive and alcoholic while raising her. She limits her visits to about twice a year because, she says, that is about all she can handle. She added that her parents are on their best behavior when she visits and that the children don't know this chapter of their grandparents' history:

"I came from a family where my father was very abusive and my mother was scared and did not speak up for her child.

Now, many years later, I can say that my father is a very sweet man that I love and adore, and we've reconciled our relationship.

"You asked me how I am able to say this today? The answer is that I set boundaries. The turning point was a visit I had with him when I was married and had two small children. I was around twenty-two years old and went to visit my father after living on a military base an ocean away. Well, he was drunk and being really mean to my daughter, who was about two at the time. I had intended to stay with them for three months while my husband was on deployment. But I left and stayed with someone else.

"I wrote my father a letter and said, 'I'm no longer a child.' I told him, 'I'm in control of the people in my daughter's life.' I went on to explain how I was going to raise my daughter and that it included the right environment. I added that it was harsh to say but, 'I can choose whether to have you in my life or not.' And I knew my father loved my daughter very much. So I added, 'What's going to change is you. So this is what it's going to look like. You are an alcoholic. I don't expect that to change. I pray that it will, but I don't expect it to. So when I do come visit…IF I come visit… this is what I expect.'

"I have to tell you that my father wrote me back three or four months later. He barely graduated from high school and writes pretty poorly, but he wrote me anyways. He apologized. This was huge for him to even express feelings. I came from a family where if you were beaten one day and the sun rose the next day, the beating hadn't happened because it was a new day. So just for him to acknowledge that something had happened was huge. Now we come and visit and when we do, he doesn't drink. He was here for New Year's, with my mother, and I can tell he struggled, but he knows. It amazes me. He does smoke a lot more when he is visiting us, and that's his way to cope. He still drinks at home but not with us.

"As a side note, it is amazing for me to be at the place I am in terms of caring for my father. I remember being fifteen or sixteen and being called to the principal's office because my father had a heart attack. At that point in life, I just didn't care. I didn't want to leave school, and I just didn't care about him in general. Now, I love him to pieces.

"You asked how I turned the corner? For me, it helped that he cut back his drinking. He became a softer person. He has kept his hands to himself for the past twenty years. He is more expressive with me. His mother passed away, and I think family means more to him now. I see a role reversal in my family, where he was very angry and mean with my mother. Now she is very ill and mean and he is taking care of her."

Supportive Others

One parent gave this advice for finding a supportive environment: "Go to the restaurant that feeds you the best." This stuck in my mind because it is such a simple but good metaphor for thinking about the people we choose to spend time with. We may find them in new or old friendships and sometimes support groups.

Friends

Many solo parents of children with disabilities described a pruning of their friendships. Either friends dropped out of sight of their own accord, or solos terminated friendships:

- "My friends give me more support than my family does. They have been there through it all; most never judged me, and they stood by me. The ones that didn't are no longer my friends."
- "It got too hard to even have short uninterrupted phone calls. Friends who had healthy kids would feel uncomfortable, or guilty, that their children were 'normal.' They would worry about their child getting hurt around mine. Their children also felt apprehensive about my child, who was not acting in a typical manner. So it would be too

stressful for them to be around my child for any length of time. One friend said, 'I love you, and I love your child, but I can't stand to be around him for any longer than half an hour, because I get so stressed out, and get such a headache. I don't know how you do it.'"

Certainly, many parents do find friends with typical kids who are able to step up in terms of friendship, as this mother comments: "Many of my friends abandoned me but those who stuck with me helped me. I know they are my true, dear friends."

Lisa, who is profiled in Chapter 7, spoke of having lost her best friend when her needs intensified due to her daughter's multiple disabilities. She added that she did not realize how much her other friends cared about her. She said:

"Wow, it is amazing that I felt that my friends who were still there really cared for me. I could see it. I learned that I really just need to speak up and say what I need. That's been a huge lesson. Also, as women, we don't always say what we need."

There is no consensus about whether or not friendship works better with other parents who have children with disabilities or not. It is clear that friends don't necessarily need to have a child with a disability to be thoughtful. For example, one solo explained the sensitivity of one of her friends:

"One of my friends likes to give parties. When my son and I are invited, her invitation includes his aide. Another friend is married and has a son who is gifted. One time after my son was diagnosed, we were swapping news about our families. She stopped for a moment and asked if I wanted to talk about something else. She understood that it can be especially painful for me to be reminded of how far behind my son is compared to others his age. I reassured her that I was happy to hear the news about her and her husband."

Another spoke of her inability to get out of the house to socialize, so she makes a regular practice of inviting friends over to sit around a backyard fire and have a drink.

Others find it harder to sustain friendships with parents of typically developing children, and some find themselves envying their friends:

> "I have one friend. There have been many times I have been angry that she has things so easy because her children are neurotypical. I have never shared this with her. There are many things I just don't share with her."

Another solo parent spoke of wanting to make friends who have nothing to do with the world of disability. She takes her time in letting them know much about her situation: "Sometimes I let them get to know me first before I tell them I'm divorced and have a child with special needs."

Being friends with other parents of kids with disabilities is invaluable to many solos. Here are two benefits they cited:

- "If your kid does something crazy in their house, you don't have to be embarrassed. No one judges it."
- "You can call and just vent rather than have someone try to 'fix it.'"

Sometimes it is only the parent of another child with a disability who will "get it."

I recently met a mother at a support group who told me about the strength and fun she has found by connecting with other parents of kids with autism on an Internet blog site. She sought a group of parents who were not what she called "warrior moms" out to defeat autism, as she felt this was not realistic and not the sort of friends she wanted. She found a group of mothers who shared their struggles with humor. With a big smile on her face, she told me that her group of mothers had a contest online for the worst "poop" story. Most of these mothers shared struggles with lack of toilet training success and feces smeared or put in the wrong places. With dark humor, she recounted a few of the photos submitted:

"No, the Fisher-Price barn from the plastic farm set (sadly) did not win. The secret deposit on the bookstore shelf did. Those friends are priceless."

Other solo parents agree that fellow parents of kids with disabilities can be the most supportive:

- "I think the thing that has helped me the most is the connection with other parents who have children with disabilities. I learned to be able to admit to them when things aren't okay and when I am scared. I was afraid to say it for a long time. But I don't have to prove anything to them. They have been there too."
- "Simply being around other parents of kids with disabilities, you learn so much—simple things too. My son was four, over seventy pounds, and still not potty trained. I was spending an arm and a leg on diapers. No professional ever told me that medical assistance pays for diapers for a child with a disability who is over three and isn't potty trained. I was coming into an office building and a woman with a child with Down syndrome was coming out, and she stopped me and said, 'Do you know your son can get this through medical assistance?' You tell them the average you use and they deliver them. I had no idea. My son had been in the hospital a million times, and nobody ever said that."

Of course, not all parents of kids with disabilities will make you feel better. You may think that you will escape competition if you surround yourself with other parents of kids with disabilities. Not so. Several parents spoke of the distress associated with this competition with some other mothers of children with disabilities. Melanie (Chapter 8) spoke at length about the common and toxic competition between parents of children with disabilities:

"I don't want to lie about my son's ability, but on the other hand, I don't want to feel bad about it. And I definitely don't want to talk to another parent of a child with a disability and feel bad about my own child. It's one thing if I don't have support from my siblings who have children who are typically developing, but I have to go into the disability world and feel like crap too."

Many solo parents lose friends in the process of getting divorced because there is often a choosing of sides. When widowed, friends may initially rally around but then keep their distance. Sometimes, when widowed, people find that it is less painful to keep some distance themselves. So, solo parents often face the task of making new friends in adulthood. I have found that being "intentional" about the goal of forming new friendships leads to more success. Reminding myself of my goal of finding new friends has helped me push past my occasional shyness and has made it easier to take the extra step and suggest "going out for coffee sometime."

Andrea Bonior (2013) offers some useful guidelines. She writes:

"First, the easiest thing to do is to maximize the places we frequent, the people we know, and the profession we have— even if some of them are new to us. In other words, introduce ourselves to our neighbors, tell some of our Facebook friends to introduce us to people they know who live in our city, or tell some of our friends we're looking to meet other mothers and try to reach out to a few people we interact with for our work. The advantages of maximizing where we already spend our time is that those relationships are easier to grow if we are in close proximity or more frequent contact."

Readers who are interested in this topic can learn more in Bonior's book, *The Friendship Fix*.

Conferences, Organizations, and Support Groups

Conferences are often wonderful sources of support on many levels. Of course, the content and the opportunities to network can be invaluable. But, on top of that, the camaraderie is so important. There is strength in numbers, and it also helps to feel surrounded by so many people who understand the joys and struggles of parenting a child with disabilities. I think this is especially important for conditions that carry a particularly high degree of stigma. NAMI, the National Alliance on Mental Illness, is a leader in fighting such stigma. One mother explained the value of this group to her and her daughter:

> "We did the NAMI walk together, and I was actively involved. My biggest thing was to teach my daughter that mental illness is no different than other illness, and we don't have to have this big stigma around it."

Other national disability organizations are too numerous to mention and easy to find on the Internet or through word of mouth, so they will not be listed here.

Solo parents' experiences with support groups vary greatly. They can provide unparalleled solidarity or be disappointing or upsetting. One mother of a young child with Down syndrome expressed her discouragement with support groups:

> "I went to one of these meetings when I was worried about her drinking out of a sippy cup. And all these people had children who had trachs and open-heart surgeries, and I thought *I'm not asking about this stupid sippy cup.* Then, I went to a group where people were almost jovial about having a kid with Down syndrome. I thought support groups were about your emotions. I kind of felt that we were on a different level. I was still hurting and wanted to talk to people about how I felt. That's what I'm still seeking, and I don't think those people are in support groups.
>
> "I would love to go to a support group where people actually talked about how they really feel. They're not out there. I think support groups should be named more accurately: 'Talk-about-your-kid's-health-issues groups.' You

can't talk about your feelings. I needed to talk about my grief, so I ended up in therapy for two years."

For many other parents, however, membership in a good support group offers a great deal. This includes being surrounded by others who "get it," the opportunity to learn from others, opportunities for advocacy, and chances to get and receive help. It is important to shop around for a group that is a good fit.

Al-Anon is a different type of support group that was mentioned by several solo parents in this book. It is a twelve-step program for anyone who has a friend, family member, or acquaintance who struggles with a substance abuse disorder. Contrary to what you might expect, meetings are very positive because the emphasis is on living well with situations that are beyond our control. Although I write of members, a person can just walk in the door and be welcome. There is no commitment. Some people just sit and listen, laugh, and maybe cry.

I have found that insights offered in the Al-Anon program apply to other parts of life and are a source of strength and growth for people even when their original reason for attending Al-Anon changes. Attendees are advised at the beginning of meetings to "take what you like and leave the rest" to reinforce the fact that there is no pressure to accept anything said at a meeting as the one right way to do something. I mention Al Anon because it is less well known than Alcoholics Anonymous (AA), although it was patterned after the twelve steps and traditions that form the foundation of that program. Unconditional support, wisdom, and help can be found in both.

Substance abuse deserves special mention. It plagues the general population, so it is also a problem for solo parents of children with disabilities. It is all too easy to become reliant on substances that provide short-term relief, but are addictive and damaging over time. This includes some medications prescribed by physicians who can't imagine that someone with a child with a disability can cope without medications. Alcoholics Anonymous, Narcotics Anonymous, and other twelve-step programs for addiction have provided invaluable help to many, but others find they need professional help. Bobby

(Chapter 5) became sober on his own, but he had a strong foundation for recovery thanks to previous mental health treatment.

Professional Help

There are times when professional help is not just useful; it is essential. These include times when depression or anxiety-based conditions result in significant distress that impede the ability to manage life and also times when anger is affecting parenting abilities. Children with disabilities are at greater risk of emotional and physical abuse by parents who lose control. Remember, angry yelling at a child affects the development of her brain's structure in a way that has lifelong effects. Verbally taking out your rage on a child is harmful and a clear reason to seek professional help.

Sometimes medical professionals point out the need for a parent to get professional help, but certainly not always. One solo mother shared her experiences with postpartum depression following the birth of her child with Down syndrome:

> "This is the kicker—you have to answer all these questions after your baby is born. They ask the questions to figure out if you have postpartum depression and to see if you will hurt yourself or the baby. I answered YES to every single of one them. Are you suicidal? YES! No one ever called me. Nothing. Now, it's comical, but at the time, no one even mentioned my responses. I got therapy for myself. I think it got me through."

Depression vs. Grief: It is important to be able to differentiate depression from "the blues" and grief itself. *The Diagnostic and Statistical Manual of Mental Disorders* (5th edition), also known as the DSM 5, provides the standard criteria used in the United States to diagnose depression as well as other conditions.

One of the key components is that there is a distinct change in mood that persists for a minimum of a few weeks. During this period, there is a loss of pleasure or interest in almost all activities throughout the day. In addition, there are several of the following symptoms:

- a change in sleep patterns: excessive sleeping or insomnia

- difficulties with concentration: foggy thinking or inability to make decisions
- increased irritability
- feeling hopeless or empty
- loss of energy or interest in life's pleasures
- unexplained aches and pains
- appetite or weight changes
- inappropriate or unexplained guilt and feelings of worthlessness
- reoccurring thoughts of death or suicide

The point of including this information is not to enable you to diagnose yourself. There are many factors to consider, including the fact that side effects of medication or some medical conditions such as thyroid problems may mimic depression. But, if these symptoms seem to fit how you have been feeling, the first step is to contact your doctor.

If you are found to have a clinical depression, medication is not necessarily the first line of treatment. Counseling itself can be very powerful if you have a skilled therapist. As a psychologist, I believe that counseling should be considered as treatment for mild depressions before an antidepressant is prescribed. Several of the solo parents interviewed for this book spoke about the help they received from counselors:

- "I have been very lonely as a solo parent at times, which has led to depression. While I have been tempted to isolate myself, I understand that this isn't helpful to me or my children. So I have sought professional help, family counseling—not just medication."
- "My therapist is doing an amazing job of helping me to process, and one of the things he helped me to do is identify what I want. He asked, 'Tasha, what would you love to do?' I started thinking about that and realized I had totally lost track of Tasha and her interests and what she likes to do. Everything had become about mental health. He said, 'You know what I need you to figure out? What it is that you like to do, and I need you to find a friend and go and do that.' So he gave me homework assignments, like going to the movies

or going out for coffee with a friend. So I started doing that, but the more I did that, the more I felt guilty because I was out having fun when I have a kid who's struggling with all these mental health issues. What I finally realized was that as I took care of me, I was able to take care of her. It was actually less stress for me when I took care of me."

Counseling may be especially useful if you are coping with multiple problems on top of raising a child with a disability. For example, Frances (in Chapter 7) had to cope with a divorce and losing her home and job. In addition, she was estranged from her family and needed help both for herself and to handle the complexities of raising an adolescent daughter who was adopted a short while before her marriage fell apart. Here is what she had to say about the value of counseling:

"I had so much going against myself. I was losing my house, going bankrupt, in the middle of a horrific divorce; there was just one thing on top of the other. So the counseling really helped me. The counselor is really neutral. Family can't be that neutral because they all have something at stake. I worry a lot about my daughter and if I will be able to take care of her. And that's where the counselor comes in. She helps me figure out who I am now. I lost my identity when I lost my job and the rest, and I'm very different than I was ten years ago.

"She also helps me with my daughter. When she acts out, I usually let loose verbally and take everything away from her. I often react first. And then I go to see the counselor, and she says, 'Remember, she's a kid; what do you really want for her?' This has helped me dial it back."

Certainly, there are times medication needs to be considered. Depressions are serious and can render a person (unnecessarily) unable to cope with daily life. If you are depressed, you often lose the ability to recognize that your negative thinking does not reflect reality. For some, this leads to suicidal thinking that can creep up in powerful ways. When lost in a depression, it may seem logical to you that everyone would be better off without you:

> "Unfortunately, I spent much of my son's life dealing with a major depression due to feeling that I was a total failure as a parent because I could not make my son well. When he started to get stable, my fears, guilt, and stress started to normalize for me. I still have days when the guilt slams me and I have to call my therapist to get through the day. Thankfully, after dealing with these issues, when I started feeling suicidal, I knew it wasn't okay to feel that way. I immediately called for help."

Others with serious depression get so stuck that they can't make the changes they often want and need to make:

> "I just had surgery this past summer, and following the surgery, I found myself in a horrible depression. I tried logic, talking, writing, praying, and acupuncture, but I just kept getting worse. Finally, I realized that I was in a severe depression, and I reached out to a friend, who gave me the name of a doctor, and I called her and got in right away. I am now on antidepressants and finally starting to believe that there may be light at the end of the long, dark tunnel."

When Lack of Insurance Is an Obstacle: Lack of health insurance or funds can be a barrier for some parents who need professional help coping with depression or other mood disorders. Some suggestions include:

- Do not hesitate to ask if a therapist has a sliding scale given your financial situation. Many do, and some do a little pro bono work. Many of my colleagues are used to providing services when people lose their insurance, so those requests are more common than you may realize. Mental health professionals are also a source for good information about low- or no-cost community services.

- NAMI (The National Alliance on Mental Illness) is another source of help. You can find contact information for local chapters on their website (www.nami.org). Although local chapters are likely to be most helpful, NAMI also has a national hotline you may call.
- Some colleges and universities offer clinics through their graduate programs, and they provide services to the general public. You may want to check with departments of social work, psychology, and counseling.
- Some of the forums at PsychCentral (www.psychcentral. com/depression) may be an option for some people who are in earlier stages of exploring treatment.
- In an emergency, the National Suicide Prevention Lifeline can be reached at 1-800-273-TALK (8255). It is a confidential service that is available twenty-four hours a day and is toll free. Local emergency rooms are another option in a crisis. They are routinely used under these circumstances.

Religion

Many parents find prayer or religion to be their bedrock. People often have mixed experiences with their houses of worship when disability enters the picture. Some learn how to accommodate the needs of all the congregants, including atypical children. However, for many, the struggle is disheartening. The art is to not become disillusioned but to find the right place and way to connect with your religion or spiritual practice. As one solo parent exhorted others:

> "We all love one another—we are all one. And *that* has been incredibly healing for me and for my kids. So to anyone who is feeling guilt from his or her church or religious group, find a new one! That has made a huge difference."

Many national disability organizations have been working on the compelling need to make houses of worship accessible to people with all types of disabilities. For readers who want to consider working with their congregation, there is a wealth of resources. The

National Organization on Disability (NOD), the largest cross-disability national organization, has been running a project called The Accessible Congregations Campaign as part of its Religion and Disability program. NOD also publishes materials that would be useful to many parents who decide it is time to push for accessibility in their congregation.

Supports for Employment

If I had a "magic bullet" to fix any single kind of problem encountered by solo parents of children with disabilities, it would be in the area of employment. Unemployment and underemployment contribute to a great deal of the distress experienced by solos, and even full employment at good pay can lead to all sorts of parenting challenges. In short, parents who are unemployed or underemployed often lack the financial resources to pay for the essentials needed to raise their families, let alone pay for therapies, medications, and other special items their children with disabilities need. And parents who are pursuing full-time careers outside of the house often struggle to find affordable childcare appropriate for their son or daughter with a disability and can be locked into jobs that don't provide them the flexibility they need to react to crises with their children.

Persistence and creativity are needed to solve these types of employment problems. This includes finding childcare as well as finding work that enables you to take time off when your child's needs are paramount.

Finding Flexible Work

A representative posting on Yahoo sets the stage for this discussion:

"Does anyone know of any real jobs where you can stay at home? I have a twelve-year-old with CP and epilepsy, and due to her health needs, I can't work outside of the home. I need to find a job that still lets me take care of her needs."

The answers the post elicited focused mostly on work that could be done at home. Although working at home is not a magic bullet, many solos find it to be one of the better options. One solo parent shared with me this comment about her work dilemma and resolution:

> "This past week I have received eight phone calls from my eldest son's school. He was suspended on Wednesday and sent home on Thursday. When he is home, I am home. So that means I am not working, and not working means bills are harder to pay. Being considered for a raise is harder. Getting used to this over the years, I have learned to make money from home, as well as work more than one job."

Parents have found work from home in a variety of ways. Ones commonly mentioned by solo parents include medical coding and billing, freelance writing or copy editing, and getting licensed for Braille transcription. Other parents have suggested medical transcription, video transcription. and tutoring. Tutoring may be an especially good option if you want to find work in the evenings after the rest of the family is in bed or doing other things. Some parents look into foster care for other children with disabilities. Some buy and sell things through eBay or other online auctions. Other have found it possible to do call center or customer service work from home.

Many online forums mention doing direct marketing. This includes work like Mary Kay and Avon. Those with special language skills may find work translating texts. If you have your own website, you can do affiliate marketing, which means you advertise a link for someone else on your website. Naturally, these are examples that may or may not suit your abilities or financial needs.

Three particularly useful websites for people who want to try to work at home are:

- Starting your own business: www.myownbusiness.com
- Home-based Working Moms: www.hbwm.com
- The Federal Trade Commission's Business Opportunities: www.ftc.gov/bizopps

Besides working at home, another possibility is to find an employer who will allow you to telecommute. The National Telecommuting Institute is one example. In addition, there are many major national companies, such as insurance companies, who hire telecommuters for substantial work.

Many solo parents interviewed were able to find understanding employers or ones that thought their value offset any inconvenience. Although working within the field of disability-service provision is not a guarantee that your employer will be understanding about child-related responsibilities, sometimes this is a good option. For example, Tasha (Chapters 10 and 12), whose daughter had a severe mental illness, found working for a disability organization to be feasible and therapeutic:

> "There were days when my daughter wouldn't sleep at all at night. We would be up all night because she would be in a place of delusion and paranoia. Every five minutes, I had to check the doors and the locks and show her that everything was locked up. And then when she finally fell asleep, it would be time for me to get up and go to work. And I would literally get up and go to work. They would look at me and say (caringly), 'Why are you here? Just go home.'
>
> "But, for me, work was my getaway. I would answer calls and talk to other families and help them through their process. That was healing for me. After hearing some mothers' stories, I thought to myself, 'It's not that bad, Tasha, because you're not dealing with this.' So I would help other people with their issues, and I found that as I helped them, it actually helped me."

Laws That Can Help

When it comes to employment supports, it is important to know about two laws that can benefit the parents of children with disabilities: the Americans with Disabilities Act (ADA) and the Family and Medical Leave Act (FMLA).

The Americans with Disabilities Act (ADA): The Americans with Disabilities Act goes far beyond coverage of discrimination in employment (although this is our current focus). It can best be thought of as a piece of civil rights legislation that prohibits discrimination on the basis of disability and guarantees equal opportunities to participate in the mainstream of life. This includes (but is not limited to) prohibiting discrimination in employment and in public accommodations such as businesses and activities that are open to the public at large. It also extends to discrimination in transportation and telecommunications. Only two provisions are discussed in this chapter, so readers are encouraged to learn more about the ADA on their own. One good source is www.ADA.gov.

An article by attorney Frank E. Stepnowski points out that most people are not aware that the ADA has a provision that extends a degree of protection to the parents of children with disabilities. He states that although these protections are limited, recent court cases have been favorable. He writes:

> "In a little-used aspect of the ADA, the law prohibits employers from discrimination against employees who have an 'association' with someone with a disability. The law would prohibit a discrimination against 'a qualified individual' because of the known disability of an individual with whom the qualified individual is known to have a relationship or association. Thus, a parent of a child with a disability."

He provides a few useful examples. One is that an employer could not retaliate against a parent who has to leave work early to care for a child with cerebral palsy (or another disability). His second example is that an employer can't fire, demote, or harass an employee who appears to be distracted by his or her family needs as long as he or she can get the job done without accommodations.

The ADA also provides important protections in the childcare arena. Title III of the ADA requires that parents and children with disabilities be afforded the equal opportunity to participate in services and programs provided by childcare centers.

Most daycare centers cannot refuse to accommodate a child with disabilities unless doing so would pose an undue burden on the center. They may only be excluded if their presence poses a direct threat to the safety of others. Even small, home-based childcare centers need to adhere to ADA guidelines for inclusion. The exception is for childcare activities and programs that are run by religious organizations.

Thanks to this nondiscrimination clause, most childcare centers cannot prohibit kids with disabilities who aren't toilet trained from attending, even if the center generally has a rule that you have to be toilet trained by a certain age. The one qualifier is that there must be at least some babies/children enrolled in the program who aren't toilet trained (of any age) and that there are facilities for changing diapers.

The same type of nondiscrimination protection holds true for after-school programs that are open to the general public. In general, centers must make reasonable accommodations to integrate children with disabilities unless this results in what is deemed a fundamental alteration of the program. Answers to commonly asked questions about the ADA and childcare can be found at www.ada.gov/childqanda.htm.

Family and Medical Leave Act (FMLA): The Family and Medical Leave Act was enacted in 1993, and protects employees from losing their jobs when they meet certain requirements and need to take a leave of absence from work. Their employers must grant them time away from their jobs and project that job for the employee to return to. Employees are typically protected when they need time off to care for an individual with a serious medical condition, to adopt or give birth to a child, or to care for someone in the military. In Chapter 7, Lisa discusses her fight to get time off through the FMLA following the adoption of her child and the onset of medical problems. Knowing the law helped her, as she was originally denied a leave of absence.

The above laws apply to jobs in the public sector, such as local, state, or federal jobs. Educational jobs also qualify. Additionally, they apply to any private employer who has fifty or more employees for twenty consecutive workweeks within a seventy-five mile radius. You have to have worked for the employer for twelve months, or a full year, in order to be eligible for FMLA protections. You also have to have worked 1,250 hours during the twelve-month period before the start of your leave. Any vacation time or paid time off you have taken does *not* count toward the 1,250 hours. Note that these are general guidelines; some states require that businesses have fewer employees and others require different numbers for public and private. Some states include domestic partners in their definitions of family.

The FMLA regulations define disability as "a physical or mental impairment that substantially limits a major life activity, as interpreted by the Equal Employment Opportunity Commission (EEOC), to define 'physical or mental disability.'" If you have problems getting your employer to give you the time off, and you believe you are covered by this law, you can go online to learn about your rights or go to your nearest district office and inquire about filing a complaint.

Respite Care

Respite care takes many forms—from having someone come to your home to take care of your child for a few hours, to sending your child out into the community with a support specialist. Its purpose is to provide parents and other caregivers with a respite or break from childcare responsibilities. Some respite programs require that you take your child to a provider's home or an agency's building. In other programs, a caregiver comes to your home. Respite might be provided for a few hours or a couple of days, during which time a trained provider feeds, entertains, and otherwise cares for your child.

Respite care has many manifestations. It may be provided by nonprofit agencies in your community such as the ARC or UCP or by a community center program. In this case, there are usually income requirements that determine how much (if anything) you need to pay for the service, as well as eligibility requirements that determine how often you may use the respite services. There are also federal funding programs such as Medicaid. If you acquire federal funding to hire your own care provider, there are restrictions on who qualifies as a respite provider (most states eliminate other family members). The type of disability that your child has may determine whether or not she is eligible. Sometimes, there are waiting lists and income requirements. Respite care is inconsistent from state to state, which can make it difficult to find and utilize.

To qualify for respite care at the federal level, your child must have one of several conditions including (but not limited to) developmental disabilities, some chronic medical conditions, and psychiatric disorders. Your child must also live with you (even as an adult). You need to be able to provide documentation pertaining to the diagnosis.

The ARCH National Respite Network (www.archrespite.org) includes the National Respite Locator, to help families and professionals find respite services in their community. Many states have State Lifespan Respite programs. You may also find respite services through your state's Aging and Disability Resource Center or by contacting private organizations such as Easter Seals, the local ARC, and United Cerebral Palsy, among many others. Veterans may find services through the VA Caregiver Services. Don't overlook possibilities through local houses of worship, as well.

Conclusion

While traveling outside of the United States, I have walked across some bridges that spanned deep gullies and were built by everyday people in small communities. Some had materials supplied by governments, but some were simply made with ropes and boards. However they were constructed, they all supported the people who walked across them on their daily journeys. That's what I envision when I think about the supports that will help you make your way: a sturdy bridge created with the help of friends, families, and professionals from materials that best suit your needs and assembled in such a way that you and your child can get where you need to go.

Chapter 5

Solo Fathers of Children with Disabilities

"I'm a good father but only a so-so mother."
—Sam

THE PHRASE "NURTURING children" is often used synony-mously with the term "mothering." Fathers are sometimes seen as be-ing essential for providing financial support for the family but more marginal in the raising of children. This bias is reflected in custodial decisions and in the tendency of educational and health professionals to automatically focus on mothers and assume fathers are not as en-gaged in child rearing.

In North America, social expectations have, to some extent, relegated men to the role of primary breadwinner and often, by default, distanced them from child rearing roles and activities. This becomes part of a negative self-fulfilling prophecy of less involve-ment. Fathers, themselves, may be vulnerable to these stereotypical roles. But the role of fathers is changing, and, according to *Single Parent* magazine, the number of single fathers has increased by 60 percent over the past ten years.

In contrast to the number of authors who focus on mothers of children with disabilities, relatively few authors write about fathers. One notable exception is Dr. Robert Naseef, who has written exten-sively about fathers of children with disabilities, particularly those with autism. Dr. Naseef, a psychologist, has an adult son with autism and went solo himself for a while. He has also worked with a very large number of fathers of children with autism. Due to his experiences, I asked him to comment on how raising children with disabilities can transform a man's views on masculinity. He wrote:

> "I think the hardest thing is rethinking our traditional ideas of masculinity and fatherhood. Fathers today are much more involved in the day-to-day care of their children; for example, the recent CDC report stated that 90 percent of fathers change diapers. This is astounding compared to the role of fathers when most of us were growing up; nonetheless, there are many vestiges of the traditional role as well.
>
> "We are problem solvers, and we certainly want to solve the problems that our child's special needs present. Unfortunately, it's not as simple as that. The diagnosis of a disability is a gritty and unwelcome reality that brings up difficult feelings that are hard to talk about.
>
> "It's okay to be angry, but the sadness and the worries that accompany the diagnosis as well as the day-to-day life of living with a child with special needs just sticks in our throats. This inability to give voice to our feelings is often the root of male depression. Not to mention, if the diagnosis is autism, and 80 percent of the children diagnosed with autism are boys, it can be a broken mirror for the father who is looking forward to having a son like himself to nurture.
>
> "These are immense difficulties, but when we accept the challenges of having a child who is drastically different from the one we expected, incredible growth is possible. Following the initial trauma of the broken dream for a 'perfect' child, posttraumatic growth is possible.
>
> "Learning to listen can bring us so much closer to our partners and our children whether they are developing typically or not. Learning to share our experiences— whether they are the heartbreaking frustrations or the little breakthroughs and celebrations—deepens our relationships.

"At the end of the day, our children with special needs and disabilities teach us profound lessons. Speaking for myself, I endured profound depression. I thought I would never laugh or smile again if my son never spoke. Indeed, I tried so hard to change him, but in the end he changed me. He helped me become the man I needed to be for my family and myself."

The fathers in this chapter are very different from one another, although they all share being in the minority as solo fathers. Without a doubt, their experiences, ideas, and strategies for handling complicated lives will benefit solo parents of both genders.

This chapter will introduce you to the following fathers:

- Sam, a middle-aged father of an adolescent daughter with autism and a son with very mild ASD. He has sole custody. His daughter is growing quickly and is still nonverbal.
- Bobby, a divorced father of an adolescent son with significant learning disabilities and a daughter. He has had an arduous path himself. He wears many hats, including those of magician and mental health advocate.
- Bruce, a military father who reconnected with his son who has autism. He now has sole custody after barely knowing his son for several years. Although he is now remarried so is not a solo parent, I could not resist sharing his story.
- Mark, a father of a college student with Asperger syndrome and a young adult daughter with Down syndrome. Currently divorced, he explains his steep path to coping with anger over the end of his marriage and custody battles as well as his very active involvement with his children.

Making It Work

The Backstory: Sam is a father in his fifties who has sole custody of his children. He made a decision to divorce due to his wife's continued drug addiction and his fear over the children's safety. To get a better sense of who Sam is, picture a man who was on crutches for about six years and didn't hesitate to bus tables at a deli during that time.

"The only person in this world that I really know loves me is my son because he tells me all the time. I think my daughter loves me, but I have never had a conversation with her. I see it in her eyes and I hope so."—Sam

Excerpts from his life story follow:
I'm a very simple guy, and all I wanted was a nice family, to be loved, and to raise our kids well. But it's all on me now. I accept that, but it makes it really hard. You see very few guys in my position, even if you forget the special needs part. I, personally, only know one.

My ex hasn't seen her kids in a year, but I wouldn't let her see my kids anyway, because she's out of control and she's done nothing to change. I'm not like her. You'd have to put me in the ground to keep me away from my kids; there's nothing on this earth that would keep me away from them.

My ex thinks that I'm "living the dream." She has no clue. Even when she was here, I took care of everything. I was your classic enabler, so I wasn't entirely innocent. For years, I used to tell my son to go see his mother while she was in drug rehab. He dealt with her during ten of those years, but now we don't do that anymore.

I believe kids are meant to be raised by two parents, although I don't believe that it has to be a man and a woman. It could be two gay parents. My son mentioned that he had a friend who was complaining about his mom, and he said to him, "At least you have a mom." It made me feel so bad. That's why I tried like hell to stick it out so that I could make it work for my kids. I miss having an adult here to bounce things off of.

I initiated the divorce when she was using hard drugs yet again. For the final six months, I could never leave the house if she was there with the kids. One of my downfalls is that I am

the most loyal person, so I put up with things. Finally, I woke up one morning and knew it had to be done and that this situation had to end.

I am all my kids have, and they are all I have. When they are gone and I have free time, I don't know what to do with myself and I miss my kids right away.

As my daughter gets older and bigger (and stronger and smarter) and I get older and weaker (and dumber), how am I going to figure out how to take care of her? What will be the best thing for her as we move forward? And what if, with all my health issues, something happens to me? I am always looking for strategies. My daughter started her period at eleven years old, and it has changed her personality. I've been thinking about puberty for years, but it is happening more quickly than I thought. She's strong as a bull and she gets very physically aggressive. I usually have marks all over my body. Now she is going into sixth grade, and these issues are at the forefront. I've lost a lot of caregivers; obviously, it's changed my life quite a bit.

My son has mild Asperger's. He has a bit of a filter problem. For example, he told the rabbi he was just going to his Bar Mitzvah for the party. I was mad because it was not respectful. I may have had the same thoughts at his age, but I knew to keep them to myself. We have a great relationship, though, and we are close and honest with each other. I used to be so controlling of him, but I've learned to let go because I was hurting his development.

My biggest concern is what will happen to my kids when I die. I think about these things because I have had medical issues, including some blood clots. I have a trust set up with my life insurance and my house. My daughter is going to need the majority of it, but I made sure some will go to my son. One day my son said, "I hope you are not expecting me to live with my sister!" I said, "No. When I'm not around anymore, I would just like you to be responsible for making sure she is taken care of." I don't want lawyers making decisions.

*In terms of daily life, there are always ten billion things
to do, and I just try to keep my head above water since I can
never catch up. So, I try to do just the most important things
and get them done. And my boss always says, "Hey, Sam,
coming to work is a relief for you." And I say, "Totally."*

*When my kids are in bed at night and everything is done
for that day, I can sit down and watch a baseball game for a
little while or read a book. I hate going to sleep because I know
once I shut my eyes I have to wake up and do it all over again.*

*One of the things that has worked for me is Al-Anon.
A lot of things at Al-Anon meetings are not about alcohol or
drug addiction—they are about life. This is the only place I
have been in my life where people have listened to me and
I have not been judged. When I first got to Al-Anon, I was
pissed off because they were laughing and enjoying themselves. Years later, I am laughing myself. Their slogan is to
"take what you like and leave the rest." That's what I do.*

*Before I went to Al-Anon, I thought that all people who
had religion were weak. I am not a praying kind of guy, so if
they pushed God, they would have lost me on the first day.
You asked what works for me when I get down. I have struggled to connect with something spiritual. I wish I could, but
I'm a literal guy so I want to see a burning bush. If I do, then
I will believe. Another thing I learned in Al-Anon is that the
only thing I can control is me. This has helped me a lot. I can
take many of their slogans (like "a day at a time") and they
totally apply to life.*

*Is this the way I thought my life would be? No, but this is
how it turned out. I accept that. Thinking about how it could
have been is a waste of time. So many people would say,
"Have you tried the gluten-free diet?" I've done all of that.*

*My daughter has autism. I don't know if it was because
my wife had a drink, or if it was because of genes. It doesn't
matter. I'm very much driven by reality, and my focus is on
what I can do to be productive. I don't have time for the bull-
shit. Through my health issues, my ex-wife's addiction issues,*

*and my kids' issues, I learned I am strong and resilient. I hate
when people tell me God only gives you what you can handle.
I believe you become who you are by how your respond
to adversity. That's how you find out who you are. I saw that
on a Dick's Sporting Goods commercial. But it's true.*

Genius Moments

I have known Sam for many years, and he is a man who
doesn't want to spend much time ruminating about what's
wrong. He puts his energy into figuring out tough problems and
guards against resentment and self-pity. He is not happy about not
having a partner and states, "In a nutshell, not having a partner is
the thing I hate worse than anything." But, he makes it work in very
practical ways.

Some of Sam's strategies and philosophies include:

- *Putting people in place.* As Sam says, "The biggest thing that's
  helped me is to surround myself with people who are bright
  so I can follow their lead." This has helped him tackle problems that could be overwhelming. For example, given that his
  daughter needed constant vigilance to stay safe, he figured
  out a way to get funding for a $6000 camera system so that
  he could watch her from every corner of the house. He has
  concentrated on searching out and engaging people who can
  help him figure out the logistics. None of them are members
  of his extended family. This is also how he is facing the major
  challenge of his daughter's transition from childhood. He has
  composed a group of neighbors, professionals, and other parents of kids on the spectrum to brainstorm and support him in
  his effort. This same group was also notified to enjoy and celebrate his son's appearance in musical theater performances.
- *Not looking back.* Sam is very aware that his original dream
  of having "just a simple family" isn't going to happen. But he
  doesn't let himself dwell on this. As he says: "That's why God
  put eyes on the front of your head—because you're going forward. I'm moving forward. I had my step back, but I'm mov-

ing forward. The alternative is to get caught up and feel sorry for yourself."

- *A day at a time.* Sam said he used to hate the advice "one day at a time." He used to think, "These people are jerks. These people are idiots. They don't know what's going on." But over time, he changed his perspective. He reflects, "You know? One day at a time is the way to be. If I get too far ahead, I don't have room in my brain to figure this all out."
- *Keeping it simple.* This is another Al-Anon slogan that suits Sam's natural style. He keeps it simple by focusing only on what matters. He described himself as developing a thought process of "not caring" about many things. He doesn't care about what caused his daughter's autism and he doesn't care that people sometimes stare at them on the street. He simply cares about his kids.

Lack of Support for Solo Fathers

Sam spoke about the isolation of being a single father: "I'm not one of the girls. When I take my kids to events, it's all moms. When I go to Al-Anon, it's all women. I'm the tiny minority."

Another father echoed this problem of feeling like "the odd man out":

> "It is different being a single father. People are always inviting my kids to stay at their house, but they are not as open to staying at our house. Because I'm a single man, there is less trust. Also, the mothers (at my daughter's school) were all getting together with their daughters, but my daughter wasn't getting invited to that. Why? It wasn't because they didn't like me; they just didn't know how to deal with me. When my daughter graduated from the eighth grade, one mother came up to me and invited me to lunch with some of the other mothers. Sitting there with a dozen mothers and their daughters, one mother said, 'Do you want to join in on our girl chat?' I appreciate that she said that because a lot of mothers don't

know what to say. I'm a parent and you can relate to me as a parent. Don't overlook that just because I'm a man."

In the United States, only 5 percent of all children with disabilities live with a single father. Throughout this book, fathers shared their thoughts on being surrounded by mothers—with rarely a father in sight. Schools and workplaces tend to overlook their needs and sometimes offer less support. Brian Tessier, a solo father who adopted two children from foster care, addressed this point in an interview for National Public Radio:

> "If a mom is in a meeting and all of a sudden she gets called because her kid is sick, nobody raises an eyebrow. But if a guy gets called because his kid is sick and has to leave, it's kind of like, 'Where's your wife?'"

Sources of Support for Parents of Kids with Disabilities

According to the Pew Research Center, solo fathers are stretched as thin as women are between work and family issues and are just as likely to feel guilty that they just can't keep up with all of their children's needs. Supports are critical to raising a child with a disability solo. Although Chapter 4 addresses this topic more generally, I have some additional suggestions:

- Make sure you are hooked up with *your state affiliate of Parent to Parent* (P2PUSA). This is a national nonprofit organization, founded more than forty years ago, that has a track record of supporting parents of children with disabilities. It is dedicated to helping parents connect and get the help and information they need in a personalized way. The organization provides a one-to-one match with a "support parent" who has personal experience raising a child with a similar disability. In this manner, emotional support can be provided as well as assistance in finding resources and information. Check out the website at www.p2pusa.org.
- Don't overlook the value of *connecting with fathers of children with disabilities* who have a partner or spouse.

Many organizations for children with disabilities have added "Fathers' night out" to their traditional offerings of "Moms' night out." If your child is part of a disability program that doesn't have a father's program, ask them to develop one. There is a good chance they will welcome this important suggestion. By doing this you will also be helping other fathers and sensitizing programs to this very common and important omission.

- Reach out and *tell others that you are looking to connect* with other fathers of kids with disabilities. Once you spread the word, you may be surprised to find out who knows someone who can lead you to a good solo father for you to meet.

- Don't overlook *the tangible help available from couples who have children with disabilities.* I have known some solo fathers to be successful in establishing platonic, helpful relationships. This is essential when you are faced with unexpected problems with child care or need information about services and issues.

- *Make an effort to extend yourself when you are out.* For example, being a little friendlier than you typically are can lead to new connections while at the park, dog walking, etc. Sam, the solo father whose story you just read, is one of the friendliest people I know. He has amassed a wide circle of people who care about him and his children and who will pitch in when needed. Knowing how tiring his daily routine is, I am certain that his friendliness sometimes takes some effort. But it has been worth it.

- *Consider joining Parents without Partners.* (www.parentswithoutpartners.org). The mission of this organization is different from ones with very similar names (that often pop up on searches and are dating sites). Founded in 1957, this organization now has thousands of members nationwide who range in age from eighteen to eighty. Although this support group is not exclusive to parents of children with disabilities, its mission may meet the needs of many solo fathers.

- Connect with *the thoughts and resources offered by Dr. Robert Naseef,* the psychologist whose personal insights appear at the beginning of this chapter. More of his work can be found at www.alternativechoices.com. Signing up for his newsletter will also help you feel more connected as well as much better informed. As you can tell, I am a huge fan of his work and don't want you to miss it.
- Visit *the website for Exceptional Parent* (www.eparent. com.), whose mission is "to develop, translate, and share information as tools for positive change for the special needs community." Exceptional Parent disseminates up-to-date information in a variety of ways including through a monthly print magazine. It is very likely you will find some information that is personally relevant, as well as comprehensive listings of resources and products.
- If you are a father of a child with Down syndrome, think about joining D.A.D.S: *Dads Appreciating Down Syndrome.* D.A.D.S. is a nationally known support, and if you visit its website (www.dadsnational.org), you can locate local chapters. The groups do not meet to discuss issues and complaints they have about their children, but rather to raise awareness, raise money for research, and support their children to the best of their abilities. As stated on their website, their three foundational pillars are support, action, and fellowship.
- *Check out the Arc,* another national organization that you may be familiar with if you are the parent of a child with an intellectual or developmental disability. The website for the national organization is at www.thearc.org. In addition to listing numerous resources, the website provides linkages to local chapters, many of which offer supports, workshops, and other types of help for families and their children.
- If you are lucky enough to live in the state of Washington, you probably know about the Washington State Fathers Network (www.fathersnetwork.org). The Fathers Network was started in 1986 and is run by professionals who specialized in intellectual and developmental disabilities. This

group dedicates much time and effort into advocating for inclusion, education, and independence of children with intellectual and developmental disabilities. I believe the group is still the only regional program in the United States and Canada fully devoted to fathers of children with special health care needs and developmental disabilities. I am including them because there is such a need for others to advocate for the development of similar programs.

Sources of Support Specifically for Fathers

There are also some websites specifically designed to provide support for fathers. Some of them include forums for fathers of children with disabilities, and others provide some parenting information you may find useful nonetheless.

- *Single Dad* (www.singledad.com) is an online support system for single fathers. The website includes resources and information available to fathers on all issues of parenting. This site also offers referrals and research-based answers to fatherhood questions such as handling a daughter's puberty. Not only does this website address many questions of parenthood, but it also allows single fathers to connect with other single fathers all over the world.
- *National Responsible Fatherhood Clearinghouse* (www.fatherhood.gov) is a "national resource for fathers, practitioners, programs/Federal grantees, states, and the public at-large who are serving or interested in supporting strong fathers and families." The site also provides fathers with helpful tips and advice, resources or programs near them, and literature on fatherhood. This is a great site for advice and recommendations.
- *Mr. Dad* (www.mrdad.com). Mr. Dad is a helpful site for fathers of children with disabilities as well as typically developing children. The author of the site has a child with numerous special needs himself and he has published eight books on fatherhood. He has helpful links, blogs, advice, and resources on being a father.

Unsolicited Advice

The advice you may crave is often very different from the advice that is offered. I'll address that next. The assumption that fathers are incompetent as parents leads to others often butting in with unsolicited advice. The essential skill of boundary setting was discussed in Chapter 4 and is useful for handling unsolicited advice from family and others who make a habit of encroaching on your parental territory. It includes a list of motives for unsolicited advice as a basis for deciding how to deal with it.

Fathers are particular targets for the unsolicited advice of strangers. Many conclude that "talking back" to strangers in pointless. Fantasizing about your perfect retort is a popular way to cope with the annoyance. One blogging father provided a good illustration:

> "Another time, a beauty product clerk in a department store asked me as I walked by with J. Bean if there was a baby sleeping in the stroller I was pushing. Yes, I replied, hoping no more conversation was necessary as I didn't want to wake said baby. You see, I had a light blanket tossed over the stroller creating a block for the light while being sufficiently ventilated. Unfortunately, the woman couldn't help herself; she asked me if the baby could breathe in there. What type of reaction to appropriate to that question? 'Babies need air?!,' 'Probably not, but I'm in a hurry right now,' 'Where's the men's department?' I had no idea how to respond to it, so I didn't" (www. dadontherun.com/2010/12/unsolicited-advice.html).

Parental strategies, polite and not, for handling unsolicited advice are easy to find. They are a matter of personal style in terms of what you want to live with. The minimalist approach is often best and involves simply saying, "Thanks, I'll keep that in mind." I have also encouraged people to learn to imagine unwanted advice literally going in one ear and right out the other.

Humor also works well to defuse the situation, since a good laugh releases endorphins. The article "8 Ways to Answer Unsolicited Parenting Advice" (www.education.com/magazine/article/unso-licited-parenting-advice) illustrates many ways of using humor to get people to butt out of your business. The author, Roberta Munoz, includes this strategic response to the stranger who observes your crying child and tells you that her child never acted that way: Say, "I know it's loud, but it's so easy to keep track of her this way." For the stranger commenting on what you feed your child (perhaps nonorganic), she suggests, "Yes, I know the orange juice has a lot of sugar, but the vodka doesn't!" Her suggestion about handling unsolicited advice from elderly strangers is wise too. She underscores that these individuals are often simply missing the days of being with their own children or grandchildren and suggests simply shifting the conversation to asking them about their own children and grandchildren.

Plunging into Full Custody—Ready or Not

The next story is from a military father I interviewed who is not technically a solo parent because he remarried several years ago. However, his story of making a decision to take custody of his son was largely a solo effort. As he said:

> "I was not nice about it. I pretty much said, 'Look, this is my son and I am not giving him up to the state. I am taking custody. If you want to be a part of it, you can, or you can leave.'"

Stepping Up

The Backstory: Bruce had made the military his career. He had little involvement with his son from his first marriage. He learned of his autism very indirectly and later found that his wife was trying to place his son with the state. He took charge at that point. His story speaks for itself:

> My son is nineteen now. When he was around two years old, his mom and I separated and then divorced. She moved to Ohio at that point, and I really didn't hear much about

what was going on. She got remarried and had two other kids. We weren't on very good terms, and I didn't really hear much about what was going on. Unless I asked very specific questions, I did not learn anything about Henry.

Later down the road, calls started coming from collection agencies about medical bills that I knew nothing about. I learned later that she did not bother to fill out the paperwork for him to have continued coverage through the military.

So I started looking at all the statements to see what Henry was being tested for. I learned he was diagnosed with autism. Apparently, he developed behavioral issues and got to the point that he was breaking things and putting holes in walls. Well, his stepfather just left. He didn't tell my ex or the kids he was going. She asked me if I could take Henry, but I was now on my second marriage with a boy and a girl in a three-bedroom apartment. So, I told her I couldn't do it until I got a bigger place. I guess she didn't like that idea and didn't want to wait.

Somehow her caseworker got hold of my number and called me at work one day. She asked me if I knew my wife was trying to give Henry up to the state. My ex-wife's grandmother thought I was reluctant to take him because of money, so she actually offered to sign her Social Security checks over to me if I would take custody of him. Money was not the problem. I did not accept the Social Security from her grandmother. I had done research and thought my son would need his own space, and at the time we did not have the room. That was the problem.

I got custody of Henry when he was ten. His mother didn't fight it. I didn't know him very well because I hadn't seen him much over the years. I was living many states away, so it wasn't easy working this out with my ex. But I did have him for three months in the summer when he was nine. He didn't speak much. He just said "momma, dada, baby, bottle, and Bubba" (the dog). These were just the normal words that he had said at two.

We figured out that summer that Henry was actually using sign. It was funny. Well, he wandered into these people's house (who had a dishwasher we were interested in buying) and came out with a glass of water. The owner said Henry had simply signed a request for a glass of water, and she recognized it.

So we began working with sign language. Then someone turned us on to using an iPad. He's using an iPod Touch and a program called Proloquo2go. So now he knows all that. I'm happier because even though he might be able to learn more sign language, he still wouldn't be able to use it to communicate with everybody.

When I first got custody, my ex told me that Henry wouldn't eat sandwiches, vegetables, or fruits. He was living off of hot dogs, raviolis, and stuff like that. We've gotten him to the point where we can tell him he has to try something; if he spits it out, that's our sign not to push it.

He likes to be by himself a lot. His room is set up for that. He has a big cushion chair where he can just sit, rock, and listen to music. He's got his own TV, VCR, and DVD player in his room, and if he asks, he's allowed to get a movie. Sometimes, he likes to put the VCR movies in and sit and watch them in fast forward. Then he gets overstimulated and starts jumping and swinging around.

Every father looks for a son to teach him to play basketball, baseball, and everything. I believe you can still do that when your son has autism. You need to do as much as you can. I know we have heard that people with autism are real smart and you've got to find that special talent. Well, unless his is eating, we haven't really found it yet. It doesn't mean that he doesn't have one.

I've read about a kid with autism who was really good at playing the drums and he just saw colors. And another girl went and got a black belt in Tai Kwon Do. We've read and heard these things, so don't quit. Continue to try to teach your kids with autism. Henry will go out and he'll shoot baskets. I can't exactly tell if he's having fun doing it. He'll go bowling, but you can't tell if he's having fun doing it or if he's just doing it to please us. If he gets to the point where he says, "I don't want to do it anymore," then we don't push it.

None of the horror stories that my ex told me came true. She used to talk about our son putting holes in the wall or rubbing poop on them as well as breaking things. She also said he'd sneak into the fridge in the middle of the night, eat to the point of getting sick, and throw up. There was all this stuff that he just never did—only a couple of holes. When she told me all that, I just said, "All right, I guess we'll deal with it when it comes." Sure, it bothered me to hear about those problems, but my larger thought was, "He's my son, so deal with it. Try to figure out a way to do something."

Although my current wife was not exactly on board when I took custody of Henry, she has been amazing with him and is a big part of his progress. In my custody agreement, there was a clause that stated if I deployed for sixty days or more, Henry would go with his mom. I was scheduled to deploy for 120 days. Henry's mom had to have major surgery, so she couldn't take him. My wife offered to keep my son while I was deployed until his own mother had recovered enough to take him. My wife kept him for almost three months by herself while also taking care of our two children. I think not knowing what to expect or how he would fit in with our other kids may have scared her at first, but she has accepted him as part of our family. My son knows that he has two moms now.

*In the military, you never know what's going to happen. So you don't just always try to plan for anything. Things are just going to happen, and sometimes you just have to work through it. You got to find a way. You got to adapt. You have to do what Clint Eastwood said in **Heartbreak Ridge,** "I adapted and I overcame." Adapt and overcome.*

Fathers Faced with Custody Battles

Bobby, the next father profiled, had to fight for custody and became a strong advocate for his children, even though it has been an uphill battle. His words on these subjects alone are of value. As a psychologist, I find his story even more compelling because he epitomizes the idea that it is possible to change our life script. The idea of a "life script" is that as children, we develop ideas of who we are, how we fit in the world, and what we can expect from life and other people. Whether or not people think about it consciously, they end up replaying patterns in life for better or for worse. Conscious examination of these patterns helps people to decide what parts of them have value and what parts need a very deep "rewrite."

Bobby rewrote his life script on many levels, including not following in the footsteps of his parents or even his old footsteps, for that matter.

A Magician Living on Reality's Terms

The Backstory: Bobby is a magician, mental health advocate, comedian, and divorced father of two. He shared his journey, which includes handling his bipolar disorder, learning from three psychiatric hospitalizations, and advocating for his children.

"I don't want to live an illusion"—Bobby

Excerpts from his story of perseverance follow:

I saw a magician in grade school, and from that day forward I knew what I wanted to do the rest of my life. I could count on magic because it brought me applause and friendship. Growing up, I had a father who was both an alcoholic and a workaholic and a mom who was never around much. My parents divorced when I was fourteen, and I fell through the gap. I was the youngest of four, so I ended up just doing my own thing and trying to find an identity for myself. When I was old enough to be on my own, I moved a few states away to pursue my dream of being a magician.

But, everything just kind of came crashing down and I made my first suicide attempt at twenty. I swallowed a bottle of sleeping pills. To my surprise, I woke up three days later, in my own vomit. I thought I was a failure at everything—even killing myself. I had not yet learned to ask for help, and for some reason I didn't know there was a reason to live. I had just taken on a lot of the same principles my mom had followed so I thought, "When things don't go right, pick up and move—maybe that will solve the problem." So I moved to California and I tried to kill myself again one day in my garage, feeling lost and alone. Luckily, I did reach out for help, and my mother got me into a facility that really helped. I recognized I had a problem. The treatment gave me structure and some tools, but it never got to the root of the problem.

Let me fast-forward ahead. Eventually, I was going all over the country performing magic and sharing my personal story at big youth conferences. When my son was born, I decided to get off the road to have some balance, and I gave up a lucrative weekly income. I have no regrets. I ended up manufacturing illusions for magicians and building a business that grew until I had hundreds of customers and was shipping fun stuff around the world. It was fun until I ended up working eighteen-hour days, seven days a week.

During this period, Jay was still very little and my daughter was born. I became an absent husband and father and ended up destroying my marriage. During the time we were splitting up, there was a point that I was going bankrupt and had absolutely nothing. We didn't even know where the kids were going to live. My wife did know that she wanted to get away. Her sister stepped in and said she'd take the kids, and she kept them for about a year. They were devastated, and it broke my heart.

After we separated and the kids went to my sister-in-law's, it felt like everything in life was gone. The kids were gone, and, of course, all of a sudden I went from having a mate to her being gone too. Alcohol was a crutch for me. I

*had a breakdown and ended up in the hospital again. I was
diagnosed at that point as having bipolar. With that diagnosis,
I finally had something I could understand. I also told myself
to get as much as I could from the hospitalization itself; I was
open to learning tools such as positive self-talk.*

*Trying to get back on track, I turned to alcohol for a few
years, but all that did was get me more depressed. Finally,
one day I just woke up to the reality of it all. I said, "Wait a
second! I have this bipolar disorder and I can't even afford the
medicine. On top of that, now I am drinking. It's time to rip
the label off. I have to be in control of my thoughts—somehow, someway.*

*It took about a year or so, but I finally got the kids back.
They were in my custody for a few years, without a formal
agreement. My ex-wife lived in the area, so she saw them
sporadically. Because there was no custody agreement, one
day my ex just intercepted them and said, "I'm taking them,
and that's that." They remained with her, but I saw them
almost every weekend. She lives fifty miles from me. If I am
working out of town on the weekend, I get to see them on
Mondays and Wednesdays instead. So I drive one hundred
miles round-trip on Mondays to see them for a couple of
hours and do it again on Wednesdays. She does have official
custody now.*

*Jay has learning disabilities. His first IEP was developed in
kindergarten. He is in the ninth grade and still struggling. They
were going to pass him in ninth grade, and I said, "No way!
Not based on his grades. If you want to pass him, you're not
doing your job." I can't really change the educational system,
but I can be an advocate for him. I've had to dig in and learn
so much about the law. I have walked into schools with a
stack of files between twelve to eighteen inches high. I have
quoted the law to supervisors of special education when they
denied the right to an independent educational evaluation. I
know all about what is (or isn't) a Free and Appropriate Public
Education. I am very "hands-on," but it has been a struggle.*

My ex-wife says it's worthless going to these IEP meet-ings, and nothing we're going to do can change it. I might not be able to necessarily change it, but I can be an advocate and I can be a voice in that process. I can teach him how to advocate for himself too. They will at least hear what I have to say and what the law says. It's a matter of getting mad at some point, but still being willing to work with the school in that process.

Over the years, I've gotten my priorities in order a little bit better. I'm not perfect yet, but they are more focused on my children. I want to have custody of them full time. I know I am better for them. Their mom still, to this day, doesn't have insurance for my children, no heat and no hot water. I called Children and Youth over a month ago, and told them about the situation. They said as long as their mom is heating water on the stove, they can get a bath that way. Let me add that was the fourth call to them, and my children's guidance coun-selor also called on their behalf. The issue was never investi-gated, and I don't think their mother has ever been contacted to discuss matters.

I actually filed for a motion for guardian ad litem, and it basically gives the children their own attorney. I just gained that this past week. Now, the attorney has the right to go to both homes, check both situations out, and interview and talk to the kids. My next step is to go back to court and file a mod-ification hearing and have my kids sit down in the chambers and talk to the judge. The judge doesn't have to agree with the children, but has to legally listen to what they have to say.

I've had to switch perspectives and say, "You know what? I failed my marriage and I wasn't around for my kids or my marriage but I can move forward."

I am on Day 477 of sobriety. Drinking was a coping mechanism and a form of self-medication for me to numb the pain of being away from my kids. I dropped my kids off at their mother's tonight. It just dawned on me as I drove back home that my old self would have wanted to swing by the bar for some drinks on a "hard to get through" Sunday night. Wow! I was on my way home and not to a bar to drink my sadness away. I commended myself and also constantly remind and reward myself. This was the first time that I recognized that old craving wasn't there. It goes to show that habits can be changed through discipline.

Nothing has replaced my empty Sunday night feeling that I always feel without my kids. But it is certainly not as intense, and having a clear head about it is making me proud. The biggest thing is keeping a balance between not being overly confident or worrying whether I am going to relapse.

I have had the kids over the past several summers, and I absolutely love it. We go all over the place doing things together and making memories. I shouldn't say I overcompensate, but sometimes I look at it and think my father wasn't there for me, and I want to be there for them.

When I am out performing, I tell people, "Everything you see me do is just an illusion but what you hear me say is all reality. What I have told you is reality." The magic is in the fact that I am still here, and I know my purpose.

Genius Moments

While thinking about my time spent with Bobby and what he shared, I realized that he fit my personal definition for *strength*. What is being strong? To me, strength is "keeping going." It is not freedom from anxiety, depression, or even the urge to drink. It is the ability to keep trying despite these feelings. He says, "I'm always a work in progress." When he gets off track, he says, "No illusion and no judgment; just get back on track." He measures his progress by how far he has come, rather than becoming discouraged by what is still not right in his life. Some of Bobby's strategies and philosophies include:

- *Changing the script.* As Bobby explained, "I've had to switch perspectives and say, 'You know what, I failed in this area, and I failed in my marriage and I wasn't around for my kids or my marriage, but I can move forward and now I can plug in.' "He has been determined to change the script for himself, which included a poor view of himself, alcoholism, and being a workaholic. The last two of these were also part of his father's script. Bobby's new script includes a new personal identity. He knows who he is now and describes himself as a "part of the puzzle." By this, he refers to his role in the world of helping others with their own recovery.

- *Refusing to be labeled and stigmatized.* Bobby often says, "I am who I say I am." This wonderful phrase reflects his staunch refusal to accept other people's labels of who he is—what role he has to play in life. When performing magic, including at the hospital where he had been an inpatient himself, he exhorts people to "rip the label off." He adds that the label of alcoholic is another label that he refuses to wear. "Although it works for others, AA is not a program that works for me because of the labeling. I feel I am no longer alcoholic (so I won't stand up and say I am one). At the same time, I find it so important to remember where I was and where I never want to go back to."

- *Reframing angry thoughts.* Bobby states it was "magical" that he lost his anger connected to visitation schedules. "I used to get really pissed off because I felt like I was a built-in babysitter every weekend for my children so that my ex could go out and do whatever she wanted to do. I finally had to get to a point in my life where I realized she's missing out. I did reframe it and knew this was actually a positive because I got to be with my kids."

- *Using positive habits to change other habits.* Bobby is a strong believer in using positive approaches to change habits. He explained how he quit smoking at the urging of his children. "I wasn't working much and I had the urge for a cigarette all the time. What happened next was almost magical; it wasn't intentional. I picked up a camera and before I knew it, every time I had an urge for a cigarette I would go on a hike and do photography. I actually did a video on it; within six months, I would've smoked 10,000 cigarettes and I ended up clicking my shutter button 10,800 times. I believe finding those positive things helps you cope."

One of the most positive approaches used by Bobby was his decision to focus on forgiveness in his relationships with his parents. His comments are included in Chapter 4, so if you didn't already read them, they are worth backtracking for.

Fathers and Custody

The custody battle experiences of Bobby and some other fathers in this chapter are not surprising. A minority of fathers (estimated at between 10 and 15 percent) have sole custody of their children. This low figure reflects several factors, including the smaller number of fathers who fight for sole custody. However, women do win the majority of cases in the legal system.

Custody has been influenced by the "Tender Years Doctrine," a historical part of family law that stated a child who is between the ages of birth and four should be raised by the mother. This was replaced in the 1970s with "The Best Interests of the Child" doctrine. Jennifer Hook and Satvika Chalasani are among those who contend that the Tender Years doctrine still operates implicitly. This belief goes so far that the motives of fathers who want custody are often suspect, including the assumption that it is to avoid child support payments.

Mark, who we will meet next in the chapter, even took out a home equity loan to pay a lawyer to fight for more custody. He made it clear that he wanted more time with his children *without reducing child support*. He concluded:

> "There is a belief out there that a lot of fathers put up an initial fight for extra time with their kids for monetary reasons. This may be true, but it should never be assumed that it is only fathers."

The expectation that men are the primary breadwinners is a complicating factor in custody. Jennifer Hook and Satvika Chalasani reported that as few as 7 percent of solo fathers with custody received any child support.

Despite the stereotypical beliefs about men, single fathers consistently have been shown to be more involved with their children than married fathers and only slightly less involved than single mothers. The slight difference has been attributed to the fact that they are more likely to have full-time employment in comparison to single mothers. However, researchers demonstrated that when controlling for employment, household composition, and care arrangement differences, single fathers are just as attentive as single mothers.

Although this discussion has focused on comparing mothers versus fathers, it is important to remember that when possible, cooperative joint custody is often best for children.

A Silver Linings Kind of Guy

The Backstory: Mark, despite a very rough end of his marriage and legal struggles over custody, has stayed greatly involved in the lives of his daughter with Down syndrome and his son who is on the autism spectrum. They are facing adulthood, and he is right by their sides while rebuilding parts of his own life. His ex-wife and his children's ex-speech therapist are now married.

"Helicopter parent, maybe, but too bad!"—Mark

An excerpt from his story follows:

She was absolutely my best friend, and we did everything together. Dating was kind of a whirlwind because you just know when it is right. Looking back, I still would have made the same choice. She had trouble having children, but after a few miscarriages, we finally had our son.

After a while, we moved up north and built a beautiful house on a lake. Three months later, our daughter Katie was born with Down syndrome and a congenital heart defect that involved all four chambers of her heart. All I wanted for my daughter was for her to survive.

When they did the amniocentesis and found the Down syndrome, I never even blinked. I thought, "This is a gift." I knew these children had to be born to someone, and I was glad it was us. I used to teach kids with disabilities horseback riding so I always had a place in my heart for kids like this. My wife did not feel the same way at all.

When Katie was about three, a speech therapist started to come over to our house for my daughter. My son, Zach, was in preschool and started to have some issues and the speech therapist suspected he was on the spectrum. Sometimes, I thought my wife was too close to this speech therapist, but I did not really suspect anything was wrong because she was a morally grounded person. And, of course, he was a professional.

I think the tipping point for my wife was when Zach got the diagnosis. She suddenly started to withdraw from me and get really disengaged. One day, I asked her when she thought we should get the house painted, and she turned around and said, "I don't know if I even love you anymore!" For the next six months, she refused to tell me what was wrong. I repeatedly told her that we had too much at stake not to resolve this problem since we had two special-needs children, the house, and a business that was really taking off.

During this period, she even assured me once that we would not get divorced. I was relieved and thought she was just going through some bad personal stuff. I suggested, several times, that she get help. A month later, it wasn't better, so I asked her if she wanted a divorce. She said, "No! But you do!" I thought she was crazy. Two days later, I was served with divorce papers. I never suspected the truth, but in the back of my mind I used to wonder about the speech therapist. So she had plotted this. I am still extremely angry over how this all went down and how I was betrayed.

My kids are more important to me than anything, but the courts think the motive for fathers is not wanting to pay child support. I wanted co-custody of my children. I even had custody evaluations done, and they came back in my favor. But do you know how much it would have cost to go to trial?! I got a new attorney and eventually got a little better than the standard visitation. People assume that the mother is always the model citizen here. They say, "Oh, you poor thing; you have these kids with special needs."

The only thing that has changed in my wife's life is me. Her mom still lives right down the street, and she has all the supports she needs. And here I am trying to find my way in the wilderness. They are actually living in my house—the house on the lake that we built. I have to pick my kids up there! She is still really condescending to me and says she never really loved me and that we got married too soon. She had to create a reality in her head to justify what she did.

Insult has been added to injury many times. When Katie was having her second surgery to correct a heart problem, it was a very tense time. I asked if I could have the kids the evening before the surgery. My ex-wife said no and picked up the kids in a car with her mother and Dick, the speech therapist. I have always taken the high road, but I said to her, "How dare you deny me time with my kids on a night like this!" I was so angry that I couldn't sleep. The next day we were in the hospital, and this guy is there in the pre-op room! I have not slept and I am furious. I have to sit there as they evaluate my little three-year-old daughter, put her in a little wagon, and wheel her off to surgery.

When Zach was about eight, he mentioned that he was going to see some caves with his Boy Scout troop. I said, "Boy, that's cool! Tell me when and I will go too." A few weeks later, when he was getting into the tub, I saw a big bruise on his side and asked him about it. He said, "That's from when I slipped in the cave. Dick took me."

I think she made me out to be some sort of monster. I really believe she told Dick that I had no interest in the kids. Last year, he said to me that I was an impressive father because I go to all their events. Why wouldn't I?

Now Zach's in college. He struggled when he first got there; I think he thought it was like going to summer camp. We went up early and met with the disability support people on campus, and although they told him to make sure and come by, I knew he would not do that. Disability support services programs need to reach out to these students, but they don't.

As the semester went along, it was clear Zach was having issues and even missing tests. He got through the first semester but was put on probation.

This winter, he got off to a better start. When I drove him back to school after a break, he had two major tests (biology and chemistry) and a paper due. I was going to stay a couple days just to make sure he settled in, but there was a blizzard coming and I knew I had to head back home. But when I saw Zach the next day, I was actually scared for him. His eyes were red, his hair all frazzled, and he said, "I don't want to be back on academic probation." This raw determination struck me and I assured him this would not happen and I would do whatever I needed to do to see to it.

This experience has been profound for me as a father. Zach knew that I was not a good student myself. I bet that I had ADHD and I had to teach myself to study properly. Suddenly, he could identify with me just like I could identify with him. He started to call me every day three or four times a day because he wanted to report back to me what he did that day. I knew that kids like him wouldn't reach out to their classmates.

In addition to establishing this closeness, another thing I did was explain to Zach why it was so important to study with other students. He started to really come around. It did a lot for his confidence. I also told him to go through his tests and then go see his professors. I gave him the advice to "make them your best friends."

So, that's my son. Now let me explain a little about my relationship with my daughter. Recently, my brother was getting married again, and I was glad that I would not have to worry about finding the right dress. I had a cool party dress we'd bought last year for a niece's wedding. At the time, it was snug, but I thought Katie could wear it again if she didn't gain any weight.

On the wedding day, I was helping Katie get dressed. That is a skill that does not come naturally and I am sometimes embarrassed to have to deal with it. This dress was not simple, but I had it all figured out and was helping her pull it on. It was not going on very easily, and then I heard the loud rip. I worked myself into a state of anger and helplessness, although I was careful to keep my feelings to myself. I called my sister to cancel since there was no time to fix the dress, and she assured me that it didn't matter what my daughter wore. But it did to me.

That's when my private and brief "poor me" slide began. I thought about the fact that it is hard enough that Katie looks different due to the Down syndrome but it would be worse to have her dressed differently than others. (While I was feeling sorry for myself, my daughter was fine and couldn't have cared less about the dress.) I felt bad that she couldn't be like other seventeen-year-old girls and look cool in the latest fashions.

I was allowing myself to run the whole self-pity spectrum, including thinking that Katie will never get married, let alone date or have a family of her own one day. Zach is twenty and hasn't had a date yet, so I added this to my self-pity pile. I ignored the fact that I actually believe he will meet a good woman one day. So I wallowed in this crappy thinking for a while; then I had a moment of clarity.

It dawned on me that we were a team and that our team would all wear casual clothes to the wedding. I remembered that we have to play the game of life with different rules and a different skill set. Together, we wore khaki shorts and matching T-shirts from the local university.

I feel like the luckiest father alive for having the kids that I have. My situation is lonely, challenging, and disappointing, yet I have a purpose. Children with disabilities are incredible gifts, and those of us blessed with them see that, even though it isn't always clear. Having the opportunity to learn and to love in a way I had never known before is quite unique.

Genius Moments

Mark is a genius at starting over, staying engaged, and forging ahead despite bad feelings about how his marriage ended and the aftermath. Some of his strategies and philosophies include:

- *Keeping the faith.* Mark explains that faith is central for him: "I am going to be blunt here. If you don't have God in your life, you won't survive. You have got to believe there is a bigger plan here. My faith is what has gotten me through this. I have believed since the day my kids were born that they are gifts."

- *Keeping discouragement away.* Mark explained his strategies for coping with discouragement: "Sometimes I get discouraged because I work seven days a week to make up for my post-divorce financial situation. I can also get a little discouraged because I want to meet a woman to bring balance to my life. But I keep thinking, 'Tomorrow is a new day, and so many good things are going to happen.' I feel uncomfortable letting things get me down. I remind myself that I am going to be horribly ashamed one day if I let these things get me down because something good is going to happen. And that will be God finally showing up yet again."

- *Taking the high road.* Mark had to swallow a lot of his own anger in order to stay well engaged with his kids. "Taking the high road simply means putting my kids' needs, wants, and feelings ahead of my own. When my ex would throw up a roadblock, I would never confront her. And I decided to let sleeping dogs lie. I felt it was better to sacrifice in the short term for a better long term. I think at the end of the day that I'm going to wake up and look at myself in the mirror and know that I did the right thing."

- *Being a helicopter dad.* Mark rejects the notion of there being anything wrong with this. "When my daughter was preparing to enter fifth grade, I had been paying close attention to what needed to be going on in school. It was becoming more obvious that the school was pretty much just doing the basics. I've spent time in the classroom and in the special education classrooms for both of my children since they were in kindergarten. I'll wear the label of helicopter parent proudly because it is very needed in elementary and secondary school. Perhaps someone being in the 'helicopter' watching is needed in college too." Mark makes a good point that there aren't enough services for students with special needs, and his determination to advocate for his children is admirable.

Coping with Inequitable Custody Arrangements

Fathers are likely to have less extensive custody than mothers for more than one reason. Sometimes there is a noncontentious divorce, and the divorcing couple continues a pattern in which the child's mother continues to be the primary caregiver. This poses different challenges than when a custodial decision seems to be skewed in favor of the mother even though this is not in the best interests of a child. This section will address those circumstances first—i.e., fathers who are relegated to the sidelines when they want to be integral parts of their children's lives.

The last two fathers we met in this chapter, Bobby and Mark, had much in common with many noncustodial fathers. They fought hard through legal channels and also evaded the common pitfalls and obstacles that cause many to slip into a less vital role. Some of these include:

- anger and resentment due to custody outcomes;
- feeling like an ATM machine or respite care provider instead of a father;
- being unaware of rights for noncustodial parents;
- frustration over a child's lack of affection or apparent preference for the other parent.

When it comes to coping with unfairness in life, the two paths are fighting injustice and finding a way to live well despite it. That is not to say that the two paths are truly incompatible; some people are able to fight legal battles for years while preserving the quality of their lives.

Providing strategies for fighting custody decisions is beyond the scope of this book, although the book is full of solo role models who have fought and won very tough battles in life. This book includes stories of many parents who have wrestled with anger and resentment for lack of "fairness" in life. They include solos whose children's disabilities occurred as a result of medical negligence, parents whose partners walked away and made themselves inaccessible, and solos whose families unfairly blamed them for their life choices or for causing their children's disabilities.

For many (other than those who continue to pursue legal proceedings), coping with unfair custody outcomes requires calling upon the same philosophies and strategies that enable people to cope with other painful, maddening circumstances that do not permit redress. As Bobby and Mark demonstrated, the key is to not let your anger and resentment be an obstacle in your parenting.

Fathers like Bobby and Mark, who can concentrate on being the best fathers possible despite negative feelings toward their exes, remind me of the wisdom of David Burns, a leading figure in the field of cognitive therapy. Burns has written about how a change of behavior can lead to a change of feelings. The feeling of wanting to withdraw due to anger or resentment is tamed by simply staying engaged despite those feelings. As Bobby portrayed, during his initial engagements with his kids, he felt as if he was being used by his ex as a respite worker. But he hung in there despite those feelings. Over time, those feelings became irrelevant.

The Educational Rights of Noncustodial Parents

Feeling powerless as a noncustodial parent about your child's education does not mean that you actually have no power. It is important to bear in mind that noncustodial parents may very well be entitled to *parent rights* under IDEA (the Individuals with Disabilities Education Act). This legislation was the foundation for ensuring that children with disabilities are guaranteed access to a free and appropriate public education (FAPE).

IDEA is federal law, so it applies in all states. It sets out the legal rights of parents during the special education process, which include the rights:

- to be members of the IEP team,

- to be provided adequate notification of team meetings,
- to be involved in plans for initial evaluation and special education placement,
- to participate in discussions about the appropriate disability label for your child, and to see results of testing the school does,
- to collaborate with teachers and therapists in determining appropriate academic goals for your child,
- to receive progress reports,
- to participate in due process during disputes about certain aspects of a child's special education program

If a couple has joint legal custody, divorce (in general) does not have a bearing on the exercise of these rights. Of course, things get complicated when parents with joint legal custody cannot agree about aspects of their child's education. Varying state laws affect the outcomes of such disputes; some allow parents to separately file for a due process hearing, whereas others require them to resolve the disagreement before filing. Some states resolve disputes over IDEA parental rights by turning to the language in the divorce decree.

Carolyn Anderson and Beth-Ann Bloom discussed some additional issues in their article, "Divorce: It Can Complicate Children's Special Education Issues." They write that even with joint legal custody, school districts may proceed with special education with the signature of one parent. They also point out that the fact that one parent may have physical custody is immaterial when it comes to deciding matters when parents share legal custody.

When it comes to advocating for your child's best educational opportunities, I want to touch on the experiences of one more solo father who serves as a terrific role model. I have never met him, but I sometimes think about him when I am tired and not feeling all that stoic:

Yu Xukang is a forty-year-old solo father of a child with disabilities in Sichuan Province in China. This man wakes up at 5 am each day to carry his son on a four-and-a-half-mile trek across rugged terrain to get him to school. Then he walks back home and works as a farmer until it is time to pick his son up from school. At the end of the school day, he walks another nine miles (round trip) with his three-foot-tall son in a basket on his back.

This father explained why he exerts himself to ensure his son receives an education: "I know my son is physically disabled, but there is nothing wrong with his mind...however, I couldn't find any school here with the facilities to accept him and was constantly rejected." So when he finally found a school that accepted his son, he vowed to get his son to school each day no matter what. He concluded his interview (published in a *Huffington Post* article by Eleanor Goldberg) by talking about his dream for his son to go to college and added, "I know he will achieve great things."

එ

Chapter 6

එ

Bereavement:
Solos and Their Grieving Children

When one person is missing, the whole world seems empty.
—*Pat Schweibert,* Tear Soup: A Recipe for Healing after Loss

IF YOU HAVE already faced bereavement, I don't need to tell you that grieving goes far beyond the loss of your hopes and dreams for what might have been. And, the hurt of your children's losses often makes the process exponentially more painful.

There is no right way to grieve and no set time period when grieving is typically complete. Although each person copes with grief through a highly personalized mourning process, it is often helpful to see how others respond. This chapter therefore includes the stories of two fathers whose wives died and describes their experiences in finding ways to live with devastating losses and help their children to do the same. These two very generous fathers were open to telling their stories for the purpose of helping others. The first we will meet is Joseph, whose wife had a sudden catastrophic medical event. We will also meet a father whose wife had been seriously ill for a lengthy period of time but had not been expected to die. Both mothers were deeply loved, as well as exceptionally involved with their children.

After presenting these two stories of bereavement and thoughts on the complexities of parenting grieving children, this chapter fo-cuses on better understanding adult grief. This includes information on differentiating grief from depression and complicated grief (since these often merit professional help). The chapter concludes with information on responding to grieving children in general, and children with developmental disabilities in particular. I have included many ideas and strategies to help readers faced with the incredibly painful situation of responding to their grieving children's needs while coping with their own anguish.

Transformations

The Backstory: Joseph lost his wife suddenly one evening a few years before my interview with him. Until that tragedy, Joseph had been the breadwinner, and his wife was very happy to be a stay-at-home mother to two children entering adolescence. Joseph's wife was devoted to helping their son with his significant communication, academic, social, and emotional delays. Life changed in the blink of an eye. Along with overwhelming heartbreak, Joseph found himself facing enormously difficult logistics. For example, for the first year and a half, Joseph drove the children to a school twenty miles away before driving an additional eighty (one way) just to make it to work each day.

"Lindsay isn't gone and her spirit is still watching over us. I told her, 'Lindsay, your dying isn't getting you out of raising these kids, and you've got to help me.'"—Joseph

Excerpts from Joseph's story follow:
That day she stayed at home with a stomach virus. As usual, I worked overtime and came home very late. She was awake and said, "I'm feeling better and I think I can take the kids to school tomorrow. I'm going to bed." I was doing some things on the computer and getting ready for bed myself when I heard her in the bathroom gagging or choking. All of a sudden, she just fell backwards and collapsed. To be honest, I thought she was joking. I'm like, "Come on, Lindsay, knock it off...I'm tired and I gotta go to bed." But, within just a minute, I was on the phone with 911 and I was doing CPR. She

had aspirated and her brain did not have enough oxygen. In my wildest dreams I never imagined that I would be in this position. I used to imagine us in an RV, traveling the country visiting our kids and our grandkids one day.

I have Marfan syndrome and two artificial heart valves and an artificial ascending aorta, so I always thought I would die first. I felt like, "Okay, God, you are not following the plan that Lindsay and I had." But I know she's not coming back, no matter how much I bargain or plead or get angry. My whole life has been turned upside down and I'm still grieving.

To understand more of what it meant to lose Lindsay, you need to understand my earlier life. When I was a kid, my dad sometimes called me "stupid." I remember one time in particular that we had to pick blackberries off a bush. I was about seven. I had those thick Coke-bottle glasses, and I missed a bunch because I couldn't see them. And my dad said, "What are you, stupid?"

The name-calling may not have happened that often, but the belief that I was stupid and unworthy sunk in. I carried that with me (even though I was a straight-A student in high school). Also, when I was younger, I was extremely introverted. I didn't express myself, and I tried to fit in with what people thought would be acceptable. With me having Marfan syndrome and being so tall, I wanted to blend in— but I still stood out. So people would make fun of me. The Adamm's Family was popular on TV at the time. You don't know how damaging it was to be called Lurch all the time, and I couldn't help it— my back looked kind of hunched. I felt ugly and bad about myself.

In my thirties, I started having heart problems, and also started changing. I (finally) thought, "I'm not stupid and I am worthy and I want to get married and have a family." That's when I met Lindsay. She was a very outgoing person, and she made me more outgoing. Boy, we meshed well together. I carry that still with me today. Here's one of the things I was afraid of when she died. I thought, "God, I can't go back to being that single person that I was." Later, I realized that I'm not that person anymore. What Lindsay had brought to the table is part of me now.

I tried to remember how it was when I was nine years old and my dad died. I've come to realize the best thing I can do is provide stability for my kids, because that's what my mom did for me. In the very beginning, I lay in my bed and didn't want to do anything but die. But after a time, I realized that the kids needed me to function. I heard, "Dad, what are we going to do for dinner?" I had to go to the store even though I didn't want to—I just did it.

As the man, I wasn't in the caregiving state of mind. I was the breadwinner. My wife loved taking care of the kids and quit her teaching job so that she could stay home with them. On the weekends, I always had daddy-daughter and daddy-son time. But, when it came to the kids, she took the lead. Whenever she wanted to do something, I'd just say, "Oh, that's good." When there were IEP meetings for our son, Lindsay would only want me to go so I knew what was going on. Now I have to think differently. If my kids have a play, then I've got to be at that play (no matter if I have to work). If I'm not, there's not going to be anyone there for them.

My son is emotionally and educationally delayed. He's in the seventh grade now, but he's reading at a kindergarten level. Now when I go to the IEP meetings, I have to participate and help make decisions. And even though I don't really know what the proper academic thing to do is, I know him better than anybody else. He is going through a rebellious stage—at least I hope it's just a stage. He is full of frustration, and it is directed mostly at me. At least he is still behaving in school.

My daughter has some issues with her heart because of the Marfan syndrome, and it petrifies me because it brings back my own issues with my heart. So now her aorta is starting to dilate, but it's not at the point where she needs surgery yet. This is in the future, and things may even improve. She broke down in tears when we talked to the doctor. She said, "Dad, I'm scared." I can't fix it, so I just held her and patted her and said, "We will figure things out: we'll talk to doctors." This is where Mom would have stepped in. I am not as good at this as she was, but I have to get better. It feels like you're carrying the weight of the world.

I was driving two hundred miles roundtrip every day for about a year and a half; finally now the kids can take a bus. It's making my life easier. I'm in the car a lot by myself. Sometimes, I turn off the radio and have a conversation or (an argument) with my wife about something. I'm sure she's saying, "Even when I'm dead, you're blaming me for stuff."

I now realize that life is temporary and is going to end. I ask myself, "What are you going to do between now and then? Do you want to do something that is significant with the kids, or are you just going to let it pass away?" Now I think about how Lindsay used to enjoy life and live like there was no tomorrow. She was a bigger kid than the kids. Sometimes that irritated me, but now I see it differently. I want to do things with the kids, and I'm looking forward to the summer. I'm renting an RV for a week and taking the kids to Stone Mountain, Six Flags Over Georgia, Gatlinburg, Pigeon Forge, and Dollywood. We have been talking about doing this since my wife died over two and a half years ago, and something has always seemed to get in the way of us going. This July we are doing it.

I'm still grieving over the loss of my wife. I still miss her. But life is moving on without her whether I like it or not. I've accepted the fact that there are things that cannot be controlled, but what can be controlled is how we respond. I never dreamed I would be a single parent raising two teens—one with special needs—but I am doing it. It's not easy, but it's also not forever. I don't want to rush through this part of life just because it is hard. I want to look back on my life one day, just as my mother did, and be able to say, "I did a good job. I was always there for my kids."

Genius Moments

Although Joseph might quibble at the idea of having some genius at living with this immense loss, I believe it is true. There are many paths to living with grief. There is a lot to be learned from Joseph and the way he handled his grief without letting it rob him of all that has been precious to him. Some of Joseph's strategies and philosophies include:

- *Continuing to seek input from his wife.* Joseph did not let the death of his wife keep him from seeking her guidance. Referring to the early weeks after her death, he described himself as not knowing what he was doing and added, "I was literally taking it day by day, minute by minute. And I would ask, 'Lindsay, what do I do now?' Things just started falling into place.'" He no longer needs this type of assistance from her, but still actively engages her when faced with weighty decisions, such as those pertaining to his daughter's cardiac care. Understanding that there is value in points of view very different from his own, he tries to incorporate his wife's style in order to make the wisest decisions. Joseph described his wife as a Taurus who charged ahead while he would advocate for a great deal of thought. He added, "Now that I'm by myself, I can't just sit and not make decisions. I've balanced myself out."

- *Opening himself to enjoyment when possible.* As Joseph explained: "I don't want to be alone but I don't want to be with anybody other than Lindsay. I feel like if I were with somebody else I would be cheating on her. I know it's not true, but that's how I feel. I don't know what's going to happen in my future. Will I get married again? I can't predict that right now. If a person crosses my path, I will try to be open to that. And I will think, 'Wow this isn't the person I thought it would be... but maybe.' In the meantime, I'm not going to be miserable. Eventually, I'll be sitting at home and my daughter will be off doing stuff with her friends and my son will be at the point where he doesn't need me much. I think that's going to be a turning point to say, 'Okay, I can't sit here by myself. I'm lonely now, and, yes, it would be nice to have a companion.' But, right now, my life is full with my kids and my work, and so I'm not lonely in that I don't have anything to do."

- *Changing but not abandoning his spiritual beliefs.* Joseph struggled with his religious beliefs as a result of this tragedy. He sought answers, in part, by reading. He explained: "Through it all, what I have personally come to believe is that God did not have a role in what happened to my wife; in other words, God didn't cause or prevent it. Life is what life is. It was created to be a certain thing, and there's uncertainty in it. We're all a part of something. You're a part of me, I'm a part of you, and we're all part of each other. Love each other and don't treat each other so badly."

- *Creating a haven.* Joseph described himself as feeling, sometimes, as if he carried the weight of the world. Like many solo parents, he emphasized the importance (and difficulty) of self-care. He said, "The first step in taking care of your kids is to take care of yourself. I'm trying to turn the house into a place that's comfortable for me. I built a front patio with plants around it because I like gardening. I put a little wrought iron fence around it, and it looks really looks nice. My next project is redoing the floors in the house. Then I want to make my bedroom a little oasis for myself. I want to make it a tropical-looking place with an exercise and reading area. It's going to be my place to get away and to just sit and read. It will encourage me to be healthier because I don't really take care of myself. I was always harping on my wife to take care of herself."

- *Allowing transformation.* Joseph appears to intuitively understand the essence of grieving and healing as described by Elisabeth Kübler-Ross and David Kessler (2007), who wrote: "The reality is that you will grieve forever. You will not 'get over' the loss of a loved one; you will learn to live with it. You will heal and you will rebuild yourself around the loss you have suffered. You will be whole again but you will never be the same. Nor should you be the same nor would you want to" (p. 230).

Joseph is not trying to get over the loss of his wife; he keeps her very present while also building a different life. T. D. Stewart (1977) wrote about identity building after massive physical injury. I think Joseph's experience with the injury of grief ran parallel:

> "My personality...was like a plate—it was shattered; I had to reassemble a new one, but I used a lot of the old pieces."

Joseph is putting together a new identity that includes changing his public persona with piercings for earrings, which his wife would never have approved of. Joseph described this change as symbolic for him continuing to develop as an individual. Meanwhile, he took his dream with Lindsay to go off in his RV with her, and, rather than totally disconnect from it, he transformed it into a goal for him and his kids.

Joseph demonstrates what many consider key elements of adjustment in bereavement. He faces, (rather than runs from) the pain of his loss. One of the most common misconceptions about grief is that if you just ignore the pain, it will go away. This will actually only make it worse in the long run. He stays connected with his wife's essence and knows that adjustment is not about trying to forget the life you had. Then there is the task of adjusting to living in an environment without her physical presence and using supports and help. He takes his time with the mourning process and doesn't rush himself. As will be discussed in more detail later in this chapter, these same elements are also important for children who are faced with the death of a parent.

Understanding "Normal" Grief Better

Many parents find models of grief useful when they are trying to make sense out of what they, or their children, are experiencing. As discussed in Chapter 2, Elisabeth Kübler-Ross observed that five stages of grief are commonly experienced: denial, anger, bargaining, depression, and acceptance. Many find this sequence of stages useful for understanding adjustment to other kinds of losses, including the "perfect" child we all imagined we would have.

John Bowlby (1980) also described different stages of response to loss. The general public knows less about this framework, but it, too, can bring some clarity to bewildering situations. The stages Bowlby identified include the following:

- numbness,
- yearning and searching,
- disorganization and despair, and
- reorganization.

While grief models offer a good place to start if you are trying to understand the basics of grieving, the reality is that grieving is more complex and that we don't "progress" through stages of grief as if we were recovering from an illness. As a close friend said to me, "You never get over it. But you do learn to live with it."

It is very important to understand that grief models only provide a basic understanding of how people *often* experience grief. You don't have to go through each definitive stage, or pass through stages in a particular sequence, in order to heal. As discussed in Chapter 2, although some find distinct stages of grief, the process is really more cyclical. People are often taken by surprise by strong feelings of grief even after they feel they have worked through a mourning process. Although it may feel as if the scab is pulled off fresh grief, emotional healing occurs more quickly than anticipated.

Differences between Grief and Depression

How can you tell if you are grieving normally or have developed a depression that may indicate a need for professional treatment? It is helpful to first look at what we know about "uncomplicated grief." This term is used by professionals for grief that progresses naturally to a point where a person can live with the loss.

Uncomplicated Grief

Uncomplicated grief often begins with gut-wrenching pain that includes a mixture of feelings such as regret, anger, loss, guilt, shock, and being overwhelmed, as well as images of your loved one popping into your mind at random times. At first, this is typically unrelenting. (Note: although typical, such pain does *not* have to be present and is not necessary to come to terms with the loss of a loved one.) After a while, there are often waves and bursts of anguish, but there are also moments of positive emotions such as joy from a memory, comfort from others, or sometimes relief. Such feelings often stir up guilt if you think you are forgetting your loved one or are being disloyal somehow.

The bursts of anguish that are intermingled are intense and frightening and often feel as if they are coming out of the blue. If you have been emotionally stable most of your life, this may make you feel scared or as if you are out of control. During acute grief, it is normal to cry intensely, have trouble eating or sleeping, and to be preoccupied with your loss.

Stress can often manifest itself in the body in the form of sickness. Symptoms such as stomach pain, headaches, anxiety, fatigue, weight loss or gain, and trouble sleeping or eating can all be common experiences during the grieving process. Memory problems are also frequently experienced and can be disquieting.

It is not uncommon for the bereaved to think they see, hear, or feel the presence of a deceased loved one. You might feel like you're going crazy if you have these kinds of experiences. Many have called them hallucinations, while others describe them in more spiritual or supernatural terms. It doesn't matter; they are common in grief. Historically, it was thought that to grieve in a healthy way, we needed to "let go" of those who have died. However, new research is suggesting that it is our way of maintaining a bond or relationship with someone incredibly important in our lives. For many, these sorts of encounters with deceased loved ones can be interpreted as a positive experience, since it can help one to cope with the loss.

Normal grief progresses to a point called integrated grief. Often, this begins within a few months. The bereaved person has an increasing ability to engage in life while also staying connected to the deceased and still missing him or her. Joseph's story offers a good example of integrated grief. A very helpful discussion of this concept can be found in Nancy Berns's TED talk entitled *The Space between Joy and Grief.* (See the reference section; I recommend listening to

Berns's thoughts on the fallacy of seeking closure and the art of carrying joy and grief together.)

Grief can't be fixed by taking medication. However, many doctors may suggest an antidepressant or other medications as a way to buffer the pain of grief. This is almost essential for some people. I believe in the judicious use of anti-anxiety and antidepressant medications, however. Sometimes they are very beneficial, and other times they are overused and block an individual's access to feelings for too long.

What helps?

- Tell your story of loss over and over again. This means talking to others and sharing your experiences, even if you don't normally do those things.
- Cry an ocean of tears if you need to (without anyone telling you to get over it).
- Be with others even if you feel like just being alone.
- Accept help.
- Find ways to stay connected with your deceased spouse/ partner.

Complicated Grief and Depression

About ten percent of the population experiences "complicated grief," following bereavement. With this type of grief, normal life doesn't resume and integration of the loss never occurs. The term *complicated grief* has been adopted to describe a state in which grief-stricken feelings remain center stage for a long time (perhaps a year or two) and an intense state of mourning disrupts your everyday routine and your ability to maintain relationships in your life.

Depression is typically considered to be normal after the loss of a loved one, as long as it doesn't last too long. Even though there isn't really a "normal" amount of time to grieve, the fifth edition of the *Diagnostic and Statistical Manual* suggests that anything past two months may be an indication of a depressive disorder. This manual is the guide for psychiatrists and other allied health professionals. The length of this "normal" grieving period was not based in science as much as general consensus, so this guideline needs to be considered accordingly.

How can you tell grief and depression apart? Grief and major depression share many of the same characteristics, including loss of appetite, trouble sleeping, and sadness. The major difference, however, is that grief tends to be "trigger related," which means those symptoms occur when you are in the presence of something that reminds you of your late loved one. In the case of depression (professionally referred to as major depressive disorder), the symptoms are constant and not related to any external event or experience. In the case of grief, a person might feel better when he or she is distracted by work or surrounded by friends and family. In the case of depression, the person is rarely able to function in day-to-day routines, no matter what is happening in his or her life.

People with clinical depression are unable to enjoy life. Sometimes, if untreated, this depression can last for many years or carry a heightened risk of suicide. The criteria for major depressive disorder found in Chapter 4 can provide readers with additional guidance.

People who have clinical depression and/or complicated grief need therapy. One reason is that thought processes are affected and self-destructive thinking that appears logical to you remains unchallenged. These thoughts are not necessarily self-healing. Talk therapy is important, and antidepressant medication may need to be considered.

Parents need to be aware that it is possible for their children to have clinical depression or complicated grief. They also need to know that depression manifests differently in children. Sometimes children express their depression through complaints of not feeling well such as frequent stomach-aches. Other common signs include new problems with refusing to go to school, acting out, and feeling listless. Depression in children leads to similar risks as in adulthood, and severe depression can lead to suicide attempts even in young children. When in doubt, consult your child's doctor or a mental health professional. Complicated grief can also occur with children and may include thoughts such as feeling responsible for a parent's death.

Counselors and Bereavement Groups

Counseling can be very helpful for people struggling with grief. There are often things that need to be said at these times that people feel reluctant to say to friends or family members, no matter how understanding they might be. Many regard counselors as supports that are natural to use during the grief process. They can help you get your bearings during the first months (or years) if you feel as if you are in a fog or as if you are sleepwalking through your life. They can also help with the guilt of moving forward, regrets, and many other facets of grieving.

Although individual grief counseling can be very helpful, some people respond better to bereavement groups. I have known people who found it invaluable to connect with others who have similar feelings. Some people also find some comfort and companionship in these groups when they cannot bear to be with those who do not understand the ongoing pain of bereavement. They may also learn important coping strategies by participating in a group.

For some, a bereavement group serves as an important support anchor in their lives, especially if the group meets on a consistent basis. Sometimes sympathy from friends and family runs out before grieving does. A group provides a place where you can let grief take its natural course, even if it is slower than others expect of you. It can be a powerful and validating experience to feel that others understand the kind of pain you are feeling and how so much of life has changed. I have known people to make lasting friendships in such groups. Some groups even get together over holidays.

Of course, not everyone who attends a bereavement group benefits. Some find them depressing. However, they offer such potential that they are absolutely worth a try. I always think it is useful to try more than one since groups vary, and you may "click" very well with one and not another. (The same holds true when looking for a grief counselor.)

You can often locate a bereavement group fairly easily by searching the Internet or by contacting local hospitals and houses of worship. Most communities have several options to choose from. For those who can't find the right fit in their community or who naturally gravitate to online support groups, there are many good possibilities. GriefNet.org is an important resource that has two websites and more than fifty e-mail grief support groups that focus on specific types of losses. They have a "widowed with kids" group, as well as many others, including one for those who are widowed and gay—although they welcome all members to all groups. Similarly, they have groups for those who have lost a spouse or partner due to suicide, substance abuse, etc.

GriefNet.org is directed by a clinical psychologist who is also a certified traumatologist. It is a nonprofit organization, and is monitored by volunteers to ensure quality of support. They do request a ten-dollar monthly fee but do not turn anyone away. They have a companion site for children, KIDSAID.com.

Before turning our focus to the grief of children, I would like to share the words of a mother whom I knew well during the time that her husband was battling a terminal illness as well as during her initial years of grieving. When she sent her account, she added a note that her daughter had just gotten married and that she had been dating a widower from her church for some time and had just gotten engaged herself.

"Learning to live again after the death of a spouse is a day-to-day lesson and is even more challenging when children with disabilities or chronic disease are involved.

"The tenth anniversary of my husband's death is quickly approaching. We were married for 15 years and 364 days, as he went to be with our Lord one day prior to our sixteenth wedding anniversary. My husband, Rick, was diagnosed June 25, 2001, with a rare brain tumor and was not supposed to live through the next three years, but by the grace of God, he lived until June 24, 2004. We were both forty years old at the time of his death. Together we have been given the gift of three beautiful children: two daughters and a son, who is the youngest. The children were thirteen, ten, and eight at the time of my husband's death. All three have various medical conditions: the oldest, Chiara malformation; the second, congenital heart defects and neurologic syncopy (three surgeries so far); the third, type 1 diabetes since age two.

"When Rick went to heaven, part of him remained with me and part of me went with him. As two become one in marriage, that "one" seems to be divided when one spouse dies. I felt as if my heart actually hurt and had a hole in it.

"I knew that I needed strength to be fully present to care for our three children. That strength came from God and Rick. I knew that I was never truly alone and had help from above. There were days when caring for our children's medical conditions, helping them to grieve, taking care of myself, and doing everyday tasks exhausted me mentally, physically, and emotionally. Unless you actually have lived this life experience, it is difficult to explain to anyone.

"When Laura asked me to write a few paragraphs, I was humbled and asked God if this was what He wanted for me to do. Then, as I began to write, my son, who has type 1 diabetes, had his first ever hypoglycemic episode, which was the result of pancreatitis. Once again I needed to be present for him.

"I, too, lost my father suddenly when he was forty. I learned a lot from watching my mom and how she raised me and three younger sisters. I knew when my husband was diagnosed that he wouldn't be on this earth long. I prayed for extra time with him so that we could make memories as a family. I knew that I wanted to be a stay-at-home mom and be present for our children as they grew up. My prayer was answered.

"The grace of God, surrounding myself with good people, reading books, and prayer are the things that helped me to get to this point in my life. An experience that happened about a month before my husband's death brought much peace and comfort. This occurred around my fortieth birthday. My husband and I were each praying in different locations of our home at the same time, but not realizing that we were doing so. We both asked God if my husband's time on earth was nearing an end. Soon after this, we were both in the kitchen looking out the window at a beautiful sunset. I told my husband that I was praying and what I was asking. As

I told him, the sun went behind clouds, and I knew what the answer was—he would be going soon.

"My husband put his arms around my waist as we were looking at the sunset and said, 'I was asking God if I was going soon. God said that my work here is almost done and that I have much work to do and many people to help and that I will be very busy when I get to heaven. I am going soon, but you will be fine. I am to save four seats at Jesus's right hand for you and our children in the future.' My husband had no recollection of saying that afterwards. I knew in my heart that everything was going to be okay. An unexplainable peace and comfort enveloped me. My husband then said that every time I looked at a sunset he would be looking back at me. When he died a month later, I knew right when his spirit left him.

"This gift of peace from God has carried me through the past ten years. Knowing that He is in control and has the greater plan is comforting to me. I know that I am never truly alone and can ask Him any questions, and He always responds. He doesn't always answer the way that I had hoped, but the challenges always end up working to prosper us and bring Him glory. I am loved and never alone. I have my husband, who also is there guiding me. God's grace is what has carried me through these challenging times."

Modeling a Life Worth Living

The Backstory: Paul and Shaina (his wife of many years) had a long and happy marriage while raising their son who has an autism spectrum disorder. Although his wife was ill for many years, her death was sudden and unexpected. He also shared breaking the news and fathering his grieving son. The second part of his story includes dating and moving toward marriage.

"When I lost my job, I remember just saying to Shaina, 'I don't know what we're going to do about my work and I was seeing all the bills coming in.' And she said, 'We're going to do

what we always do. We are going to pick ourselves up, dust ourselves off, and move forward. We always have and we always will!' It's so funny that I would keep those words a month and a half later... I actually used them in her eulogy."—Paul

The following are excerpts from Paul's life story:

I grew up in a family of disability. My mother was diagnosed with multiple sclerosis when I was in ninth grade, and it slowly progressed to where she's spent the last five years in a nursing home. We were an average family. My father sold aluminum siding for a living and traveled a lot. When he was around, he spent a lot of time with me and did a lot of things. I met Shaina just a couple months shy of her sixteenth birthday. We were friends as well as boyfriend and girlfriend. I used to joke that we got married because I just didn't feel like dating around.

Our son was the middle one of five pregnancies and the only one who made it to term. Let me tell you the story of his birth—I owe it to our dog. After getting pregnant and losing the baby yet again, my wife became very depressed. So that's when her diabetes just broke open, and she was told that she couldn't have a kid until she got the diabetes under control. This depressed her more, which made the diabetes worse, and it just kept going. It got to a point where she didn't want to get out of bed anymore.

I didn't know what to do until my sister-in-law called and said that friends had found a dog on the side of the road. So, I went down to the animal shelter and met this loveable dog that somebody had just abandoned. I took her home, and my wife said, "What am I supposed to do with this?!" I said, "Take care of her; she needs you, so you gotta take care of her." Three months later, we were given the okay to try getting pregnant again. Amazing what a little doggie will do! Eli was conceived in two months.

When it came to our son, we truly were partners. But, Shaina was the one who would go over the IEPs with a fine-

toothed comb. She'd say, "Take that out, put that in. I want it this way—this is the way it is supposed to be!" She had a bit of a temper, and I used to joke when I went to these meetings that I wasn't necessarily there to support her but to keep her from jumping over the table at you if you decide to give her a hard time. She was a momma bear. With our son, we've had a series of angels who have come along when we didn't know (after the diagnosis) what to do.

My wife had many medical problems, including adult onset diabetes. We would discover later that she was an endocrine mess and ended up with Graves disease and a very unusual kidney condition with premature aging of the kidney cells. When she finally had to go on dialysis, it was tough. She was about forty-one and our son was just about nine. She was on dialysis for about six years. Her father had had a transplant for kidney problems and died from complications less than six months after the transplant. So, this made her scared about getting a transplant.

Shaina got the call for the transplant in December. She went into the hospital and had the transplant, but there were complications. She had hemorrhaged. It wasn't until June of that following year that I could really take her home. Then everything went great until October 11, 2012. I remember the date because her birthday was October 10. That's when the train started derailing.

On the tenth, I took her and our son out, and we had a wonderful dinner to celebrate her fiftieth birthday. All the family was coming, and we were having a surprise party. The next day, I was laid off from my job. And just five minutes before that, I found out that my wife's step-dad had died. It was a double hit. We had no clue that I was going to be laid off; no clue that was going to happen to him. I got six months of severance pay, so I didn't have to rush out and get a new job, and I was able to spend a lot of time with my wife and son.

In our relationship, one would be strong while the other was weak, and then it would reverse. I always said a partner-

ship is 50/50, but it's not 50/50 at any snapshot moment. It's always fluctuating back and forth and that's what it is—you pick up after the other one.

The following December, Shaina had a respiratory virus and couldn't fight it; she was too immune-suppressed because of medication for the transplant. So they had to back off the medication and basically only used supportive measures. It was scary because they just let her fight it. And she did! But, we didn't know that it must have put too much pressure on her heart. She relapsed a few months later and had a heart attack.

She didn't survive, and I was not prepared for that at all. She wasn't supposed to go; that's not how that story was supposed to end. As sick as she was, she was indestructible; nothing was supposed to happen.

She had the heart attack when we were both home and Eli was at school. I didn't have the chance to grieve sometimes because I had to worry about my son. And I had no idea what to do. How do you tell an eighteen-year-old boy that his mother just died?! There is no good way.

First, I texted his teacher and told her what happened and that I would tell my son when he got home. My sister, bless her, had come over to the house to clean up a mess before Eli got home. She was here when Eli got home because the paramedics had just left. My mother-in-law was sitting there, and my brother-in-law and his wife were also there. Eli was playing in the family room. I just called him in and had him sit on the sofa and I just bluntly told him. And he couldn't get it. He just couldn't get it for a couple of hours. He wanted to go out to dinner like he always does. Then he broke and he was just screaming, "My mom is dead!"

I was happy because if he hadn't understood, it would have meant that he didn't know how to deal with it. But he didn't just keep his emotions pent up, so that was good. And he cried and he cried for days. I still had him go to school because I wanted to keep things as normal as possible. And I kept myself together until he went to bed. And then, I would have my time.

You ask how I parented while grieving? Well, I had to park the grief when I was with Eli. You have to be able to show children that life goes on. If you go into a vegetative state, if you refuse to handle it, then it will not benefit them at all. I had to show him that while we're missing someone, the sun will still rise tomorrow and our lives will go on. And I kept emphasizing that his mother was still watching him and that he had his memories and our pictures of her. And he's still repeating that stuff. Whenever he misses his mom he says, "I still have memories of her and I have pictures." He has a picture in his room, and I don't let myself go with grief until he's in bed. And you do move on, as cold and as awful as that sounds—you do.

Somebody gave me an idea, so on Shaina's birthday, I got some helium balloons and we went out and released them. He said, "Happy birthday, Mom. I miss you," and he let them go.

He has a moment almost every day when he says, "I miss Mom," and I say, "So do I." One of his habits, though, is hard to deal with. Whenever he sees anyone we know, he says, "Did you hear what happened to my mom?" He says it to people even if they were at the funeral. It may be good for him, but it's hard for me to hear it. But, in essence, he is working his way through the trauma, which I'm happy about.

I took the funeral as a sign that we could begin to heal, but you know, grieving never goes away. But it does get farther down the list of things you have to do that day. I still have moments that are hard, and I still miss her. Sometimes I get mad at her for leaving. Sometimes I laugh because I know that she'd find something funny. I know five minutes after she got to heaven she gave God a piece of her mind for doing this. She was good at that kind of thing. I can hear her saying to God, "I don't have time for this nonsense, ya know?"

I'd had a conversation a while ago with a neighbor who asked me, "Do you see yourself getting married again?" And

I looked at her and said, "You gotta be kidding me—who wants me? I'm an overweight, bald guy with a disabled kid and I'm old." She said she thought I was a great father and that somebody was going to enjoy that.

About three weeks later, I met Melanie at a community social inclusion group. I had just dropped Eli off, and she was sitting in the hallway when I came out. I wanted to be friendly the way people were with me when I was new in that group. Over the weeks, I felt comfortable talking to her while we were waiting for our children; she has twins.

Now I am looking forward to a new life and the challenge of being a father to two boys who've never known a father. I need to point out that I was the caregiver with my wife for many years before she died. People wonder how I can go on to love another woman. I think that they are very different women, and I have been able to keep them separate in my mind. No one is going to replace a high school sweetheart, and I didn't look for someone to replace her, because there is no carbon copy. When Melanie asks me about all of this, I say what is true. I say, "I love you very much and I plan on doing that forever at this point." The past is the past and it's not a comparison thing. These loves are just two separate entities.

Note: Interested readers can learn about how Paul and Melanie established a relationship that keeps their children absolutely front and center. Details of how they thoughtfully proceeded to the point of planning their marriage can be found in Chapter 9.

Genius Moments

Paul is a genius about using his intuition to understand what his son needed. He understood that his son required plenty of time, space, and support for his grieving process. Some of his strategies and philosophies include the following:

- *Encouraging his son's grieving process even when it was painful for himself.* There was no doubt that it was painful for him to hear his son repeat to person after person the story of his mother's death, but Paul understood that this was helpful to his son.

- *Teaching his son about staying connected to his mother.* For example, Paul made it clear that Eli could maintain a connection with his mother and that his memories and pictures were to be embraced—not avoided out of the pain of loss. Sending his mother a happy birthday wish along with the release of balloons was an important part of this. It was also a concrete, yet meaningful, expression well suited both to himself and a son with a developmental disability.

- *Showing him that life goes on.* He did this by keeping his son involved in school and his regular activities. He also maintained a regular schedule at their home. Although he was open to sharing some grief and loss with his son, he contained his emotional anguish until his son went to bed.

- *Allowing himself to heal and find a new love.* Paul has been able to commit to a new love because he understands that this does not diminish his love for his first wife. He does not want to try to forget her or replace her. He does want to commit to and enjoy the new love he has found with a woman who, like his wife, is a devoted loving mother and strong woman.

Parenting a Grieving Child

Before moving on to a discussion of the grief of children who have developmental disabilities, I want to more generally discuss grief in children in general. All kids, typical or atypical, grieve in ways that are more similar than people often acknowledge. Those with additional complications in grieving due to communication or comprehension difficulties need even more creative support.

Let's start with the fact that a parent's grieving process is often intertwined with that of his or her child. So, how we grieve affects them. This means we have to be willing to be role models for healthy ways of grieving. This includes being able to be honest about our feelings without overwhelming our children. It is important that they see parents expressing their grief rather than trying to keep all feelings inside. We don't want children to bottle up their feelings or feel ashamed of their emotions.

Children should also see parents seek or accept help and support from others and refrain from isolating themselves. In addition, they need to see that it is good to talk about memories—to understand that the goal is not to try to forget their deceased parent but to find a way to stay connected. Paul modeled this very well for his son.

People have trouble knowing what to do when a child is grieving, especially when the child has a developmental disability. So it is likely you will encounter well-intended but misguided advice. Many people think children with disabilities need to be protected from grief or that they don't have the capacity to understand it. In the end, this is harmful, and the child becomes isolated with his or her grief. Many have referred to those with developmental disabilities as disenfranchised mourners.

Parents can help their children grieve in the following ways:

- "Give permission" for children to feel their feelings. Simple phrases such as "I have sad news" or "It's okay to feel upset" start this process. As we saw with Eli, it can take a while for children to digest such news.
- Remind your children that while death is a normal part of life, most people live a long time. They don't have to worry about their own death or the deaths of most of the healthy people around them.
- Make sure your child understands that she has done nothing that has caused the death. This includes anything she may have ever "wished for" in anger.
- It is very important to help children process their grief for many reasons, including the fact they are prone to blame themselves for situations that have nothing to do with them. For example, a parent's death may be seen as abandonment due to their own lack of worth. Sometimes children may think something to the effect of "That person isn't around anymore. They must not love me."
- Be prepared to answer any questions honestly that your child may bring up, while keeping your conversation with her at a level that is developmentally appropriate.

Do's and Don'ts in Providing Information

There is a delicate balance between giving children the information they need without overwhelming or confusing them. It is hard for children and adults alike to bear the fact that eventual death is part of the natural order of life—inevitable, irreversible, and universal.

Many professionals advise *not* to use metaphors and euphemisms when discussing death with children because it can confuse them. When a child hears, "Mom went to a better place," it is easy for her to be confused. For instance, the child may wonder, "What can be better than being with me? Why is that place better? Where is this place?" We often speak about death in metaphors, but children may take these literally. For example, the idea of death being like "going to sleep" can make a child afraid to go to bed at night, or afraid to let others go to sleep.

You may find children's books useful in helping a child process a loved one's death. For good reason, many people recommend *Tear Soup* by Pat Schweibert. It presents a way to look at grieving and healing that is good for adults and children to read together. *The Invisible String* by Patrice Karst is another meaningful book that does not focus on death. Rather, it describes how love connects us with people we love "anywhere and everywhere." It serves as a natural way to discuss the bonds that survive a parent's death.

Providing the Support Your Child Needs

As Paul did, one of the first things it is important to do is to gather supports for your children. It is also a good idea to spend some extra time with your children to reaffirm that you won't leave, as abandonment fears and dependency needs may run high at this time. After all, the unthinkable has already happened and they have lost a major beloved source of support. Of course they worry about who will care for them if something happens to you.

Paul also engaged in many of the best practices to support a mourning child. He reached out and informed people in his son's life, especially those he had regular contact with over time. Letting supportive others know that your family is in the midst of grief can help increase the support your child receives. This might include teachers, extended family, friends' parents, and social groups.

To minimize the impact of the loss of a loved one, children need stability and routine to help them maintain a sense of normalcy. A large part of a child's loss experience is the fear that life will change forever. Routines also provide a sense of order and structure, which can be particularly important when faced with the chaos of loss.

Some professionals recommend not making any major changes (if possible) to your child's routine for at least a year. This includes moving, changing schools, or withdrawing from social activities or even regular attendance at a house of worship. Big changes can disrupt schedules, make it harder for your child to know what to expect, and can lead to further behavioral challenges. Most importantly, maintaining routine is also a way for a child to understand that "life goes on."

Helping Your Child Process Grief

For their own sakes, children need to be involved in the grieving process rather than sheltered from it. Without involvement, they grieve alone. As aptly put by Dr. Alan Wolfelt, "Anyone old enough to love is old enough to grieve." Even infants grieve.

Encouraging your child to talk openly about the parent she lost will help her move through the process in a healthy way. As Paul expressed, it is painful to hear your child talk about the death over and over again. However, research shows that giving children the space to tell the story of their loss is very important to the healing process. This telling of the story, usually time and time again, can help the child make sense of her loss and learn about what is really important to her. It also helps her to create a vision for what her life looks like now, without that person as part of her life. This holds true for adults as well as children.

It is important to understand that acting out is one way children respond to grief. Grief may disrupt some of your child's habits or behaviors; for example, she may not want to go to bed on time or may "regress" and engage in behavior such as thumb sucking or bedwetting. Children often show a loss of skills and become more dependent on a parent at the same time that the parent is struggling with his or her own grief. If you understand that this behavior is typical, it may help you tolerate it while dealing with your own pain and wishing that so much was not on your shoulders.

Also be aware that nonverbal behavior can reveal how your child is feeling just as effectively, if not more so, than words can. So, look for other signs that your child is struggling. Some kids express their grief through physical symptoms such as stomach aches, headaches, and complaints of not feeling well. Many others express their upset behaviorally by being increasingly agitated, oppositional, poorly behaved, or irritable. These behaviors can sometimes be misunderstood or dismissed as "senseless behavior," but if you look closely, you'll often see that the child is trying to communicate as best as she knows how.

It is also important to remember that children may have a delayed reaction to their grief—as much as six months after the loss. This is described well in a very helpful article by Randy Olin (2014):

> "A child's brain shuts down after the loss of a loved one and there's a period of numbness. About 6–12 months after the death, the brain reboots and the feelings of loss come to the surface."

Helping Your Child Manage Anger

A common reaction to loss is to have lots of anger. Your child may be angry at her loved one for no longer being there for her. Or, she may direct her anger at you. It is also possible for children to have a more generalized anger that isn't directed at anyone in particular.

It is important to help children express their anger in safe and productive ways. Dr. Darcie Sims, a bereaved parent and nationally certified expert on healthy grieving, offers some good advice on this topic in her article "Anger and Grief in Children." She wrote of the importance of helping children "dissipate the energy of the emotion of anger" in a variety of nondestructive ways. Dr. Sims adds that release of this energy does not alleviate grief but it does pave the way to be able to process other aspects of grief.

She offers the following strategies for safely and productively dissipating the energy of anger:

- Set up a stomping circle and have the child stomp around it to a one-minute timer.
- Pound cookie dough or clay.

- Have an "anger magazine stack" for tearing.
- Yell sounds and not words.

Sims suggests making an anger box by lining a shoebox and its lid with cotton balls. After cutting a hole in one end of the box, you can insert an empty toilet paper roll. Then she advises yelling into your box as much as you want and, perhaps, writing your troubles on the lid. It is hard to do justice to this excellent article, so readers are encouraged to read it at www.touchstonegrief.com. Although the article was not written specifically for parents of children with disabilities, there are enough good ideas that you can choose and modify some of them to suit your child or children.

Support Groups and Resources for Children

There is strength in numbers, and children often benefit greatly from being in a bereavement group and feeling as if someone understands them. Bereavement groups are run by professionals who understand children and grief. Many use art activities that engage children gently in the healing process. Most cities have at least a few support groups for bereaved children, and some even have day programs and overnight grief camps where children can heal together while learning to embrace life again. This embodies the concept of carrying grief and joy together, as discussed earlier.

A Handful of Websites Not to Miss: The following websites are excellent resources, although they do not specifically address the additional needs of children with disabilities. However, as a parent of a child with a disability, you undoubtedly have experience adapting activities for your own child, so I hope you make use of what they offer in your own way.

- *The National Alliance for Grieving Children* (www.childrengrieve.org) is a valuable resource. Its website includes an easy-to-use locator for grief support groups. You just click on your state and, most often, an extensive list of options will appear. The website also has lists of bereavement camp opportunities and makes registration easy with the click of a button. In addition, there is a good resource section that includes materials that may be used at home (or school) to help grieving children.

- As mentioned earlier, *GriefNet.org* has a division for children, Kidsaid.com. The organization describes its mission as providing a safe place for children to help each other deal with their grief, including via e-mail support groups. I realize that format may not be accessible to *some* children with disabilities, but the website also has a sharing space where all children can post their artwork and stories. There is also a Q and A section, games, etc. Their motto is "Kids 2 Kids understanding…coping…moving on."

- *The Shared Grief Project* (www.thesharedgriefproject. org) may be particularly good for children who connect best with video. The organization describes its mission as making sure that grieving children don't "suffer in isolation." They want to make sure children know they are not alone and to provide inspiration from famous role models who speak from the heart about their childhood losses. One of my favorites of the short videos is from Kyrie Irving, NBA superstar, who speaks with great emotion of his mother's death when he was very young and how he still feels her loss in adulthood. He is only one of many powerful models who encourage healthy grieving by validating its hugeness while also demonstrating how their lives have continued.

- The Shared Grief Project is sponsored by the New York Life Foundation, which has also established *A Child in Grief.* This website is found at www.newyorklife.com/achildin-grief. It offers excellent resources, including help finding local resources and listings of children's books. If you look through the listing, you will find a free downloadable book entitled *Something Small* [a story about remembering]. This book was produced through the Sesame Street folks, so it features Elmo. If this type of resource suits your child, make sure you also check out www.sesamestreet.org/grief.

- The *Family Lives On Foundation* (www.familyliveson. org) is a national program that relies on an extensive network of volunteers to help children continue a tradition that they shared with their deceased parent. This resource is absolutely disability-friendly, since it centers on identifying a tradition a child misses from life with his or her deceased parent and then finding ways to help the families engage in the tradition each year. The eligibility criteria include children between three and eighteen years of age who live in the United States and have either a terminally ill or deceased parent. The foundation's process involves having two trained volunteers talk with the child about special times he or she misses. Then, arrangements are made to provide the resources needed so the family can engage in that precious tradition each year until the child is eighteen. The foundation pays for and facilitates the annual tradition. Here is an example that illustrates the value of this resource:

"Malik's mother died in 2005 when he was 7 years old. When Family Lives On volunteers came to talk to Malik and his father about his favorite memories with his mother, he excitedly began to talk about the family portraits they would take at Sears every year. Malik showed the volunteer many pictures that hung around the house as proof of this tradition…He continued by telling the volunteers how the family would enjoy pizza at Old Country Buffet afterwards. Malik and the volunteers quickly decided that arranging to have him and his father's picture taken every September for Malik's birthday was the perfect way to remember his mother. He continued the tradition every year and loves seeing the volunteers when they come to deliver his request. One of the volunteers recalls how he eagerly asked if they were going to come every year. She assured him that they would be there every year until he turned eighteen, giving him the chance to continue this special tradition that his mother used to arrange."

Many other examples can be found on the foundation's website and include traditions such as going to the beach and staying in a hotel with "bouncy beds." For depleted parents handling their own grief, the emotional, logistical, and even financial help of such a caring volunteer program can be wonderful.

Family Traditions and Rituals

People in all cultures have traditions and rituals related to death because they are key to several aspects of the mourning process. These include processing grief, honoring loved ones who have died, and staying connected to the deceased. For some, rituals provide ways of expression when there are no words for the depth of the loss you feel. And perhaps most importantly, rituals can be a valuable way to connect with your child.

Rituals may help your children feel connected to the parent they lost as well as provide a vehicle for expression of their feelings. Some people choose a single symbolic ritual that occurs once, such as physically planting a tree in memory of a parent or releasing balloons, as Paul's son did on his mother's birthday. Often, this type of ritual can be extended—for example, by taking care of the tree over the years or releasing balloons every year.

Many people find that rituals help them include a deceased parent in holiday celebrations. One example is to always cook or bake a parent's favorite dish. Rituals are also important for coping with a deceased parent's birthday or the day that he or she died. Tears may be shed while "celebrating" the life of that parent in an uplifting way. Actually, that combination is very healing. Consider asking your children for ideas on how they would like to celebrate the life of their parent. This type of involvement is good for every member of the family.

Rituals don't need to be reserved for special occasions; many people find great comfort in daily rituals. They can be as simple as listening to or singing a song that a parent loved. Some light a candle each day that represents the presence of that parent at bedtime or, perhaps, at dinnertime.

Grief and Developmental Disabilities

Thomas Holmes has written that people with developmental disabilities are often "forgotten grievers" and therefore are vulnerable to prolonged grief reactions, depression, and turmoil. They are often excluded from the same practices that help others process and make sense out of their losses. This occurs for several reasons. One is a misguided attempt to "protect" them from difficult experiences. There is a common erroneous assumption that individuals with developmental disabilities have no awareness of grief and therefore do not experience loss. Without help processing their grief, they often act out. These behaviors, in turn, are often seen merely as inappropriate and in need of correction rather than unique expressions of grief. Because grief reactions are often delayed, it is easy to react punitively to unexplained anger or aggression.

Verbal expression is difficult for many people with developmental disabilities, so we need to think about how to help them "tell their stories of grief." Pictures and other visual symbols can be very useful in helping them express what they are feeling and also to process the death and to share experiences.

Thomas Holmes's article entitled "Forgotten Grief: Helping People with Developmental Disabilities Manage Personal Loss" advocates using *guided mourning* for those with developmental disabilities. Guided mourning essentially involves using pictures to help people with disabilities express feelings and concerns and to understand the death. In the appendix of his article, Holmes includes line drawings that can help those without good verbal skills to communicate their feelings about death. These include pictures of crying, confusion, and anger, as well as pictures of a grave, a casket, a flower dying, and people in hospital beds. They resemble the PECS (picture exchange communication system) that some readers may be familiar with.

You may or may not find you need to use such pictures yourself, but they are especially useful for helping others talk to your child about death. There are many things people can do with these pictures. You can show them to your child and talk about your own feelings. You can ask your child to point to pictures that illustrate how she is feeling. Better yet, you can add personalized pictures of your own. In addition, Holmes and others encourage drawing and coloring activities to help children with disabilities express their feelings. For example, you might make an outline of a person your children can color and draw to reflect their own moods.

If you have an older child in a group residence, be aware that support staff often do not provide opportunities to talk about feelings of grief. Research by John Hoover and his colleagues found that staff tend to be overprotective and to infantilize adults with disabilities when it comes to discussions of death.

I think it is important to make sure that all family members are included in family mourning, so you may consider having your adult child return home for a period of time after a death. On the other hand, this can disrupt important balance and routine. Therefore, your thoughtful consideration of options is the best approach. Also, encourage support staff to understand that your child is likely to be mourning for a long time and ask them to support her in this process. This means allowing your child to talk about her loss, checking in to see how she is feeling, and understanding that acting out may be her way of expressing her loss. You can help support staff by providing photographs, scrapbooks, or other mementoes that you are comfortable sharing for this purpose.

Conclusion

This chapter shared the stories of three adults who spoke of handling acute grief after losing spouses they deeply loved. Their highly personal approaches to living with their grief are in keeping with the words of Elisabeth Kübler-Ross, who reflected that "Our grieving is as individual as our lives."

This holds true both for parents and their grieving children.

Chapter 7

Parents and Children
Who Chose Each Other
through Adoption

IN THE PAST, single parents found it difficult to adopt any child, with or without disabilities, due to the view that they were less capable of providing a stable home than couples were. This bias still persists to a certain extent against solo parents, especially men. Although more single men have succeeded in adopting children, there is sometimes skepticism about their motives. All of these negative preconceptions conflict with research findings that support the stability of homes provided by adoptive solo parents. Today, a quarter of all adopted children with disabilities in the United States have a single parent.

Although solo parents of adopted children with disabilities have a great deal in common with other solos, they also face some relatively unique circumstances. Some of these have to do with the dynamics set into motion because of the element of choice. *You chose this* is a phrase that may echo in your own mind as well as the minds of others. Within yourself, the fact that *you chose this* may add to your dismay when you find yourself with an episode of regret. You chose this so...why am I grieving the changes in my life? You chose this... so why am I sometimes so sad...?

Solo parents who choose to adopt are often unprepared for the common slide into post-adoption depression. This is shocking to many, since they longed for and fought so long for a child. And, whether or not you expected a child to have a disability, there is often a grieving process. On top of everything else, much of this can take place in a context where friends and family don't want to hear any complaints since *you chose this*.

As described by Amy Rogers Nazarov, society often has different expectations for adoptive parents than for birth parents. For example, many people expect adoptive parents to be more prepared for the process of parenting and not need extra help with cooked meals or chores around the house: common things that friends and family do for new biological parents.

Please don't jump to the conclusion that I think solo adoption is full of distress. This is not my view, as you will see later in the chapter. But, I do believe that many unique aspects of adoption make it especially stressful and hard. (By now, you should know that I don't believe an easier life is always better.) In addition to those already touched on, the nature of many adopted children's disabilities is particularly daunting. For example, having a child with fetal alcohol syndrome or reactive attachment disorder can make it impossible for parents (single or not) to cope despite heroic efforts. Then there is the fact that school systems are not well informed on such conditions. The sheer need for knowledgeable expert help often goes unmet. And adoption, much less international adoption, spurs the public to say things that hurt: "Where is his real mother (or father)?" or "Don't worry; maybe you will have your own someday."

These issues are among those discussed in this chapter. In addition, we will meet three solo parents by choice, each of whom has a very important story to share:

- Lisa, a solo mother who adopted a baby shortly after she was born to a woman addicted to heroin
- Frances, a mother who adopted an adolescent girl with her wife shortly before she faced the loss of a job she loved and a crumbled marriage
- Lucinda, the mother of a son with Down syndrome who mistakenly expected to raise him alone forever

The main commonality is that they are all very good parents who have succeeded in meeting their children's needs while working full time.

The deep contentment that can come with solo adoption will be very clear in the stories featured here. None of you really need me to spell those out. So bear with me when I begin this chapter by writing about loss. Paula Fitzgibbons, a contributor to the online adoption archives at Scary Mommy, wrote of loss being inherent in all adoptions. Whether or not you entirely agree, I think she presents a useful perspective:

> "No matter how simple or rosy your adoption might seem, all adoption is predicated upon loss. Even if you are the lucky one-in-a-million to 'catch' baby in the hospital and you celebrate with the birth mother as she joyfully signs parenting rights over to you, your child will be affected by the adoption. Your child's birth parents and extended family will experience loss. You will feel the sting of not having carried your child. Everyone will miss the medical history if there is none available. You will have to deal with the emotional scars of adoption. Even if it doesn't look like there are any scars, there are."
> (www.scarymommy.com/category/adoption/#sthash.bWM9nDXr.dpuf)

Throughout this chapter, parents speak of an intermingling of emotions; loss is mixed in with more positive emotional states. Some of the parents anticipated that their children would have disabilities, but that doesn't mean they did not experience some of the same processes of grieving that nonadoptive parents do. So, if you have not read Chapter 1, you may want to because it addresses the process of coming to terms with many of these feelings that are shared by a wide range of parents of children with disabilities.

Lisa, the first mother profiled in this chapter, spoke very candidly about her grief over her child's disabilities. As is common, she was prepared by the adoption agency for *some* disabilities, but found her daughter's health to be *very* different from what she expected.

A Formidable Fighter and a Tender Mother

The Backstory: Lisa adopted a little girl right after she was born more than two months prematurely to a mother who struggled with a heroin addiction. Her daughter's first three months of life were spent in the NICU. Lisa was shocked by the uphill struggles that followed in almost all parts of life. Her personal story is full of battles but not defeat.

> *"I was completely taken by surprise to learn she has cerebral palsy. In fact, she would hold her hands very stiffly and I thought, 'oh, she's strong.'"—Lisa*

Excerpts from Lisa's story follow:

I was the first person the adoption agency called. They had me decide during the phone call whether I would take her. They didn't disclose everything before I adopted her, and I really had no clue about many of her conditions. The doctor simply said they thought she was "delayed." So, her cerebral palsy came as a total surprise to me. I thought her stiffness was a sign of muscular strength (not spasticity).

My nineteen-month-old girl has had quite a history in her short life. She spent the first three months of her life in the NICU, so that means that I did too. It has been quite a struggle, and I've had to fight so much over the last sixteen months.

There were many losses. One that is especially hard to talk about is how I lost my best friend over all of this. We had been friends since the seventh grade, so we were best friends for more than twenty years. She was like family to me—closer than many members of my family, even. So I called her for support and shared everything that was wrong with my daughter. I was shocked that she just said, "Oh, that's terrible...well I've got to go now." I didn't hear from her for two weeks, so I called her. It didn't go well. I shared that I was upset that I had to be the one to call her while also going to a million appointments for my daughter. Her answer was that she was busy with her son's after-school soccer games. That was not okay, so I just ended the friendship. I could have tried to work it out, but I really don't have the capacity for it. I just can't have people in my life who are not supportive.

I was shocked that work became a struggle and a big mess too. I had been at the firm for two years when I first decided to adopt. I let them know that an adoption might occur at any time and that I would need to take leave. I wanted to prepare for this together, but they kind of ignored it. When I got my daughter and I needed to take leave, my supervisor told me that they might lay me off if I took leave. I told them that was illegal, but they didn't seem to care.

I let the company know right away when Jade was diagnosed with cerebral palsy. I knew I was going to have many doctors' appointments because she also had a lazy eye that would need surgery and chronic bronchitis and a lung disease that required breathing treatments. Since she was a preemie, her immune system has always been very low, so once she is sick, she is really sick. The idea of taking Family Medical Leave (FMLA) turned out to be a joke in my office. They said their only leave was for pregnancy. I was written up for taking "too much time off." A friend who works in the field of human relations told me to get a lawyer. That advice was great, and so was the lawyer. She confirmed their leave policy was not legal and that I could sue. She warned me this would be expensive and they would quite likely retaliate.

So, I said to myself, "Great, I have a daughter who is disabled and if I find a new job, I'm not going to be covered by family leave anyway for the first year." But, I couldn't stay with my current firm, so I told myself, "Just chance it!" It took two days to move from one job to another. I took a pay cut, but the new company said I'll get back to where I was in terms of pay if I just work hard. The place is amazing. I've always wanted to work there, but they had turned me down in the past. I have been able to take the time off that I need, and it's such a positive place to be. I also found a great daycare that's been a lifesaver to me and will keep Jade when she is sick, as long as she isn't contagious.

There are times I sit and cry. Don't get me wrong—it is not all about her disabilities and her new diagnoses. It was the adoption itself and the domino effect it had on me: needing to get a new job, a new house, and even a different car. I was also wondering what friends would be there for me, and rebuilding my relationship with my mother.

I believe you have to give yourself a night to cry and to do whatever you need to do. But the next morning, it's a new day and you need to fight for your child. Jade is my baby girl, and I would do anything for her. The fighter in me has needed to come out. The stakes were big. For example, the Department of Child and Family Services (DCFS) would not consider my daughter as having a disability. Really. And without that diagnosis with DCFS, I couldn't get any other services for her. If the first person didn't give me the right answer, I learned to go to the next one. You need to do whatever it takes. I actually got the press involved and the Board of Commissioners who oversaw DCFS. I started by getting the email address of a journalist who wrote articles about DCFS, and it led to the problem being resolved. My social worker says I should become an advocate.

I could've given my daughter back until I officially adopted her. I did think about it, but not for long, since she's my baby. And I thought, "What if I really did give birth to her? I couldn't give her back then." So, for whatever reason, the moment that she came into my life was the moment she was mine. She's supposed to be in my life. It felt like a choice before I got her. But not after. I never dwelled on it, and I didn't struggle with it at all. It wasn't as if I asked myself "Did I make the right choice?" She was born in my life like every other baby. It gets better every day.

Genius Moments

There is a Dakota Indian saying, "If you find yourself riding a dead horse, dismount." Lisa is a genius at living by this principle while also honoring her emotions. She was quick to recognize when she simply had to "dismount the horse" in order to make needed changes in her life. She did not let negative situations sap her energies; rather, she focused her strength and anger on getting things changed. This worked really well for her in managing an onslaught of loss and change. Some of Lisa's strategies and philosophies include:

- *Keeping it relative.* Lisa gave issues different weights according to her new priorities, and she actively reminded herself of what mattered. For now, her daughter's ability to walk is the big issue that matters to her. She let the others shrink in size. In her words:

  "I needed to get a new house, a new job, and a new car. I reminded myself that every factor in my life was going to be better because of it. It was very interesting, because before I had a daughter, moving wouldn't have been a big issue. My last car was a huge thing and finding a new job was a huge thing. The decisions in life that would have been huge before I had a disabled baby are not new decisions but easy."

  Lisa may have felt as if she did this naturally. But a closer look shows that she allowed herself to not simply assume that she had to be anxious about things that had made her anxious in the past. She gave herself permission to change in this way by consciously being aware of what ultimately matters (or doesn't).

- *Allowing and compartmentalizing grief.* Lisa explained her approach: "For a whole year it was grief. I think you have to grieve the ideal of what your child was going to be. So I let myself cry at night. For a while, I was angry and cranky, and

I could see that it was kind of affecting my daughter. So I told myself that I could cry until morning, when my daughter would be awake. I had to tell myself, "Okay, when I wake up in the morning, the tears need to be gone; let's just do it!"

- *Refusing to take "no" for an answer.* Lisa got very far with this strategy. As you may recall, she enlisted a reporter's help in order to get her daughter what she needed. She took a lesson from her work with celebrities, who certainly don't consider taking "no" for an answer. So, why should she? In her words:

> *"I always have to find an answer; it's my job. It's really helped me in this aspect of my life. I say to myself, 'This is not working; I've got to go do something else.' Many times I've sat and cried but thought, 'Okay, I still have to go do it. I still have to do the work.'"*

The ability to cry may also give her the relief to then go do what she needs to tackle. She not only drew upon her work experience, but she channeled the fighter she was in high school. This time, rather than getting suspended for trying to avenge wrongs against others, she succeeded on her daughter's behalf.

- *Taking charge of her relationships.* One of the ways that Lisa has taken charge of her relationships is by giving her mother feedback, in an adult way, in order to stand up for her daughter. She was pleasantly surprised when her mother decided to come out for a month to help her when her daughter had surgery.

She explained:
> *"My mom and I have had a strained relationship from day one. At the time that I adopted my daughter, we had not talked for a year and a half. My mom doesn't call a lot. I suggested that we Skype, but it only happened once. She just retired, and she and my stepdad are out partying. She likes the name Grandma, but she doesn't like to be a grandma. So,*

one day we were at my mom's house and my mom was parenting her badly. It was awesome because I was able to stand up for my daughter.

I said to my mom, 'You can't parent with negative words. Saying something negative will never turn into something positive. You must be positive with my daughter.' I learned this because I had to take parenting classes when I wanted to be a foster parent. Those parenting classes made me realize how bad a parent my mother really was. It was really nice to be able to tell her that she couldn't talk like that to my daughter. She was shocked, but that turned out to be a positive thing."

- *Moving into the unknown with faith in herself.* Lisa stated that she couldn't allow herself to get paralyzed by being overwhelmed by challenges. I liken her approach to how some people cross a stream with a quickly moving current. Some people wait until they can visualize every stepping-stone. Others just move ahead (once they determine they won't drown) with the belief that they will find the steps. That style worked very well for Lisa. Whereas some people place their faith in a higher power to help them face the uncertainty that goes with such a process, Lisa places it in herself.

  Over time, Lisa learned about post-adoption depression and understood its impact on her life. This was helpful to her. Her story illustrates why it is so common, even among very strong and capable parents. The catalyst is often the cascade of changes and emotional rollercoaster that frequently accompanies adoptions.

Post-Adoption Depression Syndrome

Unfortunately, post-adoption depression syndrome (PADS) is much less well publicized than postpartum depression, yet can be just as disabling. Adoptive parents are often caught unaware, even though the term Post-Adoption Depression Syndrome has been around for twenty years, since first described in an article by June Bond.

The Diagnostic and Statistical Manual of Mental Disorders (DSM 5) is the manual used by mental health professionals in the United States to diagnose similar conditions, but still does not mention post-adoption depression (even though it just underwent a multiyear process of scrutiny and revision). I find the absence striking, especially given the fact that premenstrual dysphoric disorder was added. I would have been happy with even a mention, since professionals and the public need to be alert to PADS. Indeed, Harriet McCarthy, an expert on PADS, reported that a survey sent to about 3000 members of the Eastern European Adoption Coalition found that fewer than 8 percent of parents were informed by social workers or doctors that this syndrome existed.

PADS often begins with the "blues," and these symptoms may easily progress to meeting the criteria for a major depressive disorder. When full blown, PADS shares the same symptoms as depression. These include a pervasive change in functioning (lasting at least two weeks) that is characterized by a loss of pleasure or interest in almost all activities throughout the day. Other symptoms can vary, so it is important to be familiar with the signs of depression; these are listed in Chapter 4, in the section on getting professional help. They may include feelings of guilt, worthlessness, or irritability; insomnia; and changes in appetite. One of the dangers of depression is that thoughts become distorted, so people can become hopeless and self-critical and unable to think rationally and function normally. Depression can also lead to suicidal thinking and the belief that loved ones would be better off without us.

Amy Rogers Nazarov, a mother who has written about her personal struggles with PADS, emphasizes the critical role of therapy (along with medication). According to Nazarov, it is very beneficial to address harmful beliefs with a therapist. For her, these included beliefs that she would not be able to keep her baby safe. Her distorted thinking included seeing her struggle with infertility as a sign that maybe she was not destined to be a parent and, therefore, it was unfair to adopt a child.

It is not unusual to regret an adoption decision or fear that you have ruined your life. Melissa Fay Green wrote very candidly about the grim turn of events that followed her adoption of a son who joined their family of four children and a spouse. An excerpt from her book, *A Love Like No Other (2006),* follows:

"When I found myself weeping in the laundry room over being forced to put my children's sheets on the interloper's bed (because at age four and a half he was wetting the bed), I knew I was in trouble. Refusing to take photos of him during his first weeks in America (because it might mean he was staying, because the photos could be used as evidence that he's been here) also might have been a clue. Refusing to let anyone else take a picture of the whole family (because his presence in the family portrait, among our four kids by birth, would mar the effect) similarly sounded a warning note. Lying awake at night considering, 'If I drive all night and check into a motel in Indiana, will anyone ever find me?' I also might have signaled that I was having some issues with our son Jesse, whom we had adopted from Bulgaria...."

Parents often feel shame and guilt if they do not have an immediate love of their newly adopted child. This shame is compounded by not knowing this reaction is so common.

Harriet McCarthy has drawn a parallel between love at first sight with a potential mate and instant bonding with a child. She writes that initial infatuation (with either) quickly diminishes when we are faced with adjusting to living with another person day in and day out. She adds that families who belong to support groups for Eastern European adoptions report that it is common for it to take two to six months for attachment to blossom.

Sometimes it is helpful to think about what provides "kindling" for the flames of depression. Because caregiving is so difficult, people sometimes grieve the loss of the freedom that comes when they adopt a child. Sleep deprivation serves as kindling and so does stress. Without a doubt, both of these factors hit solo parents of kids with disabilities more often. You have no one to "tag-team" it with on nights a child won't sleep or when you must nap out of sheer exhaustion.

Stress is a known kindling for depression, and stress is greater when children who have been adopted have disabilities. Common disability-related sources of stress include worries about IEPs, bullying, and additional expenses for treatment and equipment. As Lisa's story illustrated, parenting was far harder because of the number of medical and therapeutic services her daughter needed as well as the amount of bureaucratic red tape involved in getting them. Raising children with disabilities, especially solo, is simply more stressful—no matter how great a child is.

The effect of post-adoption depression syndrome can be devastating. It has been described as lasting for a longer duration than the typical postpartum depression. So it is important to be proactive about it.

For starters:

- Enlist all the help you can from immediate family and friends to deal with the tasks of everyday life.
- Try to get out of the house every day—no matter what.
- Prevent isolation by not giving into the temptation to withdraw.
- Protect your sleep as much as possible.
- Watch out for tendencies to be a perfectionist since PADS is higher for people with those tendencies.

Support and Extended Family and Friends

It is not unusual for extended family to disappoint adoptive parents by failing to offer the same enthusiasm and support that they might for biological children or for those who don't have disabilities. Many of the websites listed in the section on Supports below have good advice from others in similar situations.

Often acceptance from friends and family comes with time, and this book is full of stories that illustrate that. To help get through to your parents or others who are struggling with acceptance, you may want to provide them with a book or two. Here are two that are often recommended:

- *Adoption is a Family Affair: What Relatives and Friends Must Know* by Patricia Irwin Johnston

- *In On It: What Adoptive Parents Would Like You to Know about Adoption. A Guide for Relatives and Friends* by Elisabeth O'Toole

I believe in incremental change, and these books may very well decrease the likelihood of thoughtless comments and increase understanding, at least to some extent.

Supports

I cannot overemphasize the need to get additional support. If you have not read Chapter 4, it is likely to be helpful when handling problems with extended family and friendships.

Research has shown unequivocally that increased social support is key to emotional coping. Yes, it is indeed "easier said than done." You are likely too busy to be spending lots of time with friends, even if you could find ones that you feel you have much in common with these days. And if you have a child with attachment issues or severe behavioral issues, it is obviously very hard to get out and see others. In these circumstances, it may be helpful to seek out help online.

Don't get me wrong, I don't think you should forgo the friends you have now or give up on getting out of the house; however, some online support groups offer valuable help and camaraderie for mothers in particular. There are things that only another parent with adopted children can "get." This includes the ridiculous questions regarding whether you are the "real" mother or father. This is not to mention intrusive comments about your being a saint for "rescuing that poor little child." Comments made to your child can be even worse. There are also the far larger issues such as connections with birth parents.

As you have probably gathered from reading this book, I wholeheartedly believe that the best approach to complicated situations is to contemplate the views and experiences of a wide number of people who have walked in similar shoes. I also factor in the views of professionals, but I never take the single opinion of any one person as the ultimate right way to handle something.

Consider visiting the following websites, which address varying facets of life for solo adoptive parents of kids with disabilities. Most offer support from other parents as well as a host of professional articles and resources.

Helpful Websites

Adopting.org (www.adopting.org) is a great resource for parents to get more information about adopting a child with a disability or one from a different culture and language. This website also offers resources on steps to take when adoption fails (so-called adoption losses: adoption reversal, adoption dissolution, how to talk to siblings). Adopting.org also provides articles about legal and community resources.

AdoptiveFamiliesCircle (www.adoptivefamiliescircle.com) gives members an opportunity to create online discussion groups. Some of those groups currently include: adoptive dads, adopting premature babies, breastfeeding adopted babies, adoption as a first choice, choosing an adult adoption, Americans living abroad with adoptive children, and LGBT parents.

Adoption.com (www.adoption.com) offers discussion boards for adoptive parents, including a very good one on special needs and attachment. I found some good quality advice and help exchanged by parents on issues such as handling red tape that makes it difficult to receive services as well as ideas on treatment and education. There are also threads where members may post on transracial adoption, single adoptive parent problems, post-adoption emotional issues, and adoption and biological children.

North American Council on Adoptable Children (www.nacac. org) offers a treasure trove of comprehensive, current information needed by many adoptive parents. For example, the section on adoption subsidies is packed with detailed but understandable information and specifics for each state in the United States as well as information for Canadian provinces. Resources on parent groups are also available.

Mothers with Attitude (www.motherswithattitude.com) is the website of Terri Mauro, the mother of two children adopted from Russia. Both adults now, one has fetal alcohol syndrome disorder (FASD) and the other has language-based learning disabilities. Her website has the tag line "Humor and help for adoptive moms, special-needs moms, any old moms at all." Let me add that it would be good for fathers too. Her work can also be found on www.specialchildren.about. com. If you follow her link to recommended reading, you will find she has written several books, including *50 Ways to Support Your Child's Special Education.* That is another important resource, especially for those parents of kids with FASD, since schools are often so unaware of the complex and often far-reaching educational implications.

When Adoptions Become Perilous

Lisa's story included the fact that, just for a moment, the thought that she could return her adopted child crossed her mind. Then she entirely dismissed it. For some, the thought is not easily dismissed. Particularly if a child has several behavioral issues, some parents fear that they may not survive the struggle with him or her.

Studies on the frequency of adoptions that are termed "disrupted" (or ended) generally report figures of close to 9 percent for younger children (under age three) and around 20 percent for older children. A comprehensive, in-depth discussion of dissolution decisions and logistics is far beyond the scope of this book. But it is a topic that is important to discuss, especially after the widely reported incident in 2010 in which a mother sent her seven-year-old adopted son back to Russia, alone on a plane, with a note saying she did not want him. The agony felt by many people struggling with such decisions is clear, and it occurs in a context in which others are prone to judge them.

I asked Ellen E. Stewart, a graduate student of mine and married mother of eleven adopted children, to share her thoughts on this issue. Based on her own struggles and perspective she wrote the following:

"Love is a messy business. Sometimes even the most heroic efforts result in loss, trauma, and irresolvable pain. So why even bother trying to achieve the impossible? Why would any sane adult choose to risk the rest of their days, financial resources, and emotional reserves to expose the rest of their family members to the tsunami of secondary stress that damages the entire unit while wreaking devastation upon the individuals within that family? Maybe because that is what love is all about. Love is a very risky adventure that promises no outcomes.

"Think about the last wedding ceremony that you attended. Did the partners promise until death do them part, or did they mention that if it seems like a reasonable decision, they can back out if it gets tough? It gets tough. We all know that. That is why the divorce rate is so great. Nobody enters into marriage hoping it will end, though. In the same vein, no parent adopts a child hoping that there will be an eventual divorce in the relationship with that child.

"I am the adoptive mother of eleven children. Some of my children were adopted domestically, others internationally. Some were older when they joined our family, and others came to us directly from the hospital. Four of the children came as a sibling group from Russia, where their biological brother remains in an orphanage. The one who was not permitted to enter into our family was assessed with psychological issues while in Russia. Two of the biological siblings we were able to bring home were later identified with those same issues.

"I never knew stress vomiting was a real thing until the psychiatrist told me that one of my girls from Russia was not allowed to return to my home. She was in a mental ward for wanting to kill herself and others when she was only nine years of age. In order for her to come back to us, we would need to provide her with her own bedroom and put buzzers on all of the doors so that we would know where she was at all times. We needed to ensure that she didn't kill anyone in our home. We couldn't do that. Our home was too small. She went to live with surrogate grandparents for the remainder of the summer while she entered into trauma therapy. Months later, she was able to reenter our family while she continued multiple forms of treatment.

"What choice did I have? Was it worth letting her live here and kill others or herself? Was it her fault? Was she simply not grateful enough that we had saved her life, fed her daily, kept her warm, loved her, and ensured that she had a good education? Or was it something else? What if her arm had been missing? People would have commented on how lucky she was to be in our family! But what if her ability to form relationships was missing? What if the traumatic events she had endured on a daily basis during her earlier years cut away at her ability to trust? What if that had left her woundedness as a potential death threat for my other kids?

"A person who has endured the shame and loss of divorce understands that some things are harder than death. Letting go of a child to another family, second-chance adoption, or foster family must be very similar. When there is a divorce, there are no flowers, sympathy cards, or condolences. There is blame. When an adoption fails, the blame is inflamed, and judgments are hurled that cut deeper than any knife. Mercy must hold the hand of love in order for those who suffer to survive."

Supports such as respite care and counseling for yourself are critical components for coping. Needed supports are typically negotiated at the time of adoption agreements; however, renegotiation is a battle that is sometimes won.

Adopting an Older Child with a Disability

To add another layer of complication on top of adopting a child with disabilities as a solo parent, some parents adopt older children with disabilities. This older age range is typically not an adoptive parent's first choice.

The solo parent whose story appears below has a lot to say about how she parented a daughter approaching adolescence. She had not expected to go solo when she adopted her.

Loving a New Teenager

The Backstory: Frances adopted her daughter, Marie, with her (soon-to-be) ex-wife. Being same-sex spouses made adoption far

harder from the beginning. For different reasons, Frances had an avalanche of personal losses that led to a serious depression. This started with harassment at work and the loss of a cherished job. This loss
resulted in a domino effect that toppled her marriage and resulted in
bankruptcy and foreclosure. Her daughter continued to mature and
heal from her earlier life experiences while living with her.

> *"Every time we were offered a child to adopt, they would
> say something like, 'He has blonde hair and blue eyes, and you
> could tackle him if he starts getting aggressive.'" —Frances*

Part of her story follows:

> *It was always my desire to have a child, so I was trying
> my best to be with guys. But it just didn't work. I've always
> loved kids, and they enjoyed me too. My office was full of
> them because they enjoyed all the cool things (and quirky col-
> lections) I had there. Many years later, my wife agreed to my
> desire to adopt. We had been married for a few years at that
> point, and we were together for twenty-one years.*
>
> *We ran into so much prejudice trying to adopt. That's
> why we were only offered children who simply couldn't be
> placed with other parents. When we finally found our daugh-
> ter, it still wasn't easy. But that is actually a good thing be-
> cause children should never be adopted by parents they don't
> connect with. The three of us spent about a year going back
> and forth. Marie would visit us and then let the agency know
> if she wanted to go to the next step of the potential adoption
> process. They also asked us every step of the way to make
> sure that this was what we wanted, too.*
>
> *When we adopted Marie, she was twelve, and we were
> told that she had both attention deficit disorder (ADD) and
> oppositional defiant disorder. She had some behaviors that
> were different. Her speech was extremely limited, and she
> didn't talk much at all because she did not have enough stim-
> ulation growing up. When she did talk, she had an accent. So
> we knew she needed a smaller educational setting that would*

be protective of her. She was used to being in a Christian environment, so we wanted to find such a setting for her again. It was hard. School personnel reacted to her labels including being a foster child and automatically assumed that she would have behavior problems.

We were successful in finding a setting connected to a religious parish that seemed like the right fit for her. I really wanted this for my daughter, but it was not easy for me personally. I was brought up Catholic and did twelve years of Catholic school. I eventually felt I needed to separate myself from the Catholic church, which was extremely hard for me. Sadly, I am not the godparent to any of my nieces or nephews. This has been very hurtful, and I suppose it is because I am gay.

The principal at this Christian school was fine with us being "different." She said, "I'm here to educate your kid. That's all I care about." It wasn't the principal who had an issue with us; it was the families in the parish who were so narrow-minded. The sad part is how they treated Marie. When they learned about us, nobody befriended her. So she spent three and a half years in a school with just one friend. Let me add that the one friend didn't speak English—only Polish. So, we had to teach her so many things that we wished she could have learned by having friends. Because she never really had a friend, she didn't know how to be one.

There were so many other things she never had a chance to experience or learn. She'd never had a birthday party. Of course, she didn't know how to talk on the phone because no one spoke to her. Nobody used to come visit her; she didn't go on play dates. She had no nursery rhymes in her repertoire and no Disney movies. It was sad, but it has also been exciting, because we have had fun together having her experience everything for the first time.

Although my wife agreed to the adoption, she became jealous that I was spending time with my daughter and didn't feel I was spending enough time with her. It wasn't only that. I also lost the job I loved through no fault of my own. Yes, I *am proceeding with a court suit, but it has been devastating. And my wife refused to work even though she knew we had a house to pay for and a child to support. One of the reasons she wanted to adopt our daughter was the child support and the subsidy for adopting a special needs child. She wanted all that so she wouldn't have to work.*

That was the beginning of the end, and that's when I filed for divorce. I was extremely scared, but I knew I had to do something, especially for my daughter. To be forty-five and need to relinquish everything I had worked for all these years in order to move on was pretty scary. So I lost my house and my job, I went bankrupt, and now I had my adolescent daughter by myself. I was lonely, and everything I had disappeared.

Now I am starting my life all over again. The divorce is still going on—it has been a nightmare. Luckily, I have my daughter with me full time. I believe my (soon-to-be) ex wanted her to stay with her for financial reasons, but I couldn't let that happen. She never did anything with Marie and just sat on the couch.

When I left my job, all my friendships and relationships were severed. The teachers at the school where I worked were afraid that if my ex-boss knew we stayed in contact, she would take it out on them next. It's very hard to find a job when you're let go on July first. It's virtually impossible when you are working at a high administrative level. But it was a real shift as to what was important to me. I had no friends, no job, no money; my family wasn't really talking to me. So I had to take a good look at my life and see what I needed to do for me and my daughter.

You asked what got me through. Counseling helped. I needed to figure out what my identity was now that all this had happened. When you have lost almost everything, what is really important becomes clear. What's been most important to me is that my daughter is happy and now has friends. It is important that she is able to live in the world and sustain herself when I'm not there. I want her to move forward in life without hesitation. I've also told her that once she finishes her college degree, she's more than free to do whatever she needs to do. That's what's important to me now.

Also, my family is back in my life. That has been wonderful, and I am connected to both of my brothers, my father, and my mother. My older brother doesn't want anybody to get in between us again. I don't have relationships with his family because his wife thinks their daughters would catch "it" from me—being gay.

Sometimes it's challenging because Marie hovers over me. She's very attached to everything I do, has a great fear of losing me, and is fearful when she doesn't know where I am. As soon as I wake up in the morning, she is next to me, and it is like this 24/7. Now that she is growing up, she answers me with a typical sixteen-year-old's mouth. That's fine. She also tries to emulate who I am and wants to do everything I do. I have said, "Listen, you don't have to be gay." She said, "Oh, I'm not sure." So I said, "You don't have to go there, if it's not who you are." But then she went to the other extreme and started texting boys inappropriate things. She doesn't have all the social skills yet.

Sometimes Marie will tell me things that floor me. The other day when we were eating at McDonald's, she said that she and her brother were always the last to eat and went dumpster diving for food too. This was when they were living with all four brothers as well as her biological mother and father. My daughter also said that they put her in an Amish home while she was in foster care. Her foster parents put her in a dress, pulled her hair back, and made her go out to work early in the morning. I wasn't surprised to hear her add, "But the food was great!"

Marie came from a violent home. Her biological parents beat the children, so the courts took them away. So I can't really raise my voice with my daughter because she gets very scared. And I also can't get into the mind-set of "oh, poor girl" because she takes advantage of that kind of attitude, and that would not be good for her either.

One of the best things we do together is laugh. We laugh about so many different things, from simple things to dumb things we both do. We are silly together, and I think that's major. Even in the midst of what has happened to us, she has learned to appreciate my humor. I like to think of stupid things to say to Marie so she will laugh.

She runs track. We made an agreement that when she stays with me, she has to do something all the time. She can't sit at home and think about things. She has to be a participant in life.

Marie's the happiest kid I've ever met, even when she wakes up in the morning. Sometimes I'm really tired and I think, "Why the hell are you so happy?" But I am so glad that she is just happy. I remind her that I love her on a regular basis so she doesn't feel like I'm going anywhere, ever.

Genius Moments:

This mother was a genius at helping her adolescent daughter thrive even though the bottom had dropped out of her own life. She compartmentalized so that her problems did not become her daughter's problems and would not detract from what she wanted for her daughter after suffering many years of neglect and abuse.

- *Transforming her own pain to empower her daughter.* She said, "I think what makes me the angriest is when Marie is hurt. I think she's experienced so much heartache in her life, I can't bear when her mom (or anyone else) hurts her. I hate when it causes her more heartache in life. When she cries, it breaks my heart and there's nothing I can do except teach Marie to stand up for herself and say what's on her mind.
- *Not personalizing it when she is hurt by her daughter's actions.* Frances understands children in general, as well as how abuse, neglect, adoption, and divorce can affect them. So she uses this knowledge to keep herself from reacting too badly when

her daughter does things that would be hurtful to most parents. She said, "There are times she makes me really angry. Such as when she tells her other mother things because she is pressured by her for information. Then I find exactly what I didn't want her to say in the lawyer's papers. It's not that there is anything that bad; it's the fact that I couldn't trust her. But she's caught and also pressured by her other mother. I process it with my counselor. I know she's a kid and she's trying to keep both her parents."

- *Learning to say what you need to say.* She explained, "I think communication is key. If you don't know what to say, reach out to someone like a counselor who can give you the strength to say what is needed. Now, I say it even though it's not always easy to do."

While I was interviewing Frances, her daughter Marie joined us. I thought about the fact that both had gone through a time where they had to let go of everything that was familiar to them. They agreed that it might be useful to readers to share what it was like for her to be adopted by two moms. She said:

> "You asked me about how I decided to be adopted? I felt like I wanted to be adopted by two moms. I had been in many different foster families. That made me not really like having both a mother and a father. So, I was open-minded about this. I'm doing much better in school down here than where I used to be. It is hard dealing with things and going through the divorce. But now that I am just living with this mom, things have changed. I got very close to her after the divorce, even closer than before. It has helped a lot. She sticks up for me and does a lot for me."

Frances adopted her daughter expecting to raise her as part of a couple. The opposite happened. The opposite also happened for the next woman we will meet. She adopted a son to raise him alone.

📖 *Spirited Devotion*

The Backstory: Lucinda was thirty-four years old when she ended up adopting her son. She was content with the idea that it would be just the two of them in life. Her son, who has Down syndrome, describes that time as being "chubby baby—chubby mom." She met her husband when her son was five.

"I didn't know how to be a mom, let alone a mom of a child with a disability. So then I have to admit to myself that I was nuts, had no business doing this, but I loved him and was mostly scared about how I was going to be able to get him everything he needed."—Lucinda

Part of Lucinda's story follows:

I still, to this day, cannot say that I went into it thinking that I was going to adopt any kid, let alone a child with a disability. I ended up going to a meeting for an organization I was curious about, and they handed me some brochures. I put them into my purse and forgot about them until months later when I was traveling. I pulled them out and was shocked to read how many kids were in the foster care system in our county. I decided it would be good to share my new house, so I called this agency to take training classes to be a foster parent.

*To say I had mixed feelings about adoption would be an understatement. I thought I would foster, until I read David Pelzer's book, **A Boy Called It**, and I was devastated, and I thought there's no way I could not adopt a child. Another part of me was doing everything not to adopt. At one point, the agency wanted me to identify what type of child I was interested in adopting. I just refused and avoided the subject. And then the stars came together.*

He was three months old when I found out about him. The agency had put his picture on TV, and they got hundreds of e-mails. But not a single person put in an application for him once they knew he had Down syndrome. It was one of those times when I said to myself, "Just do it and don't look back." That's how I am. Although I had experience spending time with adults with Down syndrome, I had no clue what I was doing with a baby with Down syndrome. I wonder if I'd had more knowledge if I would've been just as brave.

The adoption process was awful; they wouldn't give me a photo or even say that things looked good in any way. They just let me keep spending money for the process but would not commit to anything, and they made all these mistakes. This horrible process made me more determined. I said to myself, "All right, if this is how it's going to be, I'm not walking away from this kid at this point!"

When my new son arrived, my family came out to the airport. They made signs, but secretly everyone was a nervous wreck. They thought I had lost my mind. My father was assuming that this meant I would never be able to get married (are you nuts?). Even my friends thought there was something wrong with me. They were so helpful to me, but, in my nucleus, I just didn't have the kind of support that I would have had if I had a typical birth child. They helped me a lot, but the support they gave me was different.

I took maternity leave, but I had no idea what I was doing. I really didn't. I made this plan about how things would work; the plan was that he would sleep and I would get things done while he slept. By day eight, I still could not get to the grocery store. I was on the couch crying hysterically, and I called my mom and said, "I can't do it. He's got to go back! I don't know how to do this. I love him already but I can't do this." My mom said, "You've run corporations," and then showed up with Italian ice and said it would be all right. I felt very scared, very alone and isolated. I can still have some of those times.

You asked how I coped. I stuff my feelings. I think I stuffed even more in the beginning because I wasn't as connected as I could have been with other parents. I was em-

barrassed to admit that I didn't really know what it meant to have a child with Down syndrome. I almost dropped him the first time I held him because I had no idea how much support he needed. He was like Jell-O. My overachieving self got in the way of reaching out. I didn't want the families that I worked with at Special Olympics to know how much I didn't know. And I didn't want to tell my family because they already thought I was nuts for doing this.

I went into super-advocate mode. I put all my energy into thinking, "This kid is going to be okay, and he's going to get whatever he needs even if it kills me." I also put so much time and energy into proving people wrong. I thought, "He's going to be okay. He's going to go and do what every other kid gets to do." People said he is so high functioning. I think this was such bologna; I think that he had the gift of a lot of access. He also has a lot of good people in his life to say to him, "Dude just do it!"

You would never know it now, but he was a really sick little boy in terms of his respiratory system. The first year Tyler was with me, we spent literally every holiday in the hospital. Often, if he lay down, he couldn't breathe at all because he had a narrowing of his tracheal tubes and low muscle tone, so his lungs would just collapse. He spent weeks at a time in the hospital, and I was a single woman and afraid of losing my job. This went on for about four years.

It was also hard with all the early intervention services. People may think I am ungrateful for the services provided in my home, but I got sick and tired of people showing up every single morning. And I had a "need" to vacuum up all the dog hair before they came. But still, I appreciated it, and I never wanted to miss it. I was afraid if I missed it, it could be the one thing he needed. It was so awful and constant.

The second part of Lucinda's story continues in Chapter 9 on dating. It includes how she managed to change from being a happy solo to a happy duo in a marriage she had not expected.

Genius Moments:

Lucinda has fared really well in life by trusting her instincts, often making bold moves that felt mostly right to her. She progressed from feeling as if her house was too big to not share with a possible foster child, to finding herself sitting in a room of the foster care agency. She described herself as being with "all these twenty-something couples who had fertility issues, and I felt like a freak of nature." But she kept moving along and let her instincts and heart and gut rule the day. Some of Lucinda's strategies and philosophies include:

- *Trusting her gut.* Neuroscientists now believe that gut feelings often lead to wise decisions. Dr. Antonio Damasio, head of the Brain and Creativity Institute at the University of Southern California, is among them. He states, "What we construct as wisdom over time is actually the result of cultivating that knowledge of how our emotions behaved." Gut instincts draw on that knowledge. Lucinda knew more than she was consciously aware of and had a gut feeling about what would make her happy.

- *Normalizing fear.* Lucinda accepts her fear using a strategy described in Chapter 2. She is mindful of her fear so that it doesn't have to weaken her. In her words, "Being afraid is normal."

- *Connecting with other parents of kids with disabilities.* Lucinda sees this as vital for two reasons. First, calling other parents of kids with disabilities is her first "go-to" strategy when she is frustrated or scared. It took her a long time to feel comfortable, but she learned to allow herself to call them and admit to them that she was scared or that something was wrong. She said, "I know I can call and complain about something. They know that I am not asking them to fix it and that I just need to vent. That's something my husband still needs to learn." As discussed in a previous chapter, she attributes learning from other parents as key to making things work.

Conclusion

All three of the parents featured in this chapter found they had accomplished what they had wished for. Not only did their children thrive in their care, but the parents were also able to deeply love and enjoy them. It seems fitting to close with a comment Lucinda made about her son:

> "I'm not Catholic or Jewish, but he went to a Catholic school and went to a Jewish afterschool. And if there happened to be a Muslim evening program that was the best, he would go there too. He is naturally confused and used to tell the sister at the church 'Shabot Shalom.' It was so sweet. I love that concept of him growing up being everything and not having any discrimination. *I love the fact that the only time my son discriminates is if you've been a jerk.*"

Chapter 8

Conceiving on Your Own

*"I'm a mom by choice and single by circumstance.
I wanted to have this child. I could feel this soul wanting
to come out of me. So I wanted to bring this soul into the
world because he wanted to be here. I do believe he
wanted to be here. Just look at the circumstances.
Due to his medical syndrome, only one in ten thousand
actually makes it into the world. So, I went ahead and
said to myself, 'I'm having this child,' a partner would
have been wonderful but I can do this alone."*
—Amanda

THE SOLOS IN this chapter are all parents who decided they would
have a child whether or not they ever found the right partner for themselves. Although there is still some stigma about making this choice,
a look at current demographics shows that this decision is becoming
much more prevalent. As far back as ten years ago, the largest sperm
bank in the United States owed one-third of its business to single potential mothers. Solo men also often long for a child. Readers may be interested in Nicholas Blincoe's article "Why Men Decide to Become Single
Dads" about the struggles that single fathers face (see References).

Even though parents who are solo by choice are becoming more
common, they are still often faced with the strong cultural belief that

a two-parent household is more desirable, more natural, and better for the children. There is a common perception that being raised by a single parent is a recipe for disadvantage. Fathers who are single by choice face even greater stigma, skepticism, and downright suspicion.

People who are considering being single parents by choice often face worried family and friends who fear the experience will turn out badly because it is simply too much for one person to handle. If you want to talk facts with your skeptical friends and family, you can refer to a 2005 study by Clare Murray and Susan Golombok on the experiences of single versus married women who chose donor insemination (see References). The solo mothers had no higher levels of stress than the married ones, and the absence of a father was not correlated to higher levels of emotional problems. In fact, the solo mothers experienced greater joy and pleasure and lower levels of anger.

Other studies, such as one done by Judith Siegel (1998), found levels of coping and satisfaction equal to those of married women, although the solo mothers initially worried more about finances. Given that solo parents by choice were much less common fifteen years ago, these findings are especially reassuring. Much of the research on single mothers, which has historically underscored problems, is not relevant to those who made the decision intentionally because the circumstances are often very different.

In *Choosing Single Motherhood* (2008), Mikki Morrissette provides a thoughtful analysis of much of the more general research on raising a child alone. She drew, in part, from the work of Mavis Hetherington, who studied 2500 children over a period of thirty years. Morrissette explains some of the parenting implications inherent in these research findings and states that two paths often develop: a parent is either primarily overwhelmed or in control. Morrissette emphasizes that it is easy to get worn down despite the best intentions; she also firmly believes in motherhood by choice. She writes:

"As one child development expert I talked to told me, the basic needs of kids are the same in every home:
- Infants need warmth, protection, and sensitivity to their signals.

- Children need control and limit setting.
- Teens need help negotiating greater independence while remaining connected.

"'One person trying to provide all these things for a child, without backup or help from another involved adult, can feel overloaded and overwhelmed at times,' she said. 'It's harder for singled than coupled parents to do all this, but it can be done'" (p. 91).

Morrissette adds that choosing to have a child on your own does not require that you be a superhero but does require three components: 1) having confidence in the educational and childcare options you have carefully chosen; 2) establishing support networks for time when your routine is utterly thrown off due to illness and emergencies; and 3) finding outlets for stress relief that will enable you to be well engaged when you are with your children. Although having a child with a disability complicates each of these three components, it does not make any of them expendable.

This chapter focuses on coping with the additional pressures that solo parents who have conceived on their own face. It begins with information on handling the complexities of asking for help, to include ideas on setting boundaries with family members who are disapproving to the point of being emotionally harmful. Then we turn to self-imposed internal pressures that are often problematic. Guilt and perfectionism are addressed in some depth because these make parenting harder. Although many parents are vulnerable to guilt and perfectionism, these themes were especially prevalent in the stories of the solo parents featured in this chapter.

You will meet:

- Whitney, who is juggling a very demanding career and a young daughter with Down syndrome
- Melanie, who chose to conceive on her own and became the mother of twin sons, born prematurely and weighing in at two and a half and three and a half pounds.

In addition to Whitney and Melanie, Amanda in Chapter 1 also took the path of conceiving on her own.

Asking for Help

Mikki Morrissette, the author of *Choosing Single Motherhood,* highlighted the critical role of asking for help when it comes to being a choice parent:

> "Raising a baby is very hard, especially for women used to being in control and succeeding at everything—which, in my experience, describes myself and many women who consider Choice Motherhood. You lose control of your body, your life, and suddenly become the loving slave of a tiny little being. You fail at small things like staying awake or big things like learning how to breastfeed. Worst of all, you have to learn how to let other people help you. My advice is this: Don't have a baby if you don't have a support system in place. You will need parents, family, and friends to help out when you get sick, haven't slept in days, need emotional support, or are just having a difficult time. You really can't do it all by yourself, and you shouldn't. Work it out so you can pay back these people in other ways, if it makes you feel better" (p. 113).

Asking for help is harder for some people, and I suspect this is particularly true of the independent-minded people who deliberately choose solo parenthood. Furthermore, asking for help from family may be especially difficult since it may feel like it requires swallowing your pride. I am not naïve to the fact that there are indeed some parents who should not be asked for help; we'll get to them soon. But first let's address how to think in ways that make situations less anxiety-producing or onerous.

I often turn to the ideas of cognitive distortions that David Burns wrote about in his classic book *Feeling Good: The New Mood Therapy.* He defines cognitive distortions as patterns of errors in our thinking that affects how we think about ourselves, the world, and other people. These distortions are at the heart of cognitive therapy, which has been proven to help with depression, anxiety, and a host of other human problems. In other words, cognitive distortions make matters worse in all kinds of situations for most of us.

Learning to identify these common distortions paves the way for thinking in ways that enhance coping. Following is an illustration of how distortions can affect your willingness to ask for help:

1. **All-or-nothing thinking:** This type of distortion involves looking at things in absolute, black-and-white categories. Example: You may believe that asking for help means you are unable to cope. You irrationally believe (on some level) that you must be either entirely capable to handle everything as a solo parent or you are *incapable*; it is like a pass-fail test with no shades of gray.

2. **Jumping to conclusions:** David Burns explains that there are two forms of jumping to conclusions: 1) the "fortune teller error" and 2) "mind-reading." The fortune teller error is predicting negative outcomes (without a crystal ball). Mind-reading is assuming that people are thinking negatively about you. Both are better for working at a carnival than real-life. An example of both forms combined would be predicting that your family will react to a request for help by thinking you are weak and unable to cope. Without being psychic, who knows?

3. **Should statements:** These are absolutes that confer harsh judgment on anything that falls short of an ideal. Example: You may tell yourself, "A strong mother/father *should* be able to cope on their own! I *should* be self-sufficient at this point in life." Shoulds breed condemnation of ourselves and sometimes others. It would be more reasonable to say, "It *would be better* if I were more self-sufficient...."

4. **Overgeneralization:** This mistake involves regarding a single negative event as a "never-ending pattern of defeat." Example: You tell yourself that you simply can't manage your child because the last several days were filled with "meltdowns."

5. **Magnification or minimization:** You shrink the importance of something you did well and exaggerate the magnitude of what was lacking. Example: You minimize the fact that you had nerves of steel at the ER room with your child. At the same time, you magnify the importance of the fact that your house looks like it was visited by a small tornado and you need help today to simply get out to the grocery store.

I encourage you to look at the full list of distortions, which can easily be found on the Internet or in many of David Burns's excellent books.

Albert Ellis is another famous psychologist who focused on how the ways that people think can make them miserable. He used the terms *catastrophizing* and *awfulizing* to describe how people make negative outcomes worse than they actually are. Let's say you ask for help from someone, and you get the negative response you feared. Without "awfulizing" it would be fair to say that it might be very upsetting but probably far from the most unpleasant situation you have ever had. My intent is not to trivialize the types of hurt you may feel when family judges you or lets you down. But, cognitive distortions have a way of amplifying and extending the hurt. No one needs that. If you have not read Chapter 4, you may wish to do so because it includes a deeper discussion of dealing with such hurt.

Here are a few more pointers that may make it easier to ask for help:

- Remember that you did not formally relinquish your right to ask for help just because you may not have followed the advice of family or friends. After all, aren't we *supposed* to make our own decisions in adulthood?
- Bear in mind that asking for help is not an admission that you can't cope.
- Eleanor Roosevelt is credited with saying "No one can make you feel inferior without your consent." I happen to love this quote, and it can be reworded into many useful variations such as "No one can make you feel weak without your consent." Healthy coping requires a kind of internal "firewall"

that keeps us from internalizing every negative view of ourselves that others may express. This is the same skill we need to teach our children, who are likely to cope with more than their fair share of negative comments over a lifetime.

- Think about how you ask for help. I would suggest that the request be matter of fact (rather than dramatic) and specific in terms of what would be helpful. It is preferable (but not essential) to ask for help before you reach "meltdown."

Unsupportive and Sometimes Harmful Family Reactions

No doubt, many of you have heard a version of the admonition "That's what you get for fooling with Mother Nature!" You may also have been asked why you did not simply choose to adopt a child. Adoption is often seen as generous in spirit and assisted reproduction as inherently selfish. Ellen Painter Dollar (2012) addresses this in *No Easy Choice: A Story of Disability, Parenthood, and Faith in an Age of Advanced Reproduction.* She writes:

> "My preferred answer to the question 'Why don't you just adopt?' is 'Why don't you?' Those who ask this question often have biological children or don't have any children at all. When adoptive parents chime in on debates over the merits of adoption versus the use of reproductive technology, they tend to say that, while adoption is a wonderful choice that they are glad they made, adoption is not easy and not for everyone... Observers are often quick to judge adoption as selfless and biological parenthood as selfish."

Of course, there are indeed some very supportive families out there. But many families have mixed, if not negative, responses to a man's or woman's choice to conceive a child on their own. One parent shared with me the following comment about her family of origin:

"Some of my family members are disinclined to watch my daughter since they find her needs to be overwhelming. Some have a sense that since I deliberately sought out motherhood as a single woman, I have somehow abdicated my right to ever complain about the difficulties my daughter and I face."

This mother's words were echoed by several others who participated in this book. Many felt that family and friends withdrew their support because they had not heeded their warnings or admonishments—admonishments that were often rooted in the belief that assisted reproductive techniques are religious transgressions.

Some comments are so toxic that you need to put some distance between yourself and the commenter. I believe you need to prioritize protection of the well-being of you and your child(ren) above attempts to prevent waves of disruption in the family. Personally, I would tell family members who made an offensive comment that I would like to continue to see them but won't expose myself or my child to such misguided and hurtful comments. But that's my style and not for everyone. There is also nothing wrong with simply avoiding the offender. Sometimes toxic relatives change—but not always. The same holds true for relatives who make ultimatums. In fact, throughout this book you will find instances of solos who have reconciled with estranged family members and some who have found friends who functioned as family.

It is time to shift from dealing with family to dealing with ourselves. We begin with Whitney, who had very little exposure to the world of disability until her daughter was born with Down syndrome. I consider her a choice parent because she started out with IVF after deciding to pursue solo parenthood.

Starting from Scratch

The Backstory: Whitney is in her forties and a highly successful career woman who had given up on her hopes of having a child despite fertility treatments. As described in Chapter 2, she absolutely believed she was guaranteed to have a baby without disabilities because she had God's protection—partly because she went to church every Sunday.

> *"I didn't really have a lot of exposure; kids with disabilities weren't really integrated into my classroom. Even when my daughter was born I knew nothing. I didn't even take one second to think about the possibility of a child with Down syndrome."*—Whitney

Excerpts from Whitney's life story follow:

> *I was thirty-nine when I got a divorce and I started wanting to have kids. I had never wanted them before and was very career oriented. I went to a fertility doctor but did not get pregnant despite the treatments and ended up trying a second and third doctor. The third doctor did all kinds of tests and said he would not even treat me since I had* **no** *chance of getting pregnant. He said that I needed to adjust my mental state to that fact and accept that I was not going to have kids. Because it was just so final, I went through a mourning period and accepted that sad fact.*
>
> *A few years later, I walked into the doctor´s thinking I had a urinary tract infection. When the doctor insisted I was pregnant, I was crying due to shock. I think I had resigned myself to never having a kid and was at the point where I felt, "I'm forty-two years old and I have worked so hard to get thin and move on with my life like a single career woman." When I told my now ex about our pregnancy, he was really good about it from the very beginning. I was shaking, and he said, "Well, we're both good people; it's okay." We had only been dating three months at that point.*
>
> *Everyone celebrated my pregnancy because I was older, I have a high profile job, and people knew that I was trying to have a baby and couldn't. I remember walking around saying this is the biggest miracle baby since Jesus. I still do think that she is a miracle. When the doctor asked me if I wanted to have prenatal testing, I said no because I wouldn't have had*

an abortion anyway. Now I wish I had because I would have been less shocked.

I also wish my pregnancy had not had so much attention because it made it harder. When the baby's not "perfect," you're embarrassed at first. This is especially the case if you've always been an achiever because you think it's a reflection on you—as if you had failed in some way.

The day of Lauren's birth, they had to do an emergency C-section, and the birth scene was traumatic. It still sometimes replays in my mind. After we got home, we learned she had a hole in her heart and needed to be on a bilirubin light. So, nothing felt right. I had a three-month maternity leave. I couldn't get it together. I was home by myself with this baby with Down syndrome. I was thinking nonstop about it because I had nothing else to think about, so it wasn't good. My family thought I was suicidal and came to my house. The best thing that happened to me was that I went back to work.

A while after Lauren was born, I felt very strongly that I wanted another baby. Part of this was because I worried about who would take care of her when I was gone. Her father said, "You can't bring someone into this world with a job already."

I did establish a trust, so everything is set up for Lauren. But if I live another forty years, what happens to my daughter at that point? She will be an adult, and who is going to administer her funding, get her to the doctor, and help her with things? That's what gets me thinking about another kid. When I see people I know, I often start thinking to myself, "Hmm, I wonder if that person can take care of Lauren?" For instance, I have a friend who has a daughter who is seven, so I'm thinking, "Oh, she can take care of Lauren." But you never know what a kid with Down syndrome will be like when she grows up. That's the single biggest thing that keeps me up at night: Who is going to take care of Lauren if I'm not here?

It has gotten even harder to juggle work and my daughter, and there is a lot of guilt. For example, Sunday I had an

important conference call because a hurricane hit our busi-
ness region. I put her in her crib but I could hear her want-
ing attention. It was one of those impossible situations. So
then I had to take her in to work for another conference call
and I gave her the iPad and let her watch Elmo the whole
time. And then sometimes I come home at night and I'm
just really tired and I may let her watch Elmo for an hour.
I know I should be doing drawing, coloring, letters, and
sounds with her. I have a lot of guilt that I'm not the best
mother. But then, sometimes I think that I give her too much
attention and she is kind of spoiled. It is hard to ever feel I
am doing it all the right way.

If I didn't have her, I would be living downtown in a
loft condo. But now, I'm moving out to the suburbs with her
where everyone is married and I'm single. It's like I don't fit
in downtown because I have a kid; I don't fit in out there be-
cause I'm single. None of that is about special needs.

I think about dating. I think the thing with dating is
that it's hard enough to find someone who is going to like
you, particularly at this age. At age forty-six, most people are
having grandchildren, not children. Now I have a two-and-a-
half-year-old, and she has Down syndrome. It's scary to put
yourself out there and have to tell people that.

I really believe everything happens for a reason. I al-
ways thought that before, but now I really believe it. I re-
member right after she was born, I could think of a million
reasons why I had a kid with Down syndrome. But they
were negative like, "I'm such a bitch and this is my punish-
ment" or "I'm too superficial." I wouldn't say that I'm to the
point where I think it's a complete 100 percent blessing. I'm
not there yet. Well, I just continue to look at my daughter
and think she's just a living miracle. I wasn't supposed to
have a baby, and here's this baby. And I think I couldn't love
her any more than I do.

Genius Moments

Whitney is wonderfully honest about her feelings. The fact that she loves her daughter dearly is evident to anyone who knows her, yet she is honest that she struggles with the fact that her daughter has Down syndrome. She also applies what she has learned in her successful career to manage a very independent life with her daughter. If it has to get done, she will do it, move ahead, and reconfigure plans if necessary. Some of her beliefs and strategies follow:

- *Finding the balance between therapies and living life.* Whitney said it very well: "You can only do so much. I remember when all these therapists were coming to the house, and I asked how many times a day I needed to perform each therapeutic activity with my daughter. They would never give me an answer. I honestly think I wanted them to say, 'You do this for thirty minutes a day and your child will be okay.' I wanted that finite answer. I know now that it's not finite. At first, I demanded every single therapy for my daughter. But, four out of five nights a week, I was with my daughter at therapy and I recognized that was too much. It would be seven o'clock and my night was just starting! So we cut back."

- *Rethinking the role of men in her life.* She says, "Well, I think the good thing is that I will not date the type of guys that I did before. I will be different in my approach with men, and my daughter will always be my first priority. I don't think I will ever stay in a bad relationship again. Now, my attitude is, 'If you like me, let's see if it works. If you don't, then let's just move on.' That's new for me, and I think back to less healthy relationships."

- *Understanding the need for professional help with her feelings of grief.* Whitney regarded therapy as very important to handle her feelings of grief. She began therapy just a few weeks after her daughter was born. She sought out support groups but felt the members did not address their feelings. Her comments on this and professional help can be found in Chapter 4.

- *Understanding that work can be therapeutic.* As Whitney described, she turned a corner in her ability to cope when she went back to work. With hindsight she understood that sitting home ruminating while depressed was exactly what she didn't need. Of course, she was vigilant about making sure she had proper care for her daughter and still worried a great deal but also felt a great relief.

Guilt

Guilty thoughts are sneaky since they often bypass our rational mind and slip in when we are feeling tired or especially full of love for our children. For choice parents, guilt may slip in when your guard is down, and you may begin to question whether the nay-sayers are right: children need two parents. Chapter 1 discusses the fact that guilt is one of the strongest and most common emotions that surfaces when a child is born with a disability. As is clear from the stories of Whitney, Melanie, and Amanda (Chapter 1), guilt is often not far away from a parent's heart.

Guilt can drive parents to go to great lengths to "fix" a child's disability—sometimes to the detriment of the child and the family. It is kind of as if parents are softly saying to themselves, "You broke it...you fix it." Some parents wonder if they should have been more careful in the IVF process: Could something have been wrong with the sperm? Did I go to the wrong place?

Self-blame can take the form of wondering whether the critics were right—you *shouldn't* try to fool Mother Nature. The thoughts that you found so offensive when expressed by others can sneak in under the radar. For example, even though you may feel the need to distance yourself from relatives who believe that in vitro fertilization procedures are sacrilegious, in private blue moments you may wonder if some of what they say is true. This is especially the case when a child is born with a disability. Ellen Painter Dollar's book, which was mentioned earlier in the chapter, was written from her perspective as a religious Christian who used IVF but not without deep struggles with religious and ethical aspects of her choice. Some readers might find her book helpful, since she explains how she resolved these struggles for herself.

Trying to be the best parent possible is inherently guilt producing for many, and these feelings can wreak havoc with life. Guilty feelings are actually only supposed to serve as a warning system to signal us that we have done something wrong. If guilt operated like that consistently, it would be great. The problem is that the warning system may malfunction and trigger far too easily. It reminds me of a smoke detector I had that would blare an alarm if it even got a whiff of steam from a pot on the stove.

We need to determine when to heed the alarm (for healthy guilt) and when to simply silence it (for irrational guilt). Parents tend to think that if they do things just right, they can leave feelings of guilt in the dust; but this is not the case. Perfection in parenting is a moving target and simply not humanly possible. When it comes to parenting a child with a disability, it is even more elusive of a pursuit. And if you are a solo parent and working to support your family, time is even more limited.

As discussed in Chapter 2, almost all biological parents (across the world) feel, even on a subtle level, that they have somehow caused their child's disability. With few exceptions, this guilt is irrational. Robert Mittan (2005) wrote a very powerful article about coping with guilt when raising a child with a seizure disorder. He also referred to parental self-blame and extended it beyond congenital disabilities to acquired ones.

He adds that each manifestation of the disability then—in this case, seizures—becomes a personal failure of the parent.

Mittan believes that guilt also results from what he calls "the disorder of *hyper-responsibility*." Every day, we receive many messages that communicate an underlying cultural message that parents are 100 percent responsible for everything that happens to their children. We all know parents who brag mightily about their children's accomplishments as if they themselves were responsible for them. We also know excellent parents who hold themselves overly responsible for their children's problems even if they are now adults with minds and choices of their own.

Other times, guilt sensors are triggered because someone implies that we *should* feel guilty about something we have done or are currently doing. This has been called *referred* guilt. One example would be referred guilt for making the choice to be a single parent. That referred guilt may drive attempts to "make up" for there being only one parent.

Then there is the irrational guilt of being a working solo parent. So many people feel guilty because their work necessitates spending less time with their children. I have sometimes reminded myself that work is necessary, and human cloning has not been invented, so I shouldn't feel guilty. Fathers also feel this guilt, although they are less prone to being criticized for working while being a single parent.

Clearly, not all guilt is irrational. Sometimes, feelings of guilt are triggered because we did make a mistake or deviated in another way from our behavioral standards. Then, guilt can be healthy and productive if we don't stew in it and just let it positively affect our behavior.

Managing Guilt

When the guilt alarm sounds, the first step is determining if it is a genuine or false alarm. In other words, we need to decide if we actually engaged in a behavior that violated our personal standards. Some of the following strategies are useful:

- Separate irrational from healthy guilt. Decide whether you actually engaged in a behavior that violated your standards.
- Judge yourself on your *intention*. Sometimes we truly do cause harm inadvertently. I personally don't believe in feeling guilty under these circumstances. I also strongly believe we are all entitled to make some unintentional errors. I remind myself that surgeons have been known to cut off the wrong limb, babies have gotten switched at birth, and…to err is human.
- If you find that you did do something that you should feel guilty about, heed that alarm and channel the guilt into positive action. For example, if you missed a child's special event, then figure out how to ensure you won't miss future events. Make a change so that you learn from the regret. Take a moment to let go of your mistake while thinking about how you might handle things differently in the future.

- There is a great saying in twelve-step programs that people use so they won't get paralyzed by guilt and regret. It is simply: "Do the next right thing." I think it is a great mantra for all.
- Share your regrets and mistakes with someone. Finding others with whom you can share the ups and downs can help you feel not alone or overwhelmed. Some parents share "terrible parenting moments" that they can later laugh about. It helps to know you're not the only one who makes mistakes.

Paschal Baute has written a lot about the art of forgiveness, and some of his wisdom is included in Chapter 4. He also teaches the skill of apology. He says that as humans, we will invariably need this skill. He recommends four steps:

- *Step One:* Apologize as soon as possible. He adds that the longer we wait, the more we fear an apology could be turned against ourselves. It becomes progressively harder to do.
- *Step Two:* Speak specifically about the behavior that you wish to apologize for. Spell it out.
- *Step Three:* Describe your feelings about what you did. Baute provides an example: "I am embarrassed to think about how thoughtless that was..."
- *Step Four:* Explain that this is not your typical behavior. In this manner, you conclude by affirming aspects of your better self.

Of course, these are only general guidelines, and the last step may be most useful with adults (and not children) under selected circumstances.

Making a promise that you can't keep is especially harmful to children because it erodes trust. When ashamed, parents are likely to say, "I will never do this again! I promise." This makes children feel better and is often heartfelt. But, there is the risk of slipping and hurting a child more. So it is better to say, "I will try so very hard to see that I never do this again." And then, if you need to get help to ensure you don't repeat your mistake—do that.

Perfectionism

"To be a good mother, you should 100 percent focus on your kids. That's where the guilt comes in. If I am taking time for myself, they could be upset that I am gone from the house. I know it's irrational—and in reality they're playing and not even giving it a second thought—but I still get that feeling of guilt."
—Whitney

Perfectionism and guilt often go hand in hand. Perfectionists routinely feel their accomplishments are never quite good enough, no matter how well they perform or what others think. Perfectionism is a problem for the general public, and many would benefit from taking it down a couple of notches. But for solo parents of kids with disabilities, this is even more important. There simply isn't enough time or energy to burden yourself with all the ill effects of perfectionism.

The drive for perfection is sometimes motivated by the fantasy that we can ward off criticism if we do things just right. The problem is this doesn't work and also robs life of its pleasure because of the amount of effort we need to put into striving for perfection.

Research has repeatedly shown that people who are highly perfectionistic actually perform less well at many tasks when compared to people who have high but reasonable personal standards. Some people believe their own perfectionism is a desirable quality that helps them succeed. Psychologists and researchers have a different perspective. They have found that perfectionistic people tend to be more critical of others, are more guarded interpersonally, and are more prone to depression and anxiety. Furthermore, perfectionism inhibits creativity because perfectionists can't tolerate something not turning out well. For that matter, it may also cause people to procrastinate when starting a task.

The mix of perfectionism and parenting is especially hard on mothers and fathers, since perfect parenting is impossible. It's not good for children either since we are always role models to our children. When we can't accept our own mistakes, how can we teach them to accept theirs? Even if we try to control expressions of perfectionistic beliefs, children will see the subtle cues through our behaviors. We need to *demonstrate* that we can accept our mistakes as well as our performances that fall short of what we desired. This type of role modeling helps us demonstrate to children with disabilities that it is just fine not to be able to do something. Children may very well need to learn from us that it is okay if they never learn to read, run well, or drive.

As Brené Brown, the author of *The Gifts of Imperfections*, says, "Perfectionism is not about striving for excellence or healthy striving. It's a way of thinking and feeling that says this: 'If I look perfect, do it perfect, work perfect, and live perfect, I can avoid or minimize shame, blame, and judgment.'" Brown has described perfectionism as a twenty-pound shield.

The roots of perfectionism often go back to childhood, but this doesn't mean that we can't do anything about it. There are many practical strategies that are useful, and several center on daring yourself to do things well but not perfectly. This also frees up time that can be better spent on the most important priorities. Some recommendations include:

- Use time limits to curb perfectionistic behavior. Rather than focusing on completing something perfectly, set aside a specific amount of time to work on the task and when that time is up, the project is "good enough."
- If you make a mistake, embrace it as an opportunity to learn to tolerate imperfection in yourself. Your anxiety is likely to rise at first, but it gets easier and is very freeing over time.
- Think about what advice you'd give to friends. You would never suggest that they have to do something perfectly. My guess is that you would often tell them to just "do their best" when working on something. You probably wouldn't be as critical of a friend as you are of yourself.
- Observe someone you believe is very capable—and notice his or her mistakes.
- Ask yourself: Will this matter in a year? This applies both to mistakes as well as to "perfect" instances of performance.

with other parents. Our next solo parent has a lot to say about the "Disability Olympics" of parenting, among other topics:

> "Right now with the Internet, blogs, and Facebook, everyone's putting so much out there about their daily life, and there are so many groups for autism moms. There's so much comfort in that. Someone will post something like, 'My child just tried to flush the dog down the toilet—has anyone's kid ever tried that?' And sixty-eight people will say yes. It is both bizarre and good because you're not isolated. But then the judgment starts.
>
> "There's this mommy judgment that is rampant and involves variations of, 'I am a better mother than you because I do this for my kids.' It's ridiculous, but it's very real. Some parents also compete on whose kid is most disabled. It's almost like a badge of honor to have a kid who is significantly disabled and be able to handle it. It's ridiculous because we all want our kids to be as minimally disabled as possible. It's crippling because that's where a lot of the guilt comes from. Some people's mind-set is that if I'm going to be that supermom and be able to compete—I have to do everything perfectly. Taking two hours for myself is not acceptable."

Let's move on to the rest of this parent's story and find out how she handles stressors from other parents.

Trauma and Strength

The Backstory: Melanie was not sure if she wanted a husband, but she did know she wanted to be a mother. She conceived on her own and became the mother of twin sons, born at thirty-two weeks despite all efforts to delay their births and a terribly hard pregnancy. They weighed only two and a half and three and a half pounds and spent more than a month in the NICU.

> *"There's also this reaction from people. Sometimes it feels like pity or a put down. They say, 'Oh my gosh! You have*

two of them and you're by yourself. How do you do that?' If I
hear one more person say that to me...."—Melanie

Excerpts from Melanie's story follow:

I had twin boys on my own with an anonymous donor.
Several years before their birth, I almost got married, but
three weeks before the wedding, I realized that he was not
the right person for me. After a lot of soul searching, I realized
what I really wanted was to be a mom, and the marriage part
was a little bit optional for me.

On my thirty-second birthday, I had an ultrasound, and
there were two heartbeats. So I hit the jackpot! But I had a
very difficult pregnancy and multiple surgeries during it. After
holding out as long as I could, they were born at thirty-two
weeks. One was only two and a half pounds and the other
was three and a half. A few hours after birth, one had to be
life-flighted to another hospital for emergency surgery.

They were both in the NICU for thirty-three days. I have
never been through anything that stressful. I was there four-
teen to sixteen hours a day and only left to sleep. Because they
were so premature, they had apnea and would stop breathing,
so it took weeks for me to be allowed to hold them. Even
then, both babies would stop breathing and turn blue. Thank
goodness they would start breathing again on their own and
did not need to be resuscitated. But I was always so scared. I
would hold them and instead of looking at each baby, I would
look at the monitors. If their oxygen levels started to drop (or
if something beeped), I would jump out of my skin because I
was convinced the child was going to die in my arms.

Because of the entire trauma involved, I would jump
at noises, carried a sense of dread, and thought something
bad was going to happen every few seconds. Sometimes
it got even scarier. For instance, I got a phone call late one
night. The hospital said that one of my sons was extremely
ill and they didn't know what was wrong. He ended up with
an infected salivary gland, and when you're talking about a

three-pound baby, an infection could kill him. So they had to put an IV in his scalp and put him on antibiotics for ten days. During this time, he stopped breathing about ten times every hour, which was terrifying. It was true trauma and I couldn't do anything about it.

I will never forget the day I had to take the "car seat test" in order for my sons to be discharged from the hospital. The hospital staff put them in their car seats while hooked up to monitors. They had to sit for an hour because that's a very difficult position, and they could stop breathing. The numbers had to stay stable for an hour to prove they could handle the drive home. I was white-knuckling it, but they did beautifully. They unhooked them and handed them to me to take home. I said, "Are you sure?!"

It was the longest drive of my life, and I think I went five miles per hour while my mom was driving her car behind me. Because I couldn't hear them (since they were naturally asleep), it was hard not be "convinced" that they had died. I had to keep telling myself that they were okay the whole way home.

That first night, everyone offered to stay with me. I said, "No. I'm doing it on my own. I will be okay." I remember literally shaking with fear every time one of my babies cried. I was terrified that something terrible was going to happen and I wouldn't be able to meet their needs.

One day when they were nine months old, I was trying to feed one of them and the other one started to cry. I made a joke and I heard myself say, "Your cry will be answered in the order in which it was received." I remember thinking at that moment, "I'm not scared anymore; I think I'm going to be okay." I was still stressed and crazy because I had two infants with special needs who weren't growing correctly and all that. But, I was able to crack a joke at three o'clock in the morning. So, at about the nine-month point, I started to feel calmer.

Both had feeding problems, and it was taking forty-five minutes for each to eat, but they had to be fed every two hours because they were so little. So, until I found some *tricks, it was forty-five minutes plus forty-five minutes, ten minutes off, and time to begin again.*

Then I had to go back to work. The first year back in the classroom, I was just on autopilot. I don't remember the kids from that year or what I did. I was physically exhausted, and my brain was with the boys 100 percent of the time. I did find the best babysitter (by happenstance), who made this possible. I still have her.

The boys will be seven. They both have mild CP but are different. One didn't walk until he was three and needed a walker to pull himself up. The very day I asked the physical therapist if he would need a wheelchair or walker for distances, he took his first steps. He's fine now, and today he informed me he's going to run the marathon when he's older. His brother has autism and ADHD, is blind in one eye, and a few more things. His CP had been pretty bad on his whole right side, but now it is fine.

People are constantly pushing me to go out by myself or to date. I rarely do. When I do go out, one of my sons will say something like, "You don't want to be with us? Why don't you want to be with us?" My head is still 100 percent consumed by my boys, but they are just now beginning to be a little bit more independent.

I'm wondering at what point I am going to want to have somebody else to share my life with. But I also have huge fears about sharing my boys. They are mine, mine, mine—100 percent mine. I can't imagine co-parenting or having someone discipline my boys even if the discipline was totally respectful and called for. Then, I recognize that I am jumping seventeen steps ahead.

Note: the day this interview was done, Melanie had her first date. This was with Paul, whose story you can read about in the bereavement chapter. Chapter 9 describes their unique approach to exploring the possibility of a long-term relationship (or more) while putting the needs of their three children absolutely first.

Genius Moments

Melanie is a genius at understanding that a person can be totally scared and simultaneously capable of strength. As we saw when she was terrified of taking the children home from the hospital, she drives ahead (literally) with her fear. She also models how to handle the strong emotional beliefs that she knows are irrational but are very compelling.

- *Appreciating that early intervention is invaluable.* "There was a social worker in the NICU, and she said 'I don't see anything to worry about with your boys, but just make sure you have early intervention come to do an evaluation.' I bit her head off and said, 'I'm a special ed teacher, I would know if something was wrong; how dare you make dire predictions about my boys!' And she took it very well. About three days later (when I had them at home) I just called anyway because I figured I'd better. That made all the difference. I teach middle school; I can tell the kids who have had early intervention and who haven't. So I called that social worker about a year later and apologized. I said, 'Make sure you keep telling every single parent whether they want to hear it or not.'"

- *Connecting without engaging in competing parenting.* As Melanie stated, earlier in this chapter, there is often great competition between mothers of children with disabilities. In essence, the message is that they can parent far better than you can.

    Given that this was not the first time that I heard this, I asked Melanie how she handles it. She replied: "It is damaging when you are around it. You start thinking you need to be like that other mother. Now I'm able to step back from it and recognize it for what it is. It is just mothers trying to make themselves feel better by putting you down. It often starts in places like the playground. Someone starts talking about doing some aspect of parenting better or the fact that they handle more than you do. When I'm out, I've learned to recognize this kind of talk and quickly distance myself. I realize that there is nothing that I can say that will get them to lay off, so I just leave.

If the competition is on the Internet, it is easier because I can just ignore it."

■ *Celebrating her children as a strategy for fighting guilt.* Melanie said, "I will always carry the guilt of seeing everything my sons have to cope with because they were born so small. So I carry guilt, especially when they struggle with something. I see my son's balance problems, but then I see that he is funny and happy and beautiful. The day I heard he also had autism, I pulled out a picture of him playing with his twin and standing inside a cardboard box and he's clearly laughing. I looked at his happy face and said to myself that I just know he's going to be okay."

It's Complicated, So Get Informed Help

Because solo choice parents are still relatively few in number, it makes great sense to band together with others and draw upon their experiences and like-minded approaches to life.

Single Mothers by Choice (www.singlemothersbychoice.org) is an excellent organization that was created in 1981 by Jane Mattes, a therapist and solo mother. The organization has an active blog as well as a forum for registered users. In addition, there are important resources including the not-to-be-missed "celebration DVDs," which include a panel of grown "choice children" as well as the insights of mothers with grown children. There is also a DVD of a talk by Jane Mattes on how to best help children who grow up in single-by-choice households. This organization does not candy-coat issues, provides genuine help, and celebrates unconventional families.

ChoiceMoms.org (www.choicemoms.org) was developed by Mikki Morrissette, who I quoted throughout this chapter. My enthusiasm for this website has to do with the high quality of information that it offers on a variety of specific topics. It includes podcasts for the "Choice Chat for Choice Moms" radio show, including a discussion with choice mom Lori Gottlieb on her book, *Marry Him: The Case for Settling for Mr. Good-Enough.* You can also listen to a podcast from a choice mother of a child with disabilities entitled "Holly: A

High Gear Parent Slows Down." The articles are equally engaging and include the opinions of acclaimed experts in child development.

This organization also offers connections to other choice mothers from around the world. A general discussion group has more than 1200 members and is geared for mothers who have proactively chosen to have a child outside of a relationship. There are also numerous subgroups, including ones for choice mothers who are forty or older, members by geographic area, and those whose children are 100 percent donor conceived.

Creating Motherhood (www.creatingmotherhood.com) was created by Dresden Shumaker to chronicle her daily life as a solo-by-choice mother who has a donor-conceived son. Her blogs are smart, funny, and helpful. Although Shumaker's child does not have disabilities, her thoughts are often poignant in applicable ways. For example, she often wrote about loving and caregiving as related to her grandmother's Alzheimer's. Her blog entitled "Father's Day with Donor Conceived Children" contains good practical insights. In addition to discussing how she responds to questions about her son's "daddy," she speaks of the practical value of the book, *What Makes a Baby?* by Cory Silberg, the author of *The Ultimate Guide to Sex and Disability.*

Many other good online supports have forums for choice parents included among resources focused on those trying to conceive. These include the well-known Resolve (www.resolve.org). There are undoubtedly many worthwhile sites that I have not included that you will be able to locate by searching online.

Conclusion

I have had the good fortune of getting to know all three children of these two (sometimes self-critical) mothers. I hope their mothers see what I see: happy, well-loved, thriving young children.

Being a good parent is more important
than being a married parent.
—Mikki Morrissette

Chapter 9

Dating, and Sometimes "Happily-Ever-Afters"

Well, the first date is always a bit of a job interview, and among the first questions you expect when you're a parent is, 'How old are your kids?' My problem is that if I admit early on that I have a teenager who needs a babysitter, I more or less have to explain that my son is autistic.
—*Hannah Brown* (New York Times)

AS READERS, YOU know that revealing that you have a child with a disability is only *one* of the complexities to dating. The many solo parents of children with disabilities who contributed to this book were very forthcoming about their fears, strategies, and experiences in finding romantic love. Many, like the two parents quoted below, assumed that it was better not to even try:

- "I dated a few times, but was very fearful that it took my attention away from my child. I was also fearful that the person I was dating wouldn't understand my son's needs and would be judgmental of him."

- "It makes me too tired! I am so busy with my kids and exhausted both physically and emotionally that it makes the desire to have a romantic life lower and lower. There are times that I feel starved for adult affection, but it isn't strong enough to do anything about it right now."

On the other hand, when I was conducting research for this book, one of the greatest surprises was the number of solos who did find satisfying relationships—and some lasting love. This included one woman in a long-term relationship who spoke of her relative hopelessness about this prospect:

> "After he left, I was worried about being alone. My thought process went something like this: 'I'm going to take care of this child the rest of my life. I'm going to be lonely, because I'm fifty-two now. Anybody who is my age and single, their kids are grown. They don't want to take on another kid; they don't want to take on a burden like that—they are ready to retire. I have nothing in the bank.' But as of today, I've been seeing a guy for about three and a half years. He told me what attracted him to me, and he said the number one thing was how I was taking care of my daughter."

This chapter presents many facets of dating and relationships. I believe in sharing "the good, the bad, and the ugly," so nothing is sugar-coated. Some solo parents have encountered serious problems, but there are also many whose dating stories have very happy endings. In addition to discussing advice and strategies from many solos, I include comments from solos who became engaged or married. These excerpts are from people who shared their stories in previous chapters: Paul, Sarah, Lucinda, and Melanie. I am including them for those who wonder how a new committed relationship or marriage can work.

Along with much of the world, I believe in romantic love and long-term committed relationships. But I also believe that we sometimes chase it in ways that make little sense. So we will begin by briefly looking at the basics.

Love and Rationality

Immature love says: "I love you because I need you." Mature love says, "I need you because I love you."
—Eric Fromm

Albert Ellis, a world-famous psychologist, had a lot to say about what he called "the dire pursuit of love." He believes humans are prone to irrational beliefs that cause much of their own misery. This includes amplifying desires to the point that they feel like urgent needs that must be met. He states that love becomes a "dire pursuit" for all too many people, and some pay a price that far exceeds the value of what they are chasing.

Portraying humans as inherently prone to foolishness, Ellis illustrates this by looking at what we give up while chasing romantic lives. Certainly, there is the tangible cost of dating, which might include the activities themselves, purchasing clothing, getting hair or nails done, and the like to achieve the "right look." But the greater cost is that we make other, more precious sacrifices. In a video interview entitled "Conquering the Dire Need for Love," Albert Ellis (2007) said:

> "We give up other pleasures in order to be loved. Although you might not think so, persons with dire love needs don't realize that there are other pleasures. Love is only one of perhaps fifty, one hundred, or five hundred potential pleasures. We give these up almost completely to get love. And ironically, the one thing we give up to get love is other love. Because potentially we are all capable of loving and being loved, in turn, by lots of people. And yet we might say, stupidly, take one individual who we think has to love us…"

Elisabeth Kübler-Ross (2000) shared some words on love while facing her own death. Her poignant words echo what Ellis said:

> "Some of us may never find that someone special, but that doesn't mean we won't find special love in our lives. The lesson is that we don't always recognize love because we categorize it, declaring romantic love to be the only 'real' kind. So many relationships, so much love around us."

Don't Settle for the Wrong Person

Elisabeth Kübler-Ross and David Kessler (2000), the coauthors of *Life Lessons*, shared the wisdom of one woman they knew who changed her approach to finding romantic love after being diagnosed with cancer:

> "So I made a choice to stop searching. I would go (to the party) but if Mr. Right was not there, other people were. Wonderful people I could talk to. I would just talk with them, have fun. I would be open to liking or loving them for who they were, no matter what."

Don't lower the bar.

Some solo parents raising children with disabilities feel they need to lower their standards in a partner. I just heard someone say, "Who will want someone like me with an autistic child?" The answer is: probably more people than she thinks. But such fears often block people's abilities to see red flags that a relationship is unhealthy. If a person can't face his or her life without a partner, chances are he or she is not ready to choose one wisely.

Joseph Wetchler (2005) discussed dating in an article he wrote on being a solo parent of a daughter with a disability. He stated that since interested women seemed scarce, when one showed interest, he felt pressure to make it work. His fears were reinforced by one woman who told him she was "as good as he was going to find." He was not alone in being tempted to lower the bar. Olivia (Chapter 12) wrote of staying too long in an abusive relationship because she lowered the bar due to her child's disability and her desire to avoid being alone.

As this chapter continues, it will be clear that many solos can find lasting love. Those whose stories appear in this chapter were the ones who did not feel desperate. All of the solo stories featured here are of parents who came to terms well with living life as a solo parent. You will notice that all took their time to determine whether someone was a good fit for them and they consistently prioritized their children.

Many people end up in relationships with the "wrong person" time and time again. Some feel it is simply bad luck or assert that only jerks are left in the dating pool since all the good ones are taken. This can lead to either giving up or staying with a partner who simply cannot offer what you need. Often the problem is due to other factors that keep us mired in the cycle of unsatisfactory partners. If you have a pattern of picking the "wrong person" or staying in an unhealthy relationship consider the following possible reasons and suggestions:

- *You don't think enough of yourself.* Problems with self-worth often play out in a few common scenarios. The most obvious is that men and women "settle" for a sub-par relationship as if that is all they are worth. You may tell yourself, "I'm not that great of a catch myself...."

- *You may believe that you need to be grateful for a partner who is willing to be with you "despite" your children.* This is one of those beliefs that may reflect negative experiences you have encountered but that still doesn't make it a truism. This book is full of stories of solos that have gone on to find good partners who love them *and* their children.

- *You believe people will change if you love them enough.* As a psychologist, I will say that many people struggle to change themselves even when they are fully invested in the process. It is rare to be able to change a partner in major ways. My advice is not to form a marriage or partnership in hopes of change.

- *You believe immediate "chemistry" is a good way to tell if someone is for you.* Chemistry is tricky for a few reasons. The first is easy, sexual attraction can be powerful but, eventually, can't compensate for problems such as character defects. The second reason is that we often have chemistry with someone who feels "right" because he or she strikes a familiar (not necessarily good) note in our psyches.

- *You are trying to change "the end of the story."* Professionals call this *repetition compulsion*. Sometimes, traumatic events draw us back to the proverbial "do over" in ways that operate below our consciousness. By doing so, we put ourselves in a situation that evokes something in our past and try to change the ending into a better outcome. For example, if you were raised by an alcoholic parent (who never got sober), you may unwittingly be attracted to people with drinking problems due to their familiarity as well as the unconscious desire to "fix" them.

- *You are replaying parts of your family of origin without realizing it.* People often repeat dynamics that occurred while they were growing up. As a psychologist, I have seen this routinely. Examples include assertive women who end up in the same submissive role as their mothers had. Similarly, I have known men, troubled by exceedingly needy mothers, who unwittingly ended up with similar women.

- *You are seeking external validation.* If you are unhappy with yourself or with life, chances are a romantic partner will not change this in the long run. Tamara Star, a life coach and author, explained this very well:

"If we grew up in a tumultuous childhood (and who didn't?) we were unheard and unvalidated. We grew up wanting that validation from the world around us and because we never experienced it in our past, we never developed the self-validation reflex. What does this mean? It means we're vulnerable to men that lay it on thick in the beginning. We let ourselves be put on a pedestal and be lavished with false love. This false love may feel authenticating but it's not" (www.dailytransformations.com/why-women-pick-the – wrong-men/).

Just because something has been relatively unconscious doesn't mean it has to stay outside of our control. This means that people can learn to read the signs that a particular relationship has warning indicators that should be heeded.

Reading the Indicators

Good Signs	Red Flags
You are comfortable with how your partner interacts with your child, as well as his or her own child.	You experience anxiety over his/her harsh approach to discipline, lack of sensitivity, or any inappropriate interactions with children.
Your partner respects your parenting values and your decision to have your child be the top priority.	There is a resentment of your children or the time that you put into them, and this undermines your parenting. You experience a need to defend your parenting style.
You feel that you are able to be yourself without fear of undue criticism. You can drop your guard.	You feel that your partner wants you to change yourself for him or her.
Your partner has established a track record with you that engenders trust and respect.	You have discovered instances of dishonesty or manipulation.
You feel free to express yourself without negative consequences.	You feel intimidated or that you must "walk on eggshells" around this person.
You are confident that he or she is not abusing alcohol or drugs.	You have some concerns about the amount of drinking or use of other substances.
Your partner is accepting of your autonomy.	You experience your partner as exerting too much control over your choices.
You are able to discuss conflicts without getting hot-headed and yelling. There are absolutely no instances of physical force—shoving, a raised hand, etc.	You have been frightened by a verbal or physical escalation (regardless of the reason for the altercation).
The person respects your need to spend time alone or with friends and to pursue your own interests.	You feel pressured to spend all your free time with him or her; your partner feels possessive or jealous.
Friends like him or her.	Friends are worried about your relationship.
You could be happy with this person "as is"—i.e., not a "fixer upper."	You keep hoping you can get the person to change.

There are many advantages to remaining solo rather than being with the wrong person. One solo parent who graciously filled out my online survey at 1:43 a.m. (!) explained the benefits especially well:

> "I don't have to consult with another adult to make a decision. My children can sleep in my bed without anyone else complaining. I do the dishes when I want or need to. My children can always come first. There are no disputes over discipline. On top of that, there is no division of authority. I can make all the decisions over what to spend and how to budget. I don't have to wait to align vacation schedules for us to go on trips. And I don't have to worry about the emotional impact on someone else (other than myself or my children) of a diagnosis.
>
> "I can choose time with my children rather than having to juggle a partner and my children. I do not ever have to worry that a partner is harming my children. I alone choose who comes and goes from our life. I don't have to deal with in-laws. I don't have to do another adult's laundry or dishes, clean up after another adult, or feel hostility toward any other adult in my household for not pulling their own weight."

Even after finding the right person, many solo parents decide that being a daily couple just isn't for them anymore:

> "If I ended up finding a man that I became serious with, I would only want to spend two nights a week with him because I'm busy and I've become very accustomed to my own space. There's something really tranquil behind that for me."

The Role of Time

> *The art of love is largely the art of persistence.*
> *—Albert Ellis*

Often what I heard from solo parents looking for intimacy and love was that the passage of time was an especially important factor.

Many solo parents reported that they became more optimistic about the prospects of finding love as their children became older. For example:

- "My son is diagnosed with bipolar, borderline personality disorder, and schizophrenia. He was diagnosed with bipolar at a very young age. He is one of the youngest children ever diagnosed with bipolar. When I would try to have a relationship, once they witnessed his behaviors, they all decided that was more than they were willing to deal with. I gave up on trying to have a relationship and didn't for eighteen years. Now my son is almost twenty-seven, and he has been stable for five years now! I am finally in a relationship, and the man I am dating gets along great with my son. He has witnessed some of my son's weird behavior, and has not taken off running."

- "I have had a couple of committed relationships over the years, but eventually the men I was seeing simply could not cope with the challenges of dating the mother of an Asperger's child. Now that my son is fifteen and is gaining more independence, has a healthy social life of his own, and is busy with sports and extracurricular activities, I have been able to start dating again. He actually encourages it now! I think he encourages it because he knows how dedicated I am to him and he has that base of security that I will always be there for him in his successes and struggles."

- "I am too tired to have a romantic life, and feel that I could not give a romantic partner the time that he would deserve. Given my son's problems with anxiety, I'm not sure that he would adapt well if I remarried and added another person to our household. My mom found and married a wonderful man when she was a long-time empty-nester in her sixties, so I have hopes that, someday, after my son moves out, I may find someone to love who would love me back."

Being Alone Rather Than Fearing Loneliness

Loneliness can push people to be in the wrong relationship. It can lead you down the road of getting into any relationship that can "protect" you from these feelings. It is important to understand the difference between being lonely and being alone; being alone is not inherently distressing.

Two conditions turn the relative comfort of solitude into loneliness: 1) when there is a lack of emotional connection with others, and 2) when being alone feels like rejection or abandonment. All people are prone to some loneliness. Loneliness is a temporary feeling, but bad decisions made in a state of loneliness can be far longer lasting. So it is important to learn how to manage loneliness and be more comfortable with being alone.

One way is to begin to question any embarrassment you may feel about being without a partner. For example, many people feel too self-conscious to go to a restaurant or movie alone because they fear that others will regard them as a "loser." We are often conditioned since childhood to be alert to the appearance of being undesirable. (Yes, I still remember worrying whether I would be the kid with no valentines put in her box). In adolescence, it was often better to have *any* boyfriend or girlfriend than to be seen alone at weekend movies or school dances.

In adulthood, if you are still feeling like a social reject for being alone, it is time to shed this remnant of childhood. This is essential since much of the pain of loneliness has to do with feeling rejected. Researchers David Hsu and Jon-Kar Zubieta (along with a team of others at the University of Michigan Medical School) demonstrated through brain imaging that the brain responds to social rejection in much the same manner as it responds to physical pain.

The manner in which we think has a great impact on how we feel since it is reflected in our self-talk. This principle is at the heart of the work of David Burns and other cognitive therapists. In Chapter 8, I wrote about Burns's list of ten cognitive distortions that are culprits in making people feel worse than necessary. *Magnification or minimization* is Burns's term for inflating the importance of some things and shrinking others. For example, someone may inflate the importance of one particular romantic interest (that he or she may barely know) and minimize the importance of the love of children and friends.

Personalization is another one of Burns's distortions. It is defined as seeing yourself as the cause of an event that does not turn out well. When it comes to dating, self-blame is easy and often begins with, "If only I…." Often, people need to remind themselves that the end of a dating relationship does not imply that they are deficient in some way.

Then there is the cognitive distortion of *all or nothing thinking* that is reflected in self-talk such as *"I'm all alone."* Burns points out the unnecessary distress caused by *should statements*—e.g., all adults *should* have a partner who loves them. Perhaps it is better to say that having a partner is something you deeply want—but *should* elevates it to a simple imperative and adds to the feeling that you can't live well until you get it.

It is helpful to remind yourself that fewer people are seeing being part of a couple as the only acceptable way to live life well. For the first time, the 2014 census figures report that there are more singles than married adults in America. Furthermore, the percentage of never-married adults has risen to slightly above 30 percent. Clearly, the social norms have shifted and the stigma of being single has diminished.

I am certainly not implying that you should be content to remain solo; rather, that you do not let your fear of loneliness cause excessive distress or bad choices. Enjoy the love and emotional connections that exist in your life now, while pursuing romantic love. If need be, build more emotional supports such as those described in Chapter 4.

The Nuts and Bolts of Dating

When solo parents of children with disabilities feel they are ready to enter the dating arena again, they have to bear certain considerations in mind that are not issues for other single parents. These include:

- deciding when to tell the other person that you have a child with a disability;
- assessing how the person responds to your child with disabilities;

- making it clear that your relationship with your child is paramount and you are the final authority when it comes to raising him or her;
- ensuring that the other person is not a sexual predator.

When to Tell

There was consensus from the solo parents who participated in this book that prospective romantic partners should be told early on about your child's disabilities:

- "Be honest from the beginning. Don't try and hide that you have a child with disabilities. Let them know that while you would like to continue dating them, there will be times when you are not available and times that you will have to cancel at the last minute."
- "I am always upfront with the people I meet. I tell them about my daughter and her conditions so neither one of us are wasting our time. When someone is interested, I always encourage them to ask me questions or tell me how they feel about what I have told them about my child."
- "I thought about lying to someone in the early stages of dating, but made the decision to be honest and upfront with the person about my son and let them make the decision whether or not they would be strong enough to deal with it. For a long, long time, none ever felt they were, and I had decided to just stay single forever. But thankfully, my son stabilized and now I am in a beautiful relationship with someone."

It is important that you remain honest with your new romantic prospect about the disabilities your child faces and what he or she is getting into well before the relationship takes off. Wendy Helfenbaum (2013) put it well in her article "Dating as a Single Parent of a Child with Special Needs." She wrote, "I think people operate better when they know what they're operating with. Be upfront before it gets too serious. I think that parents of children with special needs need to trust their intuition on that."

The consensus to tell upfront is wise, but that doesn't mean you need to share all of your child's personal business. After all, it may not be safe to divulge too much to someone you don't really know. However, it makes great sense to give a thumbnail sketch so prospective partners can be weeded out.

Background Checks

Although most people you meet socially would never dream of sexually abusing your children, it is important to be vigilant since young people with disabilities are abused at a much higher rate. Rates for children with disabilities are at least triple those of typical children, and people with disabilities remain at high risk even in adulthood. One solo mother shared her experiences with an abusive man:

> "I did meet a most wonderful man who loved her and my other kids so very much and was an absolutely great father figure to them. But then I walked in on him molesting one of my kids. So my romantic life has been hampered by fear of whether anyone could be trusted to be around her when she can't verbalize about 'nice' behavior that could really be evil. What I mean is, I have less trust for people who are overly willing to be loving to my child. This does impact romance."

Those who sexually abuse children or adults with disabilities are generally people known to the individual. Never let anyone think you are "paranoid" for not dropping your guard. One solo parent shared her advice to do background checks on prospective dates—a strategy sometimes used by solos (even without children) for obvious reasons:

> "Always make sure to do background checks. People can always say that they're a good person but can have a closet full of secrets."

Background checks are available to the public via web searches, Megan's Law listings, private businesses, and criminal court case dockets. Many of the options don't cost anything at all. According to a 2013 article by Kim Komando for *USA Today*, online background checks can be done via numerous sites, including PeekYou, White Pages Neighbors, The Beat, and the Dru Sjodin National Sex Offender Public Website. All information found on these websites is public knowledge and consists of information (including social media postings) that comes directly from the person you are researching.

Background check websites thoroughly search the Internet for any findings on the person in question. Results can include age, addresses, relatives, even hidden or protected social media pages, licenses, misdemeanors, felonies, arrest records, bankruptcies, and more depending on the website used. Although employers are required to get permission from the person to conduct a background check, people using the reports for personal reasons, such as dating, are not. The websites are confidential, so the person you are checking up on will never be notified that someone is looking into his or her background.

Many of the background check websites claim to be free services, but once the report is generated and ready to be viewed, the site asks for a credit card number. The price for a background check varies depending on the website used.

One website that is free for public viewing is the Unified Judicial System website. This website is available for each state, but the website itself varies in each state. On this site, you can get court docket sheets from traffic violations to drug charges to other misdemeanors and felonies. This is for public view, so therefore is completely legal and confidential.

Assessing the Relationship over Time

A background check is only a start. There is a lot more checking out to do—even before the person you are seeing is introduced to your child or children:

- "Be with a person long enough to see their 'seasons of behavior.' If it seems too good to be true, it probably is. However, there are great catches out there, and we all deserve to give ourselves the opportunity to wait for a great mate, I do believe."
- "I was upfront about having a son with autism, and I encouraged my partner as we became more serious to educate

himself and to read books if he was serious about me. Then, I would randomly ask him questions about the diagnosis, in particular what he thought about handling misbehavior. I wanted to assess his views on this and punishment."

- "You almost have to treat your dates as if they are in a job interview. It is very hard to find someone who is patient and understanding of the situation. I have met many who have said sure they could handle it, but when put in that situation, it scared the crap out of them or they didn't understand the tantrums, etc. Take things slowly and suggest after a few dates that they read books or watch a movie about the disability to get a better understanding of your everyday life with your amazing child."

- "I have a rule that I won't sleep with anyone before sixty days because I need to know someone. When you're dating, I think that people don't even act themselves and are acting on their best behavior for the first six months, so if you're sleeping with someone before that, you don't even know who that person really is. And then sex changes everything. My girlfriends can't understand how I hold true to my rule, but I just respect myself that much."

Of course, when you are in the early stages of getting to know someone, you may very well be on your best behavior as well. Trying to act like a better version of yourself can add stress to your already stressful life.

Making It Clear You Put Your Child First

As your relationship with the new person deepens, it is important to emphasize that your child's well-being comes first in your life and that you are not willing to short-change your child for the sake of any other relationship. As one solo said:

"Make sure that anyone you date knows upfront that your child is always first. It is hard but can be done. Right now, I have someone who is wonderful and amazing to myself and children."

You may want to clarify what it means to put your child first. Wendy Miller's 2011 article, "8 Things to Think about When Dating a Parent of Special Needs Children," can be very helpful in this process. She is a single, homeschooling mother of two boys who have ADHD, and some of her freelance work can be found at wwwExaminer.com. This particular article can be used as a guide for when you want a potential partner to they know what he or she is getting into. I am listing her eight points followed by a brief synopsis of each. Refer to the original for additional explanation.

1. **Time is limited.** Understand that a date requires taking time away from a host of other demands that are even greater than those faced by single parents of typical children.

2. **Life gets in the way.** You will need to be flexible and be able to tolerate last-minute cancellations due to problems with babysitters, a sick child, or other unpredictable situations.

3. **Parenting requires planning.** Don't expect spontaneity. Dates have to be planned in advance due to sitters and complications related to your child's additional needs.

4. **Be open.** Be receptive to the idea of having your date bring his or her child along occasionally. This may be due to not being comfortable leaving a child behind (for a variety of reasons). As Wendy Miller points out, children are likely to "be overly excited, appear to throw a fit, or any number of other attention grabbing potentially embarrassing things." She wisely adds, "If you are bothered by the thought of dealing with this or dealing with the attention it may bring, consider that perhaps dating someone with a special needs child is not for you."

5. **Don't push.** If you are eager to meet your romantic partner's child, it's fine to ask, but don't push. Wendy Miller writes: "We know when we will be ready to introduce you and when our children will be best able to handle it. If we aren't ready, if we haven't brought it up, don't push."

6. **Be a follower, not a leader.** It's great and well appreciated if you educate yourself about our kid's disability. But each child is different. Miller suggests: "Limit yourself to asking

questions about things you don't understand or things like why we prefer one method over another. Don't try to suggest that we try some new thing, or suggest that we're not doing something right."

7. **Be a friend.** Wendy Miller underscores the importance of friendship both with your romantic partner and, eventually, with his or her child. This requires empathy for your partner's stresses as well as reasonable expectations and tolerance for behaviors that you might not accept in a more typical child.

8. **Be honest.** It is important to be straightforward about the fact that you may be a newbie in the world of disability. It's okay to be honest if you are overwhelmed. This will lead to help navigating this new territory or getting your questions answered. Of course, it is still better to be honest if you decide this just isn't for you.

You may be thinking, "Who would ever want to sign on for all that?!" As you will see, many do. Later in the chapter, you will read the stories of four solo parents who ended up married or engaged to people who loved them for many reasons, including their unwavering devotion to putting their kids first in life.

Connecting Well Despite Constraints

The question is how can you demonstrate how much you do care about the person you are seeing despite these constraints? This requires you to make the effort to shift gears so that you are fully present when you are together. This is especially important, given that time is often limited. The suggestions in Chapter 2 on mindfulness apply here. You need to temporarily slip out of the Mommy or Daddy role the best you can.

Some solos find that daily stress often spills over to their relationships. For instance, I heard from one mother who tries her best to juggle work and a few kids on the spectrum but often finds herself cranky and short-tempered. I was very impressed with her approach to setting a boundary on her bad moods. She literally does a "do over" and walks out the door and says, "Let me start over." She walks right back in with a new attitude. This is one factor that has contributed to her long-term relationship's success.

Paving the Way for Your Partner

Many solo parents feel strongly that it is a bad idea to introduce dates to their children until it is quite clear that you are dealing with a lasting, committed relationship. They think it is not fair to children to let them get attached to people who might not remain in their lives.

Generally, it is best to prepare the new person as to what to expect from your child and how to interact. Be patient and remember that most people feel awkward and will make mistakes when it comes to interacting with someone who has problems with speech or has a significant physical disability. You don't need me to tell you that the general public equates intelligence and understanding with good verbal skills and typical physical functioning. Since that is a pervasive societal belief, you may need to help your romantic interest get beyond these assumptions. Some key points to emphasize include the following:

- Presume intelligence.
- Make sure not to treat older children like young kids due to their physical disabilities or speech difficulties.
- Understand that a child's comprehension is often far greater than his or her verbal skills might indicate.
- Understand that a great deal of communication can take place with gestures and facial expressions. Lack of verbal skills does not mean a person can't communicate.

Then there are the practical ways you can provide help:

- Help your romantic interest learn to recognize a few ways your child communicates; this may include specific gestures or sounds. Help him or her learn to decode these.
- Familiarize him or her with any devices your child may use.
- Let him or her watch you interact for a while to get a feel for it.

Be patient. Fearing doing something "wrong" may lead to an awkwardness that will diminish over time. As time goes by, don't always "translate" for your child and the person; let him or her take a crack at using the communication device or at interpreting your child's nonverbal communication

Generally, it is best to prepare the new person as to what to expect from your child. For example, you may want to prepare him or her for the possibility that your child may have meltdowns or sensory issues or may refuse to eat many foods. A little bit of education on why this occurs may help. Make it clear that you have established a thoughtful way to approach these situations, and you will handle them by yourself.

Throughout this book, solos have shared their opinions that potential partners need to accept their personal approach to discipline and that this area is sometimes a "deal-breaker." Olivia (in Chapter 12) advocates giving your prospective partner an explicit example of how you parent. She emphasizes that she will always use a positive approach. A reading of her story makes it clear that she is secure with herself and can enjoy being single; therefore, she is in a position to not have to compromise on important matters for fear of not having a partner.

First Meetings

First meetings are best arranged in settings where children can have fun and interaction does not need to be forced. Outings to a zoo or park are good examples. Your romantic interest can "tag along" and interaction can unfold casually and a little bit at a time. Provide an opportunity for your child to approach interaction on his or her own terms. You will need to rein in your eagerness to get your child and romantic interest comfortable with each other quickly because that is likely to work against you.

A new person can seem very threatening to children for many different reasons, so don't expect this first meeting to go well and don't overreact if it doesn't. For kids whose parents are divorced, a new person is a very obvious threat to the fantasy that parents will reunite. Many kids also see a new person as a danger to their exclusive relationship with a parent. For instance, in Lucinda's story (below), all her son would say in the first meeting (with her eventual husband) was "no, no, no." Why would a child want to share Mom or Dad?

I recently read a quote that likened dating to making custard and warned people to "cook" it slowly so you just don't wind up with scrambled eggs. This applies even more so to children meeting your new love interest. The operative word is *slowly*. In general, a child needs to retain choice and control over how much he or she wants to interact. You will know your child best, but this may include walking that fine line between prolonging an uncomfortable encounter and being overly accommodating to your child.

Sometimes it is obvious that a new partner just isn't going to accept your child. For example, one mother said, "I have gone out with a couple of guys who needed to make sure that people realized that she was not *their* offspring, which ended the relationship."

Often it is less clear whether a match will work out. Bear in mind that the person's first reaction is not necessarily indicative of his or her ability to become comfortable with your child. Some people may be awkward at first, but gradually warm up to your son or daughter. Others may act more comfortable than they truly are. That is one reason to take it slowly when you're figuring out whether to let a relationship become more serious. You may want to invite the person to go to places like the grocery store where your child's behavior isn't always the best. In addition to providing a realistic picture of your child, he or she can see how you approach situations such as meltdowns. It may help the person decide if he or she wants to be in it for the long haul.

Long-term Committed Relationships and Marriages

The major part of the remainder of this chapter focuses on four stories from solo parents raising children with disabilities. Three of them are continuations of stories of solos you met in earlier chapters on bereavement, divorce, and adoption. We will begin with Lucinda, who shared her story of making a marriage work despite quite a few fears.

Spirited Devotion

The Backstory: Lucinda, who was introduced in the adoption chapter, was not really expecting to end up with a boyfriend, much less get married. She never went out much, and when she did, she had an 11:30 "curfew" set because she didn't want to impose on the friend who would babysit her son, Tyler. Her now-husband teases her sometimes by calling her Cinderella.

> *"It's always fear with me. I asked myself, 'Is he always going to love him?' I was also fearful of possibly having another child one day because I never wanted Tyler to feel left out and 'less than.'"—Lucinda*

An excerpt from Lucinda's story follows:

I had dated some, but not a lot. I actually met my husband in a bar and I tried to scare him away with the fact that I was a single mom. But, he found it impressive. It was a good start. We planned a second date, but I ended up in the emergency room with my son instead. I had never before let any man I dated meet my son. However, this time I did and invited him to dinner.

I didn't tell Marco about Tyler's Down syndrome—I just let him come. Tyler was a pain during this evening. Everything was "no, no, no." He wouldn't say another word, and he made us nuts. He was not thrilled with somebody else coming into the house because it was always the three of us—me, him, and the dog.

Afterward, Marco never mentioned Tyler's difficult behavior, which is one of the reasons that I went out with him again. Eventually, Marco moved in with the two of us, but I didn't really allow him much participation in my son's care and education.

It was several years before I really let Marco take an active role. I don't know if I systematically thought it through, but I chose to go to all the meetings alone and I didn't nec-

essarily talk all that much about it to him. Then I took a job that involved lobbying and public policy, so I had to travel a lot. Although Marco and I were living together, I still would have staff come to help with Tyler's care for part of the time. This changed over time with my traveling. That was huge, and Marco and my son finally had a relationship that did not include me, just the two of them. Now, it was no longer "Mommy, Mommy, Mommy." And so my being away for work actually solidified all of our relationships.

It was a change because it had always been the two of us. We never orchestrated his relationship with my husband, and we never ever pushed that this would be his dad. We were in the park one day, and my son (out of the blue) said, "Hey Daddy!" He was testing this—trying it out as if he was trying on a new coat or something. He had no concept that it was actually Father's Day.

This mother had many fears about the prospect of sharing her son with a husband. In fact, she calls herself a control freak. In her words:

"Even after my husband adopted my son, it was a long time before I would agree to let him go to a meeting without me. I did let my husband recently meet with the support coordinator without me, and I'm still cleaning up the mess. I can't tell you how many documents his support coordinator got him to sign that I would've never signed. I know we need a balance between my cynicism, my micro-managing, and my mistrust when it comes to my son and his trusting that everybody will do what they're supposed to."

She also eventually had another child, a daughter, and found this did not diminish her husband's attachment to her son. Her son is also very happy about his little sister.

Although this mother would be the first to admit she had issues trusting her husband to parent her son, the essence of her approach is very positive. She did not assume that marriage meant she needed to share all parenting responsibilities with her husband. Her approach was consistent with what Fran Prezant and I advocate in *Married with Special-Needs Children: A Couples' Guide to Keeping Connected* (2007). Although this was technically her first marriage, our comments about remarriage are applicable. A stepparent does not need to fully participate in all aspects of child rearing to be a good parent. And, in some instances, a limited role is better. This is especially true for children approaching adolescence. As noted in *Married with Special-Needs Children:*

> "A stepparent does not need to be a disciplinarian in order to have an influence on childrearing or an engaged relationship with the children. This leaves a multitude of roles including sharing activities, providing support, involvement in childcare activities, sharing interests, getting to know the child as an individual, and supporting the spouse in disciplinary decisions. This is very different than simply disengaging from the stepparent role. Stepping back from a disciplinary role does not exclude the possibility of setting some house rules mutually agreed upon by the couple" (p. 244).

Choosing What Weights to Lift

The Backstory: Sarah (Chapter 3) had only mild interest in dating because she was doing just fine as it was with her daughter, who has multiple physical disabilities and is medically fragile. In New York City, where Sarah lives, Jewish matchmakers are common and have a strong religious conviction that they are to bring Jewish couples together (even when their services have not been sought after). When a matchmaker approached Sarah, she hesitantly accepted the assistance.

"So we called the wedding off after the invitations had gone out to a hundred people and gifts were on their way."
—*Sarah*

Excerpts of Sarah's story are below:

When the matchmaker asked me if I was dating anyone, I told her that it didn't really matter to me and it was not a priority anymore. She went to her computer and searched her database of more than three hundred guys. She narrowed the list to about a dozen and handed me the printout. She said, "You're never going to call these people, are you?" and I said, "Probably not." She proceeded to call everyone on the list and say, "I got a girl for you." About six of them called me, and I found myself writing notes on each one, trying to keep track of these guys.

Ben was one of them, and we connected. And of course, I told him I had a daughter with special needs, but that's all I said. Little did I know that his mother lived with him. So it was interesting. He finally met Naomi, and I think he was a little freaked out because it was new to him.

At some point, we decided to marry. He was a bachelor in his forties. We set the date but later canceled the wedding, because he got very nervous. His friends were asking him things like "Do you know what you're getting into?" and "This is going to be the rest of your life." So we called the wedding off after the invitations had gone out to a hundred people and gifts were on their way.

I was forty-one at the time. We didn't talk for a while, and I was really mad at him. I hadn't put a gun to this guy's head to force him to get married, and I had been perfectly fine on my own. And I told myself, "If he's not ready, he's not ready and we're not going to do it." We did eventually marry with five people in my living room. My daughter and parents were there, and it was lovely. And now, of course, he will tell you it's the greatest thing (and he is such a dad to Naomi). It's really fantastic.

Just a year into this marriage, Ben's mother ended up living with us after being diagnosed with pancreatic cancer. I did put my foot down and said that I would not be her primary caretaker, although I would partner in taking care of her. This woman, who had a temper and was kind of dramatic, turned *into a lamb living with us. Maybe she knew she had to, but it doesn't matter why. And I'll tell you what—she and Naomi were amazing together. They would sit together, and eventually my mother-in-law was in a wheelchair too. The two of them would sit together holding hands watching **Jeopardy** together. It was really precious.*

Modeling a Life Worth Living

The Backstory: In his fifties and having lost his wife, Paul did not feel like much of a "catch." He met Melanie (Chapter 8) while they were both waiting for their children at a social group. Their approach to dating kept the children front and center.

"When she told me the story about how they were test tube babies and how she wanted to have them, I said to myself, 'That's a strong person to go through that.' I was so impressed."—Paul

An excerpt from Paul's story follows:

We said from the beginning that the first priority had to be the kids. If they weren't going to get along, there would be no sense in pursuing a relationship. It wouldn't mean that we couldn't be friends. But neither one of us wanted to get in a situation where there was a stepparent who was not going to be good for our children. We've seen that before with other people. And, I have had some female friends who are nice to my son but have been intimidated. So, the first time we all got together, we had lunch and then went to a kid's arcade. The kids already knew each other somewhat, but boy, did our three kids bond. And we kept doing fun things together and going places with the kids and we kept them bonding because they enjoyed being together.

It is funny to see them together since the twins are still young and small. One of her twins described my son in a way that made me happy. He just loves my son and said, "I know

Eli is really tall and he's older, but he acts just like us and he's fun to hang around with." And my son idolizes him. I get a kick out of it when he advises him about how he needs to behave: "Your mother would want you to..." They bring out the best in each other.

We started this way of "dating" in May, and it took until August for us to have our first date by ourselves. About 75 percent of the time, we have kid dates. But we have enough adult time to keep it going. The kids are at the point where they want us married tomorrow....My son and I talk about it, and he says he thinks it would be good.

And I think he understands that Melanie would be acting as his mom—that nobody is going to replace Mom, but she's there.

My mother-in-law had issues with the idea of me getting remarried. I mean, she wouldn't tell me to my face. But she said that she had to battle it herself, so she went to see her rabbi. He said, "Let me ask you this question: How do you know your daughter didn't send her there?" He asked what my first wife's number-one priority was? Of course, it was our son. And the rabbi said, "It sounds like she's taking care of him afterwards too." It's been wonderful.

This couple is moving toward marriage in a child-centric way. Yet, at the same time, they put boundaries around their relationship. They hire a babysitter on a regular weeknight to protect their relationship and go out without their children. The remainder of the time very much includes their children, and they still remain a priority.

Thank God for iPads

The Backstory: Corrine joined the U.S. Air Force when she was twenty-four and is the mother of three children. This led to the downfall of her already troubled marriage. She tells the story of how she creatively dated her current husband at long distance during temporary duty assignments and deployments.

"One of the reasons I stayed in my last marriage so long was because I had it stuck in my head that nobody's would want to be with me. I'm in my thirties, I have three kids already, and one of them has special needs."—Corrine

An excerpt of Corrine's story follows:

I love my son to death, but he will say the most incredibly inappropriate, weird stuff at the most random times. I don't even know where he gets half the things he says. He doesn't have a good concept of people's personal space; even if he doesn't know them, he will just go up to them and hug them and be all over them. He talks about death a lot, and he talks about other things that I think would freak other people. It really took a lot of self-confidence for me to realize, "You know what? The right person for me will accept all of these things."

I always have this attitude that I'm strong and can handle anything. It has been good for me, but I do think it hindered my first marriage. I got tired of waiting for my ex-husband to step up and fill a man's role. So I joined the military because he couldn't. He tried a couple of times, but he wasn't motivated enough to lose the weight necessary to get in shape. But I knew the military will pay for school, and my kids will have health insurance. It was an ugly end to the marriage and divorce because he did not have the strength to cope with it all.

I met Robert, the man I married, when we were on a temporary duty assignment. Early on, when we were just getting to know each other, I kind of warned him. I said, "I have three kids with ADHD and one is kind of autistic." I gave him a "heads up" and explained how we had a very long-distance relationship. A lot of it was by using Skype. Robert and I would Skype all the time, and he was very sweet about making it all work. He was in a time zone two hours ahead of mine, so it would be pretty late by the time I would be able to talk to him. I had to get the kids to bed, and ev-

erything was just nonstop until then. Robert accommodated that and just took naps when he was done with work so that he wouldn't be too tired to talk to me. And he simply would wake up and talk to me when I was ready.

He met my kids a few times once we got serious. At first, it was not possible to do this in person. So, he would Skype and have dinner with us. I would put my iPad at the end of the table so he could see all of us, and he would eat when we ate.

We also had Skype dates where we would watch movies on Netflix. We would try to sync up the movies on both ends and watch them together. So we'd say "one-two-three… okay…press play." And every once in a while, it would be a little off, so one of us would turn ours off and listen to the other person's.

So we did this for a long time and we would actually sleep-Skype. That helped a lot, but I know it sounds ridiculous. We would go to bed together and have my iPad there, and we could see each other sleep. Robert was great about getting ideas from blogs on long-distance relationships and ideas from a cousin of his who gave him tips.

We also would try really hard to see each other at least once a month. Sometimes I'd come out to see him. But a majority of the times, it was difficult because of the kids, so he would come out to see us.

We actually got engaged and married fairly quickly. My son was only eight, and my kids loved my husband quickly. We have four kids between us now because he had a son himself who now lives with us.

I was really surprised at how easily Robert got used to my kids. My son has a problem with empathy, so he does some things that are maddening. Like, he'll destroy something and present his version of a totally logical explanation. It makes no sense to any other person whatsoever. Robert and I both take the same approach with him and let him know, "No, no, that's not right. That's not the correct way to look at it. You need to apologize or fix it." Sometimes it's just really hard because it's like talking to an alien.

We have been married about a year and a half now, so we're pretty new yet. We've been long distance or away from each other more than we've been together. He is in Qatar right now. He's open to learning, and he's open to accepting, and he's so good with my kids. I didn't expect him to love my children right away, but it happened so fast. It worked out.

Genius Moments

Corrine decided not to get caught up in all the potential problems that could occur with dating, in the first place, and a long-distance relationship, in particular. She kept herself far away from a "what-if" mentality. She embraced the process of forging ahead and seeing what could develop while keeping her children a priority. Her strategies included:

- *Being upfront about her child's disabilities and needs.* This mother knew that she needed to wait for the right man to accept her child, so she quickly shared this information in the beginning of her relationship. She had no interest in being with a man otherwise.

- *Waiting to introduce her boyfriend to her children.* She took the time to check this man out over time before she let him meet her children. In this manner, she protected the needs of her children.

- *Picking a man who was not frightened by her strength.* As much as she wanted a man to fill a traditional strong role, she was also aware of her need to be herself—a woman who did not want to her hide her strength. Like many who have been divorced, she learned to change the characteristics she sought in a potential partner.

Let me add that as Corrine dated, there were many positive signs that she might be able to forge a long-term, healthy relationship with this man. Early on, he was sensitive to her need to prioritize her children. Their nightly phone call accommodated these needs without Robert expressing a hint of resentment or putting pressure on Corinne to put his needs first. Another good sign was how hard he worked to create opportunities to connect. In this manner, they functioned well as a team—an essential aspect of a good relationship. Of course, all initial signs have to be sustained, and in this case, they certainly were. Corinne and Robert continue to protect their relationship by using creativity during deployments.

My mother used to assure me that "there's a lid for every pot." I am not sure that I totally believe my mother's maxim, but I do think the prospects for finding a healthy love relationship are much better than many assume. Sometimes, as for Corinne and some of the other parents in this chapter, it occurs far later in life than usual. Those who are open-minded, yet proceeded cautiously over time, often (but not always) have success in love.

Anecdotally, the men I interviewed seemed to have an even harder time finding the right person. They were among the many solos who found that they could live well even if they did not find love and even if they were sometimes quite lonely. They understood that searching for that type of love could not overshadow their enjoyment of their children and the rest of life. They often took active strategies to manage loneliness while they continued to look now and then for a chance to meet the right person. There is a difference between not liking being solo and fearing it.

It's a bitch to be lonely, but it's better than feeling lonesome
sleeping next to someone you barely know.
—Judy Ford (author of Single)

㐅

Chapter 10

㐅

Parents and Adult Sons and Daughters
Letting Go and Staying Connected

BOTH THE GOOD and the bad news is that everything changes over time. There is an art to being the solo parent of sons and daughters who have entered adulthood and have some ongoing needs for support and assistance. This chapter explores how relationships are affected by the developmental needs of both parents and their adult children. Parents face many difficult questions. For example, how do they help but not enable an adult child with disabilities who still needs some support? How do they prioritize some of their own needs that have been on hold for years?

These issues are explored in this chapter with input from parents of adult children who have physical, emotional, or intellectual disabilities. I have also included some thoughts from an adult with cerebral palsy for some additional perspective on these topics. You will hear from:

- Tasha, the mother of a young adult with a severe psychiatric disorder
- Jen, a thirty-year-old woman with cerebral palsy who moved back home by necessity after living successfully on her own
- Donna (Jen's mother), who is adjusting to sharing her small house together after several years of living apart
- Charlotte, a mother who tried very hard to have her son live in the community

Making Space for Growth

The Backstory: Tasha is the mother of an adult daughter with a serious mental illness. This excerpt starts fairly far into the story. At this point, we have fast-forwarded beyond her first husband's murder and the end of her second marriage. I will also fast-forward through the first two psychiatric hospitalizations of her daughter to the time of her third. The rest of Tasha's story is in Chapter 12.

> *"I would tell her, 'I will always love you but you have to deal with whatever the issues are—whatever's in your head.' That left her with space."—Tasha*

An excerpt from Tasha's story follows:

So we got to a place where my daughter, Stephie, and I were constantly butting heads. Her paranoia and delusions had worsened, and the school did not think they could keep her safe. Residential treatment needed to be considered, but she was about to turn eighteen in a month and a half. We knew she could simply sign herself out and there would be nothing that we could do about it. So we had to figure out what to do and eventually chose a nonpublic school placement with mental health staff on an isolated campus. In addition, county mental health provided more intensive services, and Stephie had a behavioral specialist, a therapist, and a psychiatrist. So we had a whole team of people with wraparound services. They met with me once a week and they met with her two or three times a week. But there were still a lot of conflicts.

One day, things just really blew up, and she stormed out of the house. She said that she was never coming back, packed her bags, and left. She stayed with my ex-husband's sister for about ten days. Thankfully, this woman was knowledgeable about mental health disorders and was able to tell me that that my daughter was "rapid cycling" with her moods. I knew that I could not have her back in my house with this kind of volatility and conflict. It was not helping either of us.

About six weeks later, my mother called and said my daughter wanted to come home. And I said, "Only under contract," and I meant it. So we wrote up a contract for coming back that included how she was going to respect me and not use profanity in the house.

In my meditative time, I prayed, "How do I relate to this child because I feel like I'm losing her?" And that's where I came up with the two strategies that have helped so much: "mommy time" and "safe zones." When Stephie was little, I taught her that when Mommy goes into the bathroom, you don't throw a tantrum outside the door. So, she was used to me taking a "mommy time-out" by retreating to the bathroom. I would go in there just to breathe. I would look in the bathroom mirror and tell myself, "You can do this! I'm not asking you to sign up for a life sentence—all I'm asking you to do is just one more day or one more hour of this." And that is how I began to get through it. I had to constantly tell myself, "Okay, deep breath, just one more day." So, that was to help me.

I used a strategy I called "safe zone" to help her, and this is how she began to open up and talk to me. Safe zone was not really a location. It was a point in time during which different rules applied in order to create a necessary freedom of expression. Stephie needed to talk, so we came up with a few rules. First, I would be nonjudgmental. Second, I would not offer advice during the free zone. I would simply be an ear to listen. I would also help her talk out the situation if she wanted me to. Third, she was free to say what she wanted when she was in the safe zone. If she was having a problem with me, she could even discuss that without reprimand. And so she began to talk about things.

One night, we were watching a **Law & Order** episode while she was also reading a book. When the television show got to a part where a little girl was molested by her father, Stephie suddenly threw her book across the room. She wouldn't say anything at first, but she had tears in her eyes. Finally, she asked for a safe zone. Then she told me that she was molested by a family friend while at her grandmother's home. She was only eight years old, and he was around seventeen. Her grandmother would leave her and another young cousin alone with him during these court-ordered visitations.

With my daughter's permission, I called her grandmother (my ex-husband's mother). When I confronted her, she said, "Now he's such a good kid, and he's away and doing well." And I said, "But he still violated my child." She responded, "Do you want me to have him apologize?" By that time, I was livid—"It's not like he stepped on her foot!"

I later understood that Stephie's grandmother knew about the molestation but had told her that I would never let her see her again if she told me. Talking about all of this in the safe zone opened up a healing process for my daughter.

Stephie's first hospitalization was at age sixteen. I went to the hospital every single day, and I would take her food and clothes and sit and talk with her. I stayed for hours and watched her, and then I would go home and cry. She was in a very dark place and I didn't know how to reach her.

I had a conversation with my pastor that changed all of this. He said, "You're going to have to have faith," and he asked me to do something that I thought was the meanest thing in the world. He said, "I need you to find the strength to not go every single day. Let her deal with recovery and you deal with acceptance." But this was my baby! How could I not go every day? Eventually, I called and told Stephie I wasn't coming that day. She was upset. I think that was the day grieving began. My grieving process was my personal conversation with God. I said, "If you never heal her, if you never change the situation and this is what it is for the rest of our lives...I will be okay with that."

So when there were more hospitalizations, I would not go every day. I would go maybe once or twice her whole *entire stay. I would talk to Stephie on the telephone. But I al-lowed her to go through the process and deal with whatever she needed to deal with. That left her with space.*

Reflecting back on this time, Stephie once said, "I'm thankful because you never left me. You always made sure that I knew that you loved me although you didn't come and it forced me to actually deal with me." And then she said, "I thank you because you stuck in there with me even when it was difficult. And I think that's why I'm better now." And real-ly she is. She laughs again. She talks again. She tells jokes. We go for walks together. But, she still has some rough days.

Genius Moments

Tasha walked a very difficult line to meet her daughter's needs as well as some of her own. She found a way to facilitate her daughter's autonomy as a young adult while also providing the connection she needed to survive and develop well. She was also able to focus on restoring her own sense of self, which had been eroded in the process of ongoing crises. She did this by setting boundaries based on compassionate respect for her daughter as well as herself.

Some of Tasha's strategies and philosophies follow:

- *Creating space and freedom for her daughter to express herself (safe zones).* This mother altered her role with her daughter so that her role as authority figure did not squelch her daughter's ability to express herself.

- *Respecting her daughter's autonomous decisions (even if they distressed her personally).* Tasha made a decision that might surprise readers. She explained, "You may be shocked, but she continued to go to her grandmother's because she still wanted to visit. That was her choice. Believe me, I did it only for her sake, because she told me that her grandmother was the only connection she had with her deceased father. So I wouldn't sever that relationship. Sure, I wanted to. I did make sure the man who molested her was never anywhere to be found."

- *Bringing prayer and contemplation to her decision making.* This mother took the time and inspiration she needed to thoughtfully make some very difficult decisions. Impressively, she did not simply follow her feelings but sought wisdom. She explained this process to me: "You asked how I brought my 'best self' to make such hard decisions. The answer is that I spend a lot of time reading my Bible and praying. I take my first mindset and make myself sit and rethink the process. I tell myself, 'Okay, you can't make the decision out of anger. You have to make the very best decision.'"

- *Fighting guilt over enjoying herself while her daughter still struggled.* Tasha said, "I had lost track of myself. With the help of a therapist, I learned how to begin to take care of myself. He would give me homework assignments to find out what I enjoyed doing. He made it clear that he expected me to start doing those things again. That became my homework. I felt guilty at first, because I'm out having fun while I have a kid who's struggling with all these mental health issues. But I realized that as I took care of me, I was able to take care of her."

- *Allowing her daughter to face some of her struggles without her.* She bravely took the advice of her pastor not to visit her daughter daily during the first psychiatric hospitalization, and she continued to limit her visiting in the ones that followed.

Support and Encouragement

Tasha's understanding of her pastor's wisdom echoes the points made by Abraham Maslow, a psychologist famous for his writings on the hierarchy of human needs. Maslow (1968) wrote about the fact that some grief and pain is unavoidable in life as well as part of necessary growth and development:

"If these things [grief and pain] are, to some extent, necessary and unavoidable, then to what extent? If grief and pain are sometimes necessary for growth of the person, then we must learn not to protect people from them automatically as if they were always bad. Sometimes they may be good and desirable in terms of the ultimate good consequences. Not allowing people to go through their pain and protecting them from it may turn out to be a kind of over-protection, which in turn, implies a certain lack of respect for the integrity and intrinsic nature and the future development of the individual" (p. 18).

Decisions to pull back to let a son or daughter struggle are painful and complex. After sharing her pastor's advice with another mother, Tasha took the opportunity to talk with her daughter about how she felt when she decided to minimize her visits during the psychiatric hospitalizations. Tasha related what her daughter had to say:

> "She acknowledged that it made her angry when I did not visit and said, 'I was angry, but Mom, it was better that way. When you were there every day, I could pretend that I wasn't in the hospital and I didn't have to face any of my issues. When you were there every day, I just pretended I was sleeping at a camp or something. I didn't really deal with it. When you stopped coming, I was forced to actually have to deal with it.'"

It takes bravery not to jump in. It is one of the hardest things for a parent, but often, as in this case, very loving. We also saw Tasha practice this principle during their "safe zone" time together where she agreed to listen without giving advice—unless her daughter wanted to talk something through together.

Helping vs. Enabling Your Child

Tasha's story brings us to a few very complicated but important issues. Namely, how do we determine what is helping and what is enabling? The starting point is consideration of what is best for a child's development. If Tasha's child had intellectual disabilities that made her unable to understand her mother's absence during much of her hospitalization, Tasha's action would not have been helpful. In Stephie's case, however, Tasha helped her grow.

Debbie Pincus, a life coach and author, has written about adult children living at home and addressed some of the complications that occur when the child has a disability. According to Pincus (2011):

> "Launching can be a very difficult process for kids with ADD, ADHD, or other issues. Some kids really need help cooking and taking care of an apartment and doing housework.
> No matter what, I believe the goal is for your child to be as autonomous as possible. I think the answer is to have a plan of action to motivate your child towards independence."

Finding a balance between protection and fostering independence gets harder when you have a child with a condition that impairs judgment and self-regulation even more. A good example can be found in the situations of parents raising older children with fetal alcohol spectrum disorder. Debbie Michaud and Valerie Temple (2013) researched the perspective of mothers in this circumstance and quoted one who expressed the exquisitely painful dilemma very well:

> "I don't even know how to let go, there ought to be training… after years and years of having been that intensely involved in another's life, how do you let go? How do you do that? 'Cause I don't think that is going to be very graceful. I can tell you that much, it's going to be pretty ugly" (p. 97).

Sometimes simply defining the problem needs to be our starting point. My own parenting has required making tough judgments under conditions that sometimes obscure the correct path of action. My rule of thumb has been to ask myself a few key questions and do my best, knowing there may not be a correct answer. Important questions include the following:

- Am I over-functioning by doing something for my child that he could do for himself?
- Am I encouraging dependency simply because it makes me anxious for him to face risks?

- Does he need to learn from the negative consequences of his own behavior? At what point does the damage of negative consequences overshadow the potential gains?
- Am I feeling taken advantage of or manipulated?
- Am I overreacting to his feeling depressed or anxious?

When it comes to this last point, sometimes how we react to a child's emotional pain is bound up in our own childhood histories. Some parents who did not receive adequate support as children from their own parents swing the proverbial pendulum too far in the other direction with their own children. They may end up being emotionally overprotective and interfere with their children's ability to develop their own resiliency.

> What lingers from the parent's individual past,
> unresolved or incomplete, often becomes
> part of her or his irrational parenting.
> —Virginia Satir

Singular Lives Together, Part 1

I could not do justice to the discussion of going solo with adult children without including the interwoven perspectives of the mother and daughter whose story appears below. They bring depth to this complicated discussion and lead us into the territory of balancing a parent's needs along with an adult child's needs.

Throughout my personal and professional life, I have been presented with this issue. I have met many parents, especially mothers, who believe in a 100 percent sacrifice for their children. Do I believe in making large and sometimes huge sacrifices for children? Absolutely.

But, I also think *all* lives matter and that there are times when our personal needs also need to be seriously factored into decisions. One example would be the extent to which limited finances will be used to enhance *your* life rather than buying something your child really wants. Another, more difficult one is when out-of-control behavior from an adult child routinely poses emotional or physical risks for you. At what point does a child need to move out of the family home? I can only reiterate my guiding principles that *all* lives matter; this includes your own life and those of your child's siblings.

The Backstories: Donna and her thirty-year-old daughter, Jen, spoke candidly about the process of Jen moving almost two thousand miles away from home for graduate school as well as her return home when she completed her master's degree. Their lives were complicated by Jen's cerebral palsy and their cramped living quarters in a very small house that can't yet be made accessible.

> *"My daughter said, 'You know, Mom, as hard as it is living together in such close quarters, we really do okay.' I said, 'We really do, but it's just tough on both of us.'"*—Donna

Excerpts from Donna's perspective follow:

> *Jen had been away from home for four years for undergraduate school, but it was easy for me to keep in touch or get together since she was only a few hours way. So when she said that she wanted to go to graduate school almost two thousand miles away, I told her it was entirely too far. Of course, she said, "I'm going anyway!"*
>
> *Let me answer your question of how I got such an independent, high achieving, and strong-willed daughter. When she was young, I used to be in therapy clinics with her about five days a week doing occupational therapy, physical therapy, and the rest of those things. While in those clinic waiting rooms, I got a chance to talk to a lot of other parents and also just observe. I saw a lot of parents who didn't think their kids could do anything, and I saw a lot of parents who babied their children and did way too much for them. I decided that was not how I wanted my child to grow up.*
>
> *I wanted Jen to understand that she could do anything, and I really did not want her to be helpless. I knew there would be a day when her father and I weren't here to help her. She needed to be as independent as possible for that.*

Her going to college was never an issue because she was very bright. I didn't see any reason why she couldn't do it. There are 10,000 things you can do in life, and if you can only do 8,000, let's go for the 8,000. That was my attitude.

She's back home now and almost thirty. I know she's older than I'm treating her. When it's the dynamic that you've had for so long, it's a hard habit to break, and sometimes you don't realize that your kid is actually growing up and has become mature.

I always had fear with Jen in the house while she was growing up—what if there was a fire and she couldn't get out? That fear still petrifies me and has been there since she was a baby. Another fear is that someone might take advantage of her when she is living alone. The worry is probably the worst part of being me.

I worry about her health because of what happens to your blood flow and muscles when you sit in a chair all day. Even though they say cerebral palsy isn't progressive, it is. I don't want to see Jen at forty not being able to stand up anymore and make a transfer. So, I try to get her to exercise and will say things like, "Let's go around the house on your crutches and just get your cardiovascular system going." She doesn't want to hear about it from me. I talked to her about it since she's been home a couple of times. Then, I had to draw the line and say, "She's made her decision, and it's her decision. It's her body and there's nothing I can do about that." She will still make her own choices when I am gone.

When Jen went away to college, I cried for two days and then I went in her room and totally cleaned it. After that, I didn't know what to do with myself because I'd spent my whole life taking care of her. Every time she went back to college, there was a cry fest, followed by relief mixed with sadness.

When Jen is living on her own, I don't have to be home at any specific time and can stay at work all day. So when I learned she was coming back to live, I was upset for a couple

weeks and my stomach churned because my life was chang-
ing again. I felt like I had to get my last bit of freedom and
independence in before she got here.

I love my daughter and I'm just helping her get to the
next step, but I don't have a life. This is partly my fault be-
cause my thinking completely changes when she is home.
For example, when I am at work I feel a need to get home
and feed her even though there is food in the fridge. The
longest I have left her since she moved back home is eight
hours, even though she lived far away from me on her own
for many years.

It's hard on Jen too. When she lived away from home,
she really liked her apartment. She felt very good about living
alone and doing things for herself. She could go to the super-
market and she could fix some of her meals. In my little place,
she can't do that, and she can't even get in and out the front
door by herself. We both know it's temporary, but it is so
hard. It's a one-person house and there's not a lot of privacy
there. I'll say to her, "If you want a private phone call, go in
my bedroom and just face the front wall because I really can't
hear anything when I'm in the living room."

I could worry about 50,000 things because she's a vul-
nerable person, but aren't we all? I could go shopping down
at the strip mall late at night and somebody could mug me
or steal my car. Who knows whether anything could happen?
All this worry! It's not good for me, and she's doing just fine.
I think I felt like I had so much responsibility as a parent that
I always needed to make sure that my daughter was okay. I
know I need to break that cycle.

Genius Moments:

This mother has a deep desire to provide the right support
for her daughter. This has meant handling her fear when her
daughter moved several thousand miles away. But it has also meant
adjusting to having her daughter back to live in her little one-person

home. She also has continued encouraging her daughter to be independent despite her own very high anxiety about risks and vulnerabilities in life.

Some of Donna's strategies and philosophies follow:

- *Reminding herself it is her daughter's life—not hers.* Donna repeatedly reminds herself that her daughter has the right to live with as much autonomy as anyone else. She is aware that her fear is her own problem, not her daughter's, and that she must work hard to contain it. She explained how she handled it when her daughter wanted to move thousands of miles away from home: "I thought about this for a few days. I said to myself, 'What's the worst thing that can happen? She had been independent at college. If she doesn't like it, she'll come home. It's just a plane ticket.' Of course, I knew it could be worse than that. I knew that I wouldn't see her more than once or twice a year because it would be expensive to get there. But I let her go. It wasn't my life. It was her decision, and it was what she wanted to do."

- *Trying to keep her advice to a minimum.* She explained, "She's smart, she understands it, she gets it. It's not like she doesn't understand what I have to say. So, I can't keep pounding on something, because it just makes the relationship a little more strained. I really have to put a leash around my mouth. And I try to keep it to a minimum—she already knows."

- *Preparing for her daughter to outlive her.* Donna is very aware of her own mortality and of her daughter's need to continue on without her or her father someday. Donna said, "I'm going to die someday, and she's going to be here without any brothers and sisters. I've asked one person I know to help my daughter get situated when I am gone and help with whatever needs to be done, and there are a few more people that I want to bring into that process. I need to make it easy for Jen to contact everyone she will need: the legal people, those dealing with the trust, my friends, and my sister. I want to give her a list and be able to say, 'Here are the people that are going to help you get through this.'"

- *Educating herself (and others) on caregiver health risks.* She explained, "I think you have to take care of yourself as a parent. I used to give talks at the university on being a parent of a child with CP. The research shows caregivers are extremely at risk for all kinds of health problems, along with depression and isolation. Caregivers often don't see their friends anymore or do the fun things they used to do because their responsibilities are so heavy. They don't take the time or get someone to give them relief. They don't keep a life that has friends and fun and gives them that surge of endorphins they need."

- *Pursuing a right-brain creative hobby.* This mother not only found an engrossing hobby, but she found one that uses her right hemisphere—rather than the left brain that we use to think about life and figure things out. She said, "I do mosaics and it takes me to a place where I don't think about anything but what I'm doing on a project. All the responsibilities go away for that hour and a half when I'm working on cutting glass on the front porch. I'm really a creative person."

Singular Lives Together, Part 2
Excerpts from Jen's perspective follow:

[My mother] did a really good job, and she wanted me to do things that other people did. She did a good job making me independent, and a lot of parents don't do that. However, my mom and I get along much better when we don't live together because it is easier for her to treat me like an adult. My dad is better at treating me like an adult because he wasn't the custodial parent since he was working so much.

I don't think my mother and I ever had good boundaries with each other. Now that I am back home, we are in a really small house that is not big enough for two people. I have two chairs and a walker and all kinds of stuff that are taking up the room in the house.

My mother said that when I was five, she told herself that she was never going to have a fat girl in a wheelchair. I get it, but she needs to stop trying to control what I eat. I am thirty and capable of making my own food choices, including bad ones, just like everyone else. She is also very opinionated on how I dress. She hates these blue Doc Marten shoes that I'm wearing and tells me they are ugly so that I won't wear them. I can't wear girls' shoes because they make my feet hurt in my chair and then I'll have a bad day. I think she should keep her opinion to herself unless she is prompted for it.

You asked me if I think the appearance thing has anything to do with disability. I do. I think she doesn't want me to look any more weird, but I've never been able to get her to admit it.

I think that my mother feels like she was always a single parent even before the divorce. She used to say things like "If I had let your dad handle it, you would have drowned in a bathtub." Which I don't actually think is true. Now, when he is late picking me up, she wants me to be angry with him. I spent a lot of time in my twenties (and before) being angry that he wasn't who we wanted him to be. I have figured out and accepted who he is, and I don't want anger to eat me up.

My mom was always really focused on my health. When I was in high school, it was like a second job. We were working on my physical functioning, my mobility, and my strength. We spent so much time going to occupational therapy, physical therapy, conductive education, and sports. I know she is afraid that I am going to wind up with less function, and I am a little bit afraid of that too. But I am doing a sport and I am working on it my own way.

You asked me what advice I would give to parents whose adult children moved back home. I would say, "Butt out with your opinion"—especially if they had autonomy in an area before they came back home. She always has an opinion. But I will say that she is my biggest advocate.

The occasional conflict between this mother and daughter is part of their growth process. They are trying hard to reconfigure their relationship, keeping in mind their own needs as two autonomous, loving adults with interwoven lives.

The Dignity of Risk

Several decades ago, Robert Perske (1972) coined the phrase "the dignity of risk" to remind society that people with disabilities have the right to full involvement in community life rather than being segregated in institutions. Although the passage below was written for a professional journal and focused on broader societal issues, it has retained an important message for parents as well:

"Overprotection may appear on the surface to be kind, but it can be really evil. An oversupply can smother people emotionally, squeeze the life out of their hopes and expectations, and strip them of their dignity. Overprotection can keep people from becoming all they could become.

"Many of our best achievements came the hard way: We took risks, fell flat, suffered, picked ourselves up, and tried again. Sometimes, we made it and sometimes we did not. Even so, we were given the chance to try. Persons with special needs need these chances, too. Of course, we are talking about prudent risks. People should not be expected to blindly face challenges that, without a doubt, will explode in their faces. Knowing which chances are prudent and which are not—this is a new skill that needs to be acquired. On the other hand, a risk is really only when it is not known beforehand whether a person can succeed.

"The real world is not always safe, secure, and predictable. It does not always say 'please,' 'excuse me,' or 'I'm sorry.' Every day, we face the possibility of being thrown into situations where we will have to risk everything…

"In the past, we found clever ways to build avoidance of risk into the lives of persons living with disabilities. Now we must work equally hard to help find the proper amount of risk these people have the right to take. We have learned that there can be healthy development in risk taking…and there can be crippling indignity in safety!"

Perske's words are compelling, and many of the solos in this book, including Donna, have tried to follow these beliefs. Still, parents are rarely able to let an adult child with disabilities take risks without fear and the struggle to change the innate desire to protect our loved ones. As my friend Shelly said to me, "When you have children, it is like wearing your heart outside of your body. You are that vulnerable to heartbreak forever."

Living Life on Life's Terms

The Backstory: Charlotte described herself as raising five children "with the youngest being my husband." Divorced for many years, she is living with an adult son who requires 24/7 care.

> "Being married to a physician was difficult. In his profession, he fixes things and makes people better, but he couldn't fix his child. Besides that, he was not cut out to be a doting father. I remember being at a picnic with him. I had four young babies with me (one was in a wheelchair and another in a stroller). He went up and got his dinner and sat down to eat, leaving me to take care of the four kids. So I raised five kids with him being the youngest of them all."—Charlotte

A portion of Charlotte's story follows:

> Since my other kids are now grown and have left the house, I'm on my own with my thirty-year-old son who has cerebral palsy and seizures. Nate has caregivers now because I can't lift him anymore. I need help all the time. The plan was that he was going to move out from our home just as my other children left the house when they became adults. It did not go according to plan.
>
> For residential placements, there are waiting lists and more waiting lists, so I put our name on a list and expected to wait a long time. A spot came up much more quickly than expected, so I found reasons to delay. I just wasn't ready and neither were my other children. Finally, I couldn't

stall any longer and had to make a decision. I reminded my-self that this was our initial plan and that this facility had a very good reputation.

My daughter put up a huge fight when it came to even considering residential placement for her brother. She told me that she and her boyfriend would find a bigger place so Nate could live with them. I told her that I appreciated it, but that I would not let her do that. It was hard on her because she has always been very attached to him and has been his fierce "defender" in life. When they were little, if someone stared at him, she'd put her hands on her hips and say, "What are you staring at?!"

I remember the night before Nate was to move out, my two youngest sons, both teenagers then, came into my room and the three of us sat on the bed and cried. We were all a mess. Our lives would change dramatically. No caregivers in the house. It would be very quiet. We would be free to go and get ice cream at 9:00 p.m.! That would be an unexpected perk. It would be very different.

Initially when Nate moved, I wanted to be there for everything to make sure it went smoothly. The staff assured me that I could, but in reality, this wasn't true. I have never had professionals shun my assistance and treat me so poorly. It was clear they wanted nothing to do with me.

All I wanted was proper care for him, and since he is nonverbal, someone had to guide the staff for a smooth transition. I had legitimate problems with the place. For example, the eye doctor would go from one patient to the next without washing his hands. I'm not asking for too much; all I wanted was good hygiene. The doctor at the residence would change my son's medication without asking me, and Nate would have horrible reactions. All they needed to know was that we had already tried that medication, and things would have been much better.

I would say to the staff, "Let me show you how I put him on the toilet." And they'd say, "You can't go in there! That's a private space." Are you kidding me?! I gave them a whole notebook written about my son—but do you think they would read it? Never!

It's hard to feed him. He loves to eat and will eat a lot because he's always moving and burns calories off so quickly. I wanted them to feed him whole food, but I conceded to their need to puree it in order to make feeding him easier. At that point, my goal was for them to simply get the food in him. They showed me a therapeutic spoon for infants that they wanted to use for feeding him. It was so tiny that it would take forever to finish a meal. They insisted on using this tiny little spoon because they said they liked that spoon.

Nate lost ten pounds in the first three months there, from 105 pounds to 95 pounds! I would bring him home every weekend. He was dirty and his teeth needed cleaning so badly they had fuzz on them.

I would bring him back on Sundays, and he would cry. It was obvious that he did not want to go back. He may not be verbal, but you can tell what he wants. Sometimes, he'll make a "I don't like it face" or an "I'm happy" sound. You really need to know my son to understand all of this. We read to him things like Harry Potter and the newspaper. He really understands a lot, but it's not complex thoughts.

On Sunday nights when we would bring him back to his new home, it was often a NEW caregiver who would open the door. They had never met Nate before, and I probably could have dropped off someone else and they never would have known it was the wrong person! As bad as all that was, it was the seizures that finally ended it all. Nate was seizure-free for five years when he went to live away from home. But when they started again, I knew it was time to bring him home. I don't know if it was because he was so stressed or because he didn't always get his meds as needed.

In the eight months that we tried to make it work there, Nate regressed so much. When I told them I was taking him and not coming back, their mouths dropped open. These spots are in such demand that I don't think they ever had anyone leave. Because my son's needs are so complex, he really needs more continuity of care. Such care as could be provided by a supervisor who knows him well (like me!). If he were verbal and ambulatory, I think he might have been okay there. Along the way, we even tried a wonderful place outside of the United States.

My latest goal is to move to a smaller house. My house is twenty years old with a leak here and there. It has eight bedrooms. It is just the two of us since my other kids are gone. I would like to move. To remodel another smaller house so it's accessible and has more privacy for me would be ideal, but honestly, I just don't have the energy. Besides, it's only avoiding the issue. The issue is that I won't be here forever and the plan for the future needs to be to find a residence and ensure quality of life for Nate without me.

I have several friends who have children with severe cerebral palsy. The son of one of these friends died last month just shy of his thirtieth birthday. He spent the last ten years of his life in bed. She devoted her whole life to her child. I think I read somewhere that 50 percent don't make it to twenty-five. At times, I am acutely aware that my son has outlived this statistic. He is not as strong as he used to be. I always have it in the back of my head that things could go wrong. You have to cross your fingers and leave it in God's hands.

Genius Moments

Charlotte has moved heaven and earth in order to give her son a good life, and she does this without a trace of martyrdom. She knows she is entitled to a good life herself and is aware of her needs even if she most often prioritizes her son's over her own.

Some of Charlotte's strategies and philosophies follow:

- *Accepting her best effort.* Charlotte worked exceedingly hard to give her son a high quality of life. One small example (of many) is that she wanted Nate to have the same sled-riding experience that other children got to have; she arranged it even though it took four people to get him on the slope. She was also able to accept that she did her best in pursuing residential living for Nate. In her words, "You know you have to give yourself a break. You do the best you can. It wasn't what it was supposed to be."

- *Not losing sight of personal happiness.* Charlotte explained, "Here I am. I've been single for a long time. It is easy to wonder for a moment how life might have been different. What if my son had not had CP? What if I were still married? But I don't think about any of that for more than a moment. You can't waste your time on that stuff. When I was having a lot of problems with my husband, I was miserable. You have to just get out there and be happy with what you have. I am sixty now and thinking about what I want and how to continue to make myself happy at this point in life."

- *Going with life's flow.* The philosophy of accepting life on its own terms runs throughout Charlotte's story. She is very proactive about shaping her life and her son's and is anything but complacent. Yet she accepts a lack of control over ultimate outcomes. "Looking back, you think your life's going to turn out a certain way. You imagine yourself doing this and that with your children. And a lot of it didn't happen. But I am looking forward to what will happen in the next chapter in my story."

Conclusion

Tina Calabro, a freelance writer and expert on disability issues, shared with me a presentation she did in 2014 for parents of transition-aged sons and daughters on "letting go." Her presentation included the following insight provided to her by one parent:

"One time I heard someone compare parenthood to flying a kite. Sometimes we have a short string and run to keep the kite up, taking on most of the load. Sometimes we let the string out, letting the kite fly on its own up in the wind, every once in while pulling in the string or giving it a tug when we see it falling. Sometimes the kite fights against us testing our strength to hang on. The thing is we never cut the string, we never let go. The string is always there.

"Parenting individuals with disabilities is much like parenting any child. The only difference is usually children without disabilities push us away and 'get caught up in the wind' a little sooner. Parents of children with disabilities sometimes have to do 'more running, more holding the kite up' themselves, which feels wrong, but is necessary. I find parents who have children who are medically fragile have the hardest time with this. It's scary and 'the kite keeps getting caught in a tree.' Parents feel that 'letting out the string' has way more risks than for other children.

"Parenting any child is a balancing act of safety and the young person's freedom. I guess that is the balance in how tightly we hold the string. If we hold on too tight the kite can't fly on its own."

Chapter 11

On Your Own for Long Stretches
Military Solos

THIS CHAPTER IS devoted to solo parents who are in families that are serving their country in the military while raising children with disabilities. The parents whose stories are included in this chapter are either active military themselves or married to military spouses. If you are a civilian solo parent, you may wonder why I think about these military parents as solos. But as you read their stories and experiences, this will become clear. In military families, the active duty spouse is often deployed for a year or more, and the parent remaining at home has to consolidate all of his or her strength, make changes, and be creative in order to stay afloat in many situations. In this chapter you will read about:

- Alyssa, a mother whose story includes being airlifted with her newborn son to the United States while leaving her husband and toddler daughter behind in Japan
- Mary, a mother who began going solo when her daughter was born surprisingly early, weighing less than two pounds
- Tanya, a mother whose daughter has Sanfilippo syndrome, a rare and typically life-shortening disease
- Rashaun, a military spouse living off base and raising four children, including one who is on the autism spectrum
- Trixie, a woman with a long, successful marriage whose youngest son has a dual diagnosis of Down syndrome and autism

Insights and stories from military solos can also be found in other chapters. This includes Corrine (Chapter 9), Bruce (Chapter 5), Jasmine (Chapters 2 and 3), and Julia (Chapter 12).

There is a great deal of wisdom shared in this chapter for civilian and military solos alike. It begins with stories of parents who are coping with huge medical challenges, mostly alone. The chapter then moves into a discussion of finding support and staying connected over long stretches of space and time while doing very high intensity parenting.

Coping Emotionally

The first solo parent highlighted is Alyssa. I asked her husband to share his thoughts about being away during deployments while his wife was home with their medically fragile son. While on deployment, he wrote:

> "It's difficult. I love to be with my family, but I have a job that requires me to be gone a lot and for a long duration. I feel sometimes that I am not fulfilling my duties as a father and a husband. It's hard knowing that stuff is happening at home while I'm on the road and I can't be there to help, comfort, and support my family's needs. While I'm gone, I wait for the phone call or e-mail that says, 'We're headed to the hospital. I'll keep you informed with what the doctors say.' There is so much unpredictability in our lives that I am always worried about what the next day will bring.
>
> "There is so much pressure put on Alyssa while I'm gone to take care of the kids and the house and manage all of the appointments for our son. I appreciate all that she does every day to keep the family on track. That help alleviates my worries for the kids while I'm deployed but shifts it to her. Then there is the problem of her finding time to relax and decompress. There are a lot of stressors that I have to deal with, and it helps that I have a spouse who is strong and can hold down the fort while I'm gone. It helps keep my focus on the mission at hand."

Walking with Her Grandmother's Love

Their Backstory: When their first child was six months old, Alyssa and her husband moved to Japan as part of his military service. Alyssa loved being there, but in the blink of an eye, almost everything that was familiar to her changed. Her second child was born with a life-threatening illness that required immediate specialized treatment in the United States.

"Do you know those mechanical claws that you see in kids' arcades where you get the toys? I felt like a giant claw just picked me up and dropped me."—Alyssa

Excerpts from Alyssa's story follow:

We had to be airlifted when my son was only days old. It was rough. I had to say goodbye to my daughter, who was barely two years old at the time. I could not even take the time to say good-bye to friends. Cole was born with Potter's sequence, so his kidneys stopped developing at about twenty-four weeks, and his lungs also stopped developing. At birth, he was intubated and put on an oscillator. They told us that there was no way that he would be able to survive and that the only chance was getting him to Stanford University Medical Center in the United States.

Ambulances in Japan are different than in the United States, so they had to handbag Cole for four hours as we tried to make it to the airport. Then they had to put us on a K loader to get us on the plane while my baby was hooked up to life support and worked on by a medical team. I had a heavy pack on and I was in so much pain from recently giving birth. It was all surreal.

We made it to Stanford Medical. But, of course, it was just the two of us alone. My husband, Tom, and our little girl had to stay behind for two months. I'm a believer. There was a lot of praying going on from all kinds of people. Prayers were even said by some of the doctors and nurses, people at the front desk of Stanford, and even some of the security guards. So we were not entirely alone with this. It was the same at the Ronald McDonald house. It has sort of been like military life because you are all in it together and you are all each other has. You have to rely on each other like a big family.

They tease me at the hospital, and they used to say that I had a mythical husband. When Tom comes, they pretend to be surprised that he really does exist. He is gone a lot and sometimes my mind plays tricks on me. The devil can stir up resentment. I used to be active military myself, and I loved it. Sometimes, I find myself resenting that Tom gets to go somewhere and I don't. It helps to remember that I signed on for this life and I knew I would be the one at home during deployments and remotes. He is in a highly deployable unit, which is actually a good thing because they are so willing, for the most part, to work with our family.

When Tom is home, he knows that I need to go out. So he doesn't consider this as "babysitting." I am luckier than some others this way. Also, I go once a year to the Women of Faith conference.

I think it is also important to spend time together as a couple. My in-laws came up and watched the kids, which was huge because they had been really hesitant. I understand their hesitancy because Cole's meds keep him alive and are delivered through his port. Then there is also his g tube and a central line that dangles from his chest. As nervous as they were, I told them that they had to learn. This was not just to help us. I told them, "If something happens to us, they're yours, so you need to learn." The first time was rough; my father-in-law got the g tube caught on the crib by mistake. He freaked out, and yes there was blood. But, it popped back in and everything really was fine.

It's a tough life; I'm not going to lie about it. But, I wouldn't change it for the world. You have to make do with what you have. The grass isn't always greener on the other side, you know? Or it may be greener, but it may be full of thorns and weeds.

I owe my positive attitude to my grandma; she raised me and was an amazing woman. She had such compassion and was the glue that held community and the family together. Not only did she found the food bank, but she was also the fire chief at the volunteer fire department. She recently passed away, but she's alive within me. Whenever I do anything like cooking or something around the house, I say to myself, "Oh, Grandma taught me that." The last time I saw her, everyone but my husband got food poisoning, and Cole ended up in the hospital. My grandma was eighty-eight and took care of both me and my daughter. We were sick as dogs! And you know what? I am thankful that I got food poisoning because she took care of me and I got that one-on-one time.

Cole has been in organ rejection for about three years now. He has lots of medical problems, including epilepsy and chronic lung disease. He coughs all night, so I don't get much sleep. I try not to think too much about his medical problems because then I get more stressed and it is hard to keep the worries and "what-ifs" from coming. "What if we have a natural disaster? Then what would I do about his meds? And then what would I do about his food?" Our insurance does not allow us to stockpile; in fact, it is scary even without a disaster because I barely have enough medicine at the end of the month to get me through until I get my next shipment.

You have to handle your fears and all the "what ifs." I used to fear that Tom would die or that the kids or I would be in an accident. I had to stop thinking like that because it becomes all-consuming. I would be horribly devastated if something did happen to my family, but I can't keep worrying about what **could** happen. You need to try to enjoy every minute of life because it is a gift. You never know when you might lose your child or your spouse or when your child might lose you.

The main way I cope is to do a lot of crying. Crying cleanses the soul! I always feel better afterward. The bottom line is that I can't let sadness and fear own me. I won't let it happen.

Genius Moments

Alyssa staunchly refuses to let fear and resentment own her. Through faith and a desire to protect the gift of life, she relegates negative emotions to the sideline by putting the value of her family life front and center. She can embrace her sadness, feel her fears, and then contain them so they don't dominate her life.

Some of Alyssa's strategies and philosophies include:

- *Embracing her gratitudes.* Alyssa illustrated this beautifully when she spoke of being glad she had the terrible bout with food poisoning so she could be taken care of by her beloved grandmother one more time. She spoke freely of her gratitude for other things that occurred along the way. This included meeting the Dalai Lama and receiving his blessing at the Ronald McDonald house.

- *Shutting out fear.* Alyssa said, "I do suppress my fear when I can, although it doesn't always work. You know, sometimes that 'closet door' comes flying open. But I say to myself, 'I can't control this. I'm just going to have to let it go and trust in God.' If you don't believe in God, just trust that it will work itself out."

- *Using Military OneSource for counseling.* Alyssa understood the hesitancy of military parents to use counseling services, but she felt very strongly about its value as well as its safety. "The best advice I can give is to look into a therapist. Talk to someone, and even if you don't think you need to go, think about getting a 'checkup' with a counselor. You could also think about it like going in for a tune-up on a car. It was the best thing I ever did. People are very afraid, but military OneSource is an amazing outreach because it doesn't go on your file in the military. It is completely separate. A lot of active duty people are hesitant because admitting to having mental health problems could be considered career ending. But if you go as a spouse, your partner can come too and nothing goes in the file for him or her. They can talk about anything."

Finding Strength from Necessity

The Backstory: Mary's baby weighed in at one pound and eleven ounces. She was born at twenty-six weeks after Mary had left Japan and her baby's father behind. Her daughter has multiple disabilities. Now she is married, but her husband is often gone for long deployments.

> *"The first three years, I think I was doing everything by myself, even when he was here."—Mary*

An excerpt from Mary's story follows:

I grew up as a military brat. I went back to Okinawa to visit my family and to help my mother out with the younger kids while my father was deployed. I got pregnant while I was in Japan. When my father got back from deployment, he sent me back to the states. I wasn't scared of him, although he was strict since he was a marine. But I just didn't know how to say, "Hey, Dad, you just got home from deployment and I'm pregnant." I wasn't super young at the time. I was twenty, but he still saw me as his baby girl. I just didn't know how to tell him, so I left Japan, my daughter's father, and my family, and went back to the United States.

To make a long story short, I was staying at my aunt's house when I suddenly and unexpectedly went into labor. My grandmother and my aunt rushed me to the hospital and put me in a wheelchair while they went to park the car. I had my daughter before they had finished parking the car! Sissy was one pound, eleven ounces, and was in the NICU for almost four months.

We did everything backwards. Sissy's father and I actually got married a week after she came home from the NICU. When I was pregnant, he decided he wanted to join the military to support us. We both thought this was the best decision for us financially and as far as medical benefits go. This was especially the case when we found out she was premature. Carl went to boot camp seven months after she came home from the NICU.

Sissy is six. She was initially diagnosed as having cerebral palsy when she was about two and a half years old. She was diagnosed with autism two years ago. That's not all that she has. Because she was such a preemie, her lungs were underdeveloped, so she also has chronic lung disease and asthma. She doesn't eat by mouth and has a g tube now. She is nonverbal, but I did teach her to sign.

I counted, and I think it's about thirteen specialists and therapists that she needs to see. This does not even include the dentist, the pediatrician, or the two surgeons we still need to go back and see.

For a while, Carl didn't know how to cope with all of this. During this time, I was a super advocate for Sissy, and he just didn't do much. For the longest time it was just me telling him, "She needs this" and "She needs that." He would just look at me like he was bored. But he does work between ten and twelve hours at a time.

Anyway, it came to a head when I had to have my appendix removed and Sissy needed emergency care at the same time. I was super drugged up, and Carl was trying to talk to me about our daughter. She ended up being transferred to Children's Hospital. He called me every time that he couldn't answer any of the doctors' and nurses' questions. This was at least four or five times. Finally, he asked, "What was she diagnosed with again?!" That was a low point, and I knew it had to change.

Also, I learned that Carl consulted his parents (before me) about some decisions related to his military career. This led us back to marital counseling, and we straightened out some things. I have told him that he can no longer make decisions without me and that we are a team.

Carl's now been gone for more than a year in Turkey. It's not that I am miserable when he is gone; it's just that I am aware of how alone I am with this all. So, I worked on making friends and found a really close friend by bumping into her at medical appointments. Her husband is also military and her son has CP, so I saw her at physical therapy appointments, occupational therapy appointments, and even at the pulmonary clinic when we would see the doctors there every three to six months. I simply told her that we had to become friends. Later, when she was going through a divorce, I said, "I'm coming over and bringing some wine." This turned into what we now call "Wine Wednesdays." This grew into such a good thing and we don't even always drink wine.

You asked what helped me the most. Honestly, I think I found out a lot about myself, about being an advocate. It has really helped that I have been working with the special-needs task force and talking to all the women who have special-needs kids. I reached out to a lot of other moms in the Exceptional Family Member Program whose kids were sick, needed a specialist, or simply needed to talk. During the year that Carl has been gone, I've found out how strong I am. No matter how much anxiety I have, I am strong and I have a lot to offer.

Genius Moments

Mary was a genius at finding her voice and using it well. She went from being unable to explain her pregnancy and desire to stay in Japan to using her voice to better the lives of her daughter, herself, and other moms, as well as to strengthen her marriage. Some of Mary's strategies and philosophies include:

- *Learning to accept help.* At first, Mary was unwilling to ask for help. But she learned to share some of her particular strug-

gles and to accept the help that was readily offered. Once she
opened up, her friends spoke of similar problems with anxiety
and pitched in to help her. In her words, "My home had become a bit of a mess because I kind of hoarded a little bit, but
they helped me sort through it."

■ *Creating a group for fun and a sense of family.* Despite the
name *Wine Wednesdays,* this is not your regular drinking
group. Yes indeed, it got its name from how it began. Then it
grew into a very diverse group that crosses ethnicities and ages
and includes military and civilian parents from different countries. Mary commented on the group's scope:

"I feel kind of cool about the fact that I started this club. We do
potluck, and we don't always drink wine. In a way, it is like my
family, and I was pretty much the baby of the group. Many
people are my parents' age. Often, there are up to twenty
people at a time with about fifteen in the main family. We try
to get as many of us together as possible every Wednesday, and
we even have wine glasses with our names on them. We also
have some Fun Fridays and may go off to the movies or do
something else; we've even had a tour of Napa Valley.

"We celebrate birthdays and holidays as well. It's an
international family because we come from all over. We
are open to any new friends—black, white, green, orange,
and yellow, whatever! Umm… moms, dads, no kids, single,
everyone! The people in the group are friends who help each
other cope with being alone together. I have received some
advice from everyone and vice versa."

Connecting with Others in the Same Boat

Mary is one of many military wives who emphasized that connecting with others is essential for living well under the tough circumstances that come with deployments, military relocations, and
raising children with disabilities. Solos who participated in this book
through the online survey offered the following advice:

- "It truly takes a village to raise a child. I have found comfort in joining the special-needs community at my base. The advice and experience of others has been priceless. I would encourage spouses to utilize the benefits of EFMP (Exceptional Family Member Program). The resources that are available in this program have changed the way my son with autism functions on a daily basis."
- "Please become friends with other military families. This way you will have a support system. Most women take turns doing things for each other. Like, one day, you take her kids for a few hours, and the next week she will take yours."
- "Good friends are always there to help you. You just have to swallow your pride and ask for help."
- "I have found time to go to the YMCA and work out. This helped me meet other military wives in our new surroundings who have children that attend the same school as my own."
- "Hobbies that can be done around the kids' schedules are good. Gym time, knitting time—the key is taking a break. It also helps if you ask for help. So many people want to help but don't know how."
- "The respite care offered through our military base and our Exceptional Family Member Program is a lifesaver. I also searched for a support group for other special-needs parents, and when I couldn't find one, I started one myself. It has been wonderful to connect with other parents who have children with rare diseases."

STOMP (Specialized Training of Military Parents) is an important resource. This organization is a federally funded Parent Training and Information (PTI) center that was established to assist military families who have children with special education or health needs. STOMP's mission is to empower parents by providing information and resources related to many facets of raising children with disabilities. This includes in-depth information about parents' rights related to special education services. The organization provides assistance in accessing resources, both for current duty stations and for future assignments.

To find a STOMP specialist in your area, call 800-5-PARENT (572-7368) or send an e-mail to pave@wapave.org. You can also connect through the group's Facebook page. The website can be found at http://wapave.org/programs/specialized-training-military-parents-stomp.

Growing with Grace

The Backstory: Tanya and her husband have a young son, Brandon, and a daughter, Lucy. Lucy has Sanfilippo syndrome, a rare genetic condition. Presently, the disease is considered life-shortening and progressively impairs the ability to walk, talk, and swallow.

"We don't want our daughter's disease to define us. We also don't want it to define her. The disease is not who she is."—Tanya

Excerpts from Tanya's story follow:

You ask how we cope. We just focus on the little things. My husband and I tell each about the little daily things, such as "Oh, Lucy smiled today."

It is hard on us, and I worry about my son Brandon. He is young. We need to think about only sharing what is age appropriate while also answering his questions. You can tell that he is trying to figure out what may happen in the future. One day he said that when he grows up, he is going to drive Lucy to get ice cream. I don't know if he was trying to see how we would react or not. Later, we went to visit a little girl while she was hospitalized with the same disease as Lucy.

Brandon started to piece things together when he saw that she was struggling to breathe even with assistance from a machine. He asked me if she was going to be okay, and all I could say was "I hope so." He then asked me if Lucy was going to end up like that little girl. My answer was, "I hope not, and every child is different. But, there is always a possibility that she will because she does have the same disease."

I haven't told Brandon anything about the people we know who have died. But on Lucy's birthday, he asked, "Is Lucy going to live a long life?" He added, "She can die early, can't she?" And I just said yes. My husband and I just cried! We cried so much. We've tried to be graceful about the whole thing.

Brandon is going to be the only child I have left, and I worry about him. When my husband is deployed, he will sometimes say to him, "Dad, why can't you just come home already?" He's happy when we're all together. We used to do all kinds of outdoorsy things as a family, but we can't do them anymore like that. As my daughter has gotten older, we have had to slow down. When possible, my husband takes Brandon on camping trips by himself since Lucy can't tolerate the cold anymore. My daughter has done more in her lifetime than most adults have done.

I've had anxiety attacks that have gotten worse, and this has really been the toughest year of my life. But I try to live in the moment. I do this by telling myself, "She's here now" and "She's happy." This has always been our goal, just to make sure she is happy. We are doing well with that goal.

Deployments are hard. There's the normal deployment stuff that everyone has about missing your husband and being alone with the kids. But then there is dealing with the life-and-death stuff. You know, I joke that my goal for the year is to just keep my kids alive. Some wives say things like, "I'm going to lose weight when my husband's gone." They'll ask, "What's your goal?" I tell them my goal is to survive.

I keep telling my husband that I don't want to resent him at the end of this deployment. I have to remember that he's not there by choice. He doesn't want to be in Korea, but that's what he needs to do. And I have to remind myself that it's just as hard on him mentally as it is on me. We have to be a whole unit to get through this.

The way other wives complain irritates me, although I try not to let this happen. I can think of one time in particular that it really got to me. My husband had just left for Korea, and this wife was on Facebook complaining and crying and carrying on because her husband would be gone for two weeks and miss Thanksgiving. She wanted to go to the commander. Those of us with exceptional children found it really insensitive. We said to ourselves, "She has a normal kid— just suck it up for two weeks!"

I don't usually compare myself to others. I got a lot of my strength from my father. He had his issues, but he also had his beliefs. He'd always say, "You're a Diaz, so you need to be strong. Don't settle, don't stop, and don't compare yourself to other people." When I was a kid, if we got picked on, he'd say, "Those people aren't worth your time." I also don't usually feel the need to conform and be part of a clique. I think these lessons from my father served me well. I've seen other people just not continue to grow, and I don't ever want to stop growing. I haven't yet.

Some people hate the saying "What doesn't kill you makes you stronger," but I like it. I actually learned that while running track, and I think about it a lot. I try to think something positive has to come out of every bad thing that happens. My daughter's disease is devastating, but it's opened us up to this whole new world of people and way of thinking and opportunities that we wouldn't have had. I remember in high school seeing kids in wheelchairs and the special-needs groups, and I didn't think much about them. Our lives were separate. And now I see people look at my little girl who doesn't walk or talk. And I see them close themselves off to her and miss who she is. She is such an amazing little girl.

I've grown a lot. I'd never thought of myself as being smart or really capable. I look at all I have accomplished and I'm like, "Oh, my gosh! How did I do that?" But I don't like recognition, because I think people should do things just because they're supposed to do them—not to get an award. That's probably the thing that drives me crazy about the military. They want to give you gold stars for everything.

If you would have asked me four years ago what I wanted to do with my life, I never would have said what I would say today. Now, I want to be a criminal profiler and get a PhD. Being a profiler involves dealing with all kinds of scary stuff. You know, if you've been told that your child is going to pass away, there's not much else that's going to scare you.

Genius Moments

Tanya manifests a notable grace with life. She believes that life is to be lived fully and that our responsibility is to grow into our best possible selves. Some of Tanya's strategies and philosophies include:

- *Practicing mutual interdependence.* Tanya and her husband both express a need for each other. Daily contact is a priority for both of them, so they make it happen. Tanya explained, "I tell him that I don't care what time of night it is, I want him to call me. I want to hear his voice and know that he is safe. We often end up talking for hours. At first I think, 'Oh crap! I have to get to bed.' Then I tell myself that sleep can wait a while longer. Sometimes he says that he feels bad that he is keeping me up late talking, but I tell him that I need him—and need to talk to him. He replies, 'I need you too.' Throughout the day, he tries to send her an instant message, even if it is only a smiley face. She said it reminds her that he is thinking of her.

- *Not losing herself in her daughter's illness.* Tanya states it very clearly, "You are more than your child's disorder. My advice to other parents is, 'Don't lose yourself and don't forget who you are.'" She makes plans for her future, embraces her strength and intellect, and enjoys her marriage.

- *Allowing her life to transform her.* Tanya does not run from the future or dwell on how life could have been different.

She accepts that this is the life they have and is quick to see the positives, even while acknowledging the parts that have been devastating.

Staying Connected

In military marriages, there is a heightened need for spouses to be self-reliant that can be a double-edged sword. Self-reliance is essential, but it can also lead to disconnection within the couple. There is a line to walk between not burdening your partner when he or she is deployed and distancing him or her from you and your children. Rashaun, whose story appears later in this chapter, spoke of this difficult line:

> "He's always gone, so we always have that disconnect. Then we are faced with having to reconnect when he comes back. He doesn't talk about his work at all. I do know that he works with computers and that it's secretive. Sometimes that's okay with me and sometimes it's not. Because I find that I don't talk about my life either. It's just a natural reaction for me. I parent by myself. I do not really include my husband when he's away."

In contrast, another mother who contributed to this book gives ways that she involved her partner while he was on long and frequent deployments.

> "We would Skype almost every day. He was usually on twelve-hour shifts, and he would try to get up early enough so he could Skype with the kids before they went to school. And then we'd have our separate time to Skype. My daughter would take the iPad and shout, 'This is Daddy!' as she ran off for some privacy. When she finished, my husband would ask for my son. I would be next. So, all three of us would have our private time with him.
> "I am one of those who believe it is important to share what is going on with my husband. I know some wives tell you

they don't want to bother their husbands, but I don't agree. He always asked me about the kids' day and I never lied to him. So, if my son acted out in school, I would tell him what the teacher said. His response was usually something like, 'Let me speak to him.' I would give my son the iPad, and after my husband spoke with him, several days of good behavior at school would follow. This has been my husband's way of staying involved, continuing his role in the family, and helping me not to worry as much."

Another spouse underscores that she personally needs the connection with her husband to cope, but has also worked on strengthening her individual coping skills:

"One of the things they tell you when your husband's deployed is to keep everything good. Don't tell him the bad stuff that's happening at home. They say that spouses don't need to know about anything because they are in a situation that is hard enough.

"My husband is not on the frontlines, however. Our son can have a thirty-minute tantrum over what has happened to his toothbrush. He sees the letters on the electric brush are starting to rub off, and it makes him mad. So it takes him thirty minutes to brush his teeth before bed. It is hard for me because it is the end of the day and I just want him to go to bed so that I can have one hour to myself. My husband is the only one who knows how a thirty-minute tantrum about a toothbrush affects me and my son. I don't think the wife should have to bear it all by herself and deal with it internally. We need to vent to people who understand. It's true that I can talk to Elaine at the Exceptional Family Member Program, and it helps a lot. But I also think my husband needs to know that I had to pull my kid out of drum class because he was going to hit the teacher with the drumstick.

"I've learned to deal with these tantrums differently over time. These days, I'll just go sit on the couch and be like,

"Okay, well, I've got a moment to myself." You learn to use these moments well. I home school him now, and if he doesn't want to do his schoolwork, he has to sit in his room, and since there's no toys in his room, he just reads. While he reads, I sit on the couch and catch up on my DVR. I have found a way to make it okay for both of us."

So far, I have touched on ways to stay connected that require access to the Internet or phone lines. Of course, not all military spouses are able to stay in touch this way during deployments. When necessary, it's important to come up with alternate ways to stay in touch for the sake of everyone in the family. Coping and parenting are both easier during deployment when children feel connected to their deployed parent.

Erin, a Navy wife and the blogging author of the *Deployment Diatribes*, shared some of the ways she helps her four sons, including one with autism, stay close to their father while he's away. I especially like her suggestions because they are sensitive to the needs of children with disabilities who may need visual reminders. She writes:

"A daily way we stay close to Dad is that we keep a large bowl filled with Hershey's kisses. Each evening, the boys each got a "kiss" from Daddy before they brushed their teeth. As his return date drew closer, and we had an exact reunion date, I made sure the number of kisses was right so that the last ones were taken the day before he came home. It's a visible reminder for the kids that homecoming is approaching....

"There are lots of ways to help your kids and spouse stay connected. In our family, before my husband left, he bought several Lego minifigures and let each son select one to represent himself. Then, my husband took the minifigures with him on deployment. He attached them to magnets and they attached to his bunk. He took them with him sometimes when he left the ship and took their pictures at various spots."

Often, spouses who are facing deployment record bedtime stories to be played regularly after they have left home. Others take very creative approaches such as leaving behind a home-based scavenger hunt complete with clues to help the children locate hidden objects.

Sometimes differences in emotional reactions to a child's disability threaten a couple's ability to stay connected more than actual distance due to deployments. Tanya and her husband shared their grief and tears together at times. More often, however, partners react differently than each other due to gender and individual styles of emotional coping. For example, one parent may grieve openly while the other appears stoic and expresses little emotion. Such differences in a couple are natural and fine under many circumstances. The problems develop when one or the other is upset that his or her partner is not reacting as he or she is.

Fran Prezant and I (2007) discussed this topic in depth in *Married with Special Needs Children: A Couple's Guide to Keeping Connected*. Let me share a few excerpts from that book as a way to pass on some parental wisdom on this topic:

- "I would say that husbands and wives need to give each other the freedom to cope with and express feelings differently. My style of coping is to gather as much information as I can about the disability and treatment. At first, when my husband didn't behave the same way, I thought he didn't care. Now I realize his focus is more on how our son is like other children. I think that gives our son a healthy balance" (p. 30).

- "We don't see eye to eye on a lot of things. When I grieved for a long time about our daughter's disability, my husband (who grew up on a farm in Kansas) just shrugged his shoulder and said it changed nothing. He just loved her and did whatever he had to do for her. Only when I get him all liquored up can I get deep emotions from him, but even then, he is very calm and at peace with her condition. I've always commented that farmers take everything in stride—a tornado, hail, drought— they don't get upset, they just go back to work. That seems to be his motto in life. I guess this is good because I'm a hot-tempered Irish woman who emotes, cries, laughs, gets angry, yells, and hugs with great abandon. Maybe I did the feeling for both us while he held down the fort" (p. 30).

Resentment

There has been a lot of discussion about resentment throughout this book. This is because it is an emotion that often accompanies parenting children with disabilities—especially solo parenting. It also rears its head in marriages when, for a variety of reasons, one parent is largely responsible for a child with a disability.

One mother, whose marriage is now sound but was almost ruined after she had a child with a severe physical disability, shared her insight. As they say, "hindsight is 20/20" and hers most certainly is valuable to others:

> "It all started with resentment. My husband felt helpless and overwhelmed. I took over caring for our son, and my husband pulled away. I resented him for this and did not show any care toward him. I was angry that here was so much on my shoulders. So, I told myself, 'He's a big boy. He can take care of himself!' Then he began to resent our son because I took care of him."

I have seen variations of this dynamic so often in my work with couples that I have dubbed this the "resentment dance." In the resentment dance, one partner rushes full force into taking care of the child's needs. This 100 percent immersion is sometimes necessary, such as when there is a medical crisis. Other times, it can be more of an obsessional approach driven by fear, guilt, and grief. As the very active parent gets more and more involved, the other parent tends to get less and less involved, and the dance (and relationship) spirals down.

The mother who shared her hindsight succeeded in changing the resentment dance. She mustered up all her self-discipline in order to encourage her husband's involvement without her typical expression of anger and resentment or cold shoulders. Although this mother was entitled to her resentment with her husband, these feelings were not making daily life even a little bit better. You know the saying "Do you want to be right or happy?" She was not wrong to feel the way she did, but getting stuck in those feelings made a bad situation even more entrenched. So, she focused on ways to shift more of their son's care to her husband while helping her husband be successful and refraining from criticism. In essence, she was creating new space and providing the help and encouragement that a long-time passive partner needed to step up. I realize some of you will say that you have given up on getting help from a spouse. But the dance can still change, as it did for that woman after many years.

Without exception, each parent that I interviewed for this chapter spoke of his or her resentment and the need to manage it. Sometimes, resentments had little to do with the parents' marriages. For instance, one military wife with a happy marriage spoke of her need to manage resentment for her own sake. She also shared her strategy:

> "I try not to dwell on it, but I feel resentment when I think of an activity I would like to do as a family and then it seems impossible because of my son's problems. Sometimes, my husband will discourage me by saying everything will be too hard and not worth the effort. I have learned over the years that I will be less resentful if I try to do that thing. Then, if it doesn't work out, I can accept it. For example, we might drive forty-five minutes to go to the beach and when we get there, my son can't tolerate any more and he's ready to go. It's the same way with bowling. One game later—he is more than done. It's hard, but I think if you try, you're least likely to be resentful. At least that is how it works for me."

A Little More about Coping in a Military Home

Keeping Order and Faith

The Backstory: Rashaun's husband is typically not home due to his military career. This mother of four children created a structure that benefitted her kids and enabled her to complete two master's degrees—while going solo.

"Sometimes when you feel like it is too much, that's actually okay because it actually is too much."—Rashaun

An excerpt from Rashaun's story follows:

My husband has been gone a lot. Now he works three or four hours away and comes home on some weekends. Before that, there were several years of deployments when he would only be home for a few weeks. So I set up a very structured routine. My child with autism knows what to do every morning since the routine doesn't change. The routine is great for him and benefits all the rest of us too. I even found a structure for the kids' activities. Each child chooses a season for activities. Then I can run that child around, but at least it is only one child at a time.

It is a very difficult transition when my husband comes back; I start picturing it in my mind at least a week before. I know that the structure I have is no longer going to be in place, and that is very hard for me. I like things to be a certain way in order for the kids to behave in a certain way and for me to handle everything that's on my plate. I work on my attitude so that I won't get mad about these changes since he is only trying to come back and reconnect.

Being in graduate school helped me a lot because it kept my mind off things and focused on a goal. This really helped when he had deployments in Afghanistan and Iraq. During those times I could not bear to listen to the news.

My oldest child was the most scared. My husband said that if I reacted, the kids would react even more, so I didn't show any feelings and kept a stone face. Sometimes they'd have to go to bed earlier if it was an emotional time for me.

I don't have family that helps much. My father is not a part of my life anymore and my mother is very busy helping my sister with five kids. My side of the family doesn't understand that I need time to regroup, and my husband's side doesn't even think my son has a disability. They don't want to acknowledge it because of the stigma of these kinds of things. So they prefer to think that he is just spoiled. He's not, but they see me let him do some things differently; that is how we do it in our home. We have the rule that everyone has their own special needs. They are my elders and they're my husband's parents so I don't want to disrespect them. When they say something that bothers me on the phone, I pretty much just say "thank you" and excuse myself from the phone as quickly as possible. Then I call my best friend to talk.

I have to keep busy in order to not think about the chaos going on in my life. You'd think being too busy would cause more chaos, but it actually creates order because you have to stay on a schedule so you know when you have something due. It helps keep everything in line. I actually earned two master's degrees while parenting the four kids mostly on my own.

Genius Moments

Rashaun has learned to streamline family life so that a great deal can get done. Her kids pitch in to help their brother, but they also get their own needs acknowledged. When I interviewed her in her home, the dining room was full of balloons that they had just used to celebrate one of her children's birthdays. With the help of strong daily coping strategies, she lives well on her own.

Some of Rashaun's strategies and philosophies include:

- *Using a toolbox of daily coping strategies.* She said, "I have lots of different ways to cope every day. Sometimes I play gospel music really loudly. I also find that writing helps. I don't use my journal just to complain. Instead, I write a prayer about what I want to change. And I call my best friend and sister almost every day."

- *Changing churches.* Rashaun explained: "It was very important to find a church that welcomed my son. Our first church did not work out well. He was more disruptive, ran around, and talked loudly to himself. Even though the church people were saying, "It's okay, he's fine," their behavior indicated they were just tolerating it—and not all that well! We switched to a church that looks at him really differently."

- *Staying on top of her resentment.* Rashaun said, "I have some resentment because my husband can pick up and go whenever he wants, and I have to maintain four schedules—five, if you include my own. When I'm feeling resentful, I try to think about the joy that I have in my children because they are such blessings. Since my husband's overseas, he doesn't get a chance to go to the awards assemblies when they make straight As or when they make the honor roll. If I was over there, I wouldn't be able to do that and other things."

Holding the Line

The Backstory: Trixie has been happily married for more than twenty-six years. Her husband is a chaplain who often deploys. She has three children, the youngest a teenager with both Down syndrome and autism.

"It is hard not knowing what is going on inside of him. It may be his hormones and all. But one thing I do know is that you can't carry a hundred-pound kid to the bus stop."—Trixie

Part of Trixie's story follows:

My son Simon is not as social as other children with Down syndrome. His communication is very limited, and he doesn't smile. He was doing great at school for a while in an autistic classroom. Most of the boys in his class were higher functioning than he was.

Now and then he had trouble going back to school after breaks for holidays. After the long weekend for President's Day, we really began to have troubles with him. He started taking his clothes off in the classroom and he would just plop himself down on the floor. Simon wasn't aggressive, but they couldn't move him. He was suspended twice;

one suspension was for taking his clothes off and the second one was for trying to do it again.

There are still times now when Simon doesn't want to go to school. You can't carry him to the bus because he is 109 pounds now. So, if he decides he doesn't want to go to school, he gets nothing all day. I mean he gets no computer, no videos, no nothing.

He may have Down syndrome and autism, but he "gets" it. He's learned. There were days last year where he wouldn't go to school for three days in a row. Finally, he began realizing that he had to go or he would get nothing that he wanted.

I know I have to keep a consistent routine so he will learn. I know a lot of parents would just give up and give in. Some would just say, "It's not worth it." They say things like "My kid is driving me nuts and he can't do anything." I want to tell them that's part of the process, and once you get through that part, they know you mean business. But, if you give in all the time, your child can't learn what they need to learn.

My husband was deployed to Afghanistan with the marines from 2010 to 2011. He was deployed again in the spring of 2012, and I had to close on the house we are in myself and then move us (literally the next month). Military wives often have to do things without their husbands. So I just do those kinds of things because I am doing it for my family and supporting my husband. I think that and my faith keep me going.

I just graduated from college last year. My husband supported my plans for education. I think my mother was the only one who questioned whether I'd be able to handle it with my husband deployed. But, my parents are also the first ones who will drop everything and come if I need them. My oldest son, Alex, and I were in college together. By the way, I ended up making a better grade point average than him.

I try to let my daughter be the typical sibling. There are times she does get mad at her brother Simon and resents him. I think it is important to let her express it. Sometimes *she will accuse me of doing things for Simon that I don't do for her. The redhead in me says, "Do you want me to have to wipe your butt too? Or give you a shower?" because that's what I still need to do for him. I want her to understand, but I also try to understand what she is feeling. Typically, I do something like get the neighbor to watch Simon on a Saturday night, and then we have a girls' night out together.*

I decided to go back to school for graduate school around the same time that Simon was getting his autism diagnosis and while I was trying to get the proper educational services and supports for him. My negative experiences with an administrator got me so fired up that they empowered me to go back to school. So I am doing my master's degree online in the area of special education. My goal is to be able to help parents with IEPs and other things.

A lot of times when my husband is deployed and my kids are in bed, I go into my garden tub and relax. While I am doing that, I listen to old Frank Sinatra music. I cry and have my moments and try not to let the kids see me. Sometimes my daughter has seen me cry; it may happen if a song comes on that makes me think of her dad. But I try not to have this happen.

I am a redhead, and I have learned to cope with my temper. As you get older in life, you realize what battles to pick, what upsets you, and what not to let upset you. I walk away a lot and then come back and try to face something with a different attitude. I don't want to get my blood boiling.

I think if parents can get past what they want their children to be and accept them for who they are, they can enjoy life. I do see more women doing this more easily (than their husbands), but I've also seen a couple where the men have stepped up more and they're on active duty.

Without a faith in God and a strong marriage, I don't know how people do it. I need those supports. I meet a lot of young wives who don't seem to understand that it's a two-way street when you're married—it is not just about your side of the road. This kind of support for each other is what makes our marriage and family work.

Genius Moments

Trixie is a genius at understanding the importance of supporting each individual in the family—herself included. Neither her son's dual diagnoses nor her husband's frequent deployments overshadow the needs of the rest of the family. Each person's identity and desires are clear. For example, when the family needed to relocate, she explained, "We looked at all the variables—not just for my son or my husband—but for my daughter too."

Some of Trixie's strategies and philosophies include:

- *Creating a family climate of mutual encouragement.* Trixie explained that encouragement flowed freely in her home: "When I was trying to get my degree, I was thinking about quitting, but my teenage daughter told me I couldn't quit. So if you're an encourager to your kids, you become a role model for being supportive, and they'll be there for you too. My older kids have been wonderful and have helped me out lots of times. If it wasn't for them, I don't know how I would have finished my education."

- *Finding the right support groups.* Trixie spoke of searching for the best resources. She stated that she found more help from autism groups than those devoted to Down syndrome. Her advice would be to keep looking for groups that can help you get well educated about how to help your child and connect you to the best resources. Like so many others in this chapter, she sang the praises of Exceptional Family Member programs.

Conclusion

As we have seen, parents who are on their own for stretches of time have unique circumstances and complex stories. While they are not prototypical solo parents, they have much to share about how to cope in difficult life circumstances. They remind us that finding support outside of a marriage or other partnership is one of the most important strategies for maintaining self-care.

Finding creative ways to adapt to parenting alone is something that any solo can do to help create a more manageable life. Many of the military solos talked of finding a sense of family outside their biological family and noted that this sense of belonging and support was crucial to their success as temporarily single parents. For those of us who are not in the service, these strategies and stories can shed light on our own lives.

෧෨

Chapter 12

෧෨

Resilient Solos Creating New Life Stories

Faith is the bird that feels the light and sings
when the dawn is still dark.
In effect, the people who change our lives the most begin to
sing to us while we are still in darkness. If we listen to
their song, we will see the dawning of a
new part of ourselves.
—Rabindranth Tagore

ONE OF THE many things I want you to take away from this book is faith in the ability to live well, on your own, while raising children with disabilities. If we see others do it, it is easier to believe that it is possible; this is especially important for those stretches of time when we are feeling overwhelmed and exhausted from what we are facing.

This chapter includes stories from four more solos whose lives I want to share. They have all persevered and reshaped their lives in ways that have great meaning, autonomy, contentment, and sometimes lots of fun. They all demonstrate resilience—adapting in the face of adversity. I hope at least some of their stories get "stuck" in your mind in case you encounter times where you doubt that anyone can cope with what you are facing. Perhaps Christopher Robin expressed this same sentiment (a little better) when he said to Winnie the Pooh:

Promise me you'll always remember:
You're braver than you believe, and stronger than you seem,
and smarter than you think.
—A. A. Milne

In this chapter, you will read about the experiences of some solos who each perceived new possibilities in their lives despite an onslaught of problems that were beyond their control. I doubt that any of them were exceptional in the sense that they were innately blessed with unusual abilities. You will hear the words and stories of:

- Bea, a solo grandmother who found herself suddenly raising four grieving grandchildren on the autism spectrum
- Olivia, a woman who ended up thriving after the suicide of a husband, an acting-out child with bipolar illness, an escape from an abusive relationship, and more
- Julia, a divorced mother of twins whose parenting and service to veterans demonstrates daily resilience
- Tasha, who simultaneously cared for a terminally ill father and a suicidal daughter and needed to flee from a threatening marriage

Understanding Resilience

To outsiders, resilience looks like the ability to "bounce back" after prolonged hardship or crisis. Some think resilience is partly inborn, but psychologists have concluded that resiliency is a capacity we can develop throughout life. We develop resilience as we acquire coping skills and learn to look at ourselves and situations differently. This may include tapping into our own strengths and being surprised at what we found. It often includes forming supportive relationships and using resources. Reorganizing and adapting to daily life while managing distress are hallmarks of resilience.

Embracing the Inevitability of Change

Bea's story wonderfully illustrates many of the factors that contribute to being able to live with resilience. As you will read, she responds to challenges gracefully because she understands that she must reorganize her life and mind-set to cope with drastic changes in her life.

A Graceful Woman

The Backstory: Bea is a grandmother in her sixties who is now the solo parent to four young grandchildren who are all on the autism spectrum. Their mother died from breast cancer and their father was not capable of parenting them due to his ongoing battle with drug addiction.

> *"I was around sixty-four at the time this all happened, and I remember a girlfriend saying, "You know you're going to have to raise those kids." I remember saying, "No I'm going to get a nanny." I was so clueless; I thought I was going to have Mary Poppins fall from the sky."—Bea*

An excerpt from Bea's story follows:

The kids were three, five, seven, and nine. They were young and vulnerable. Three of them are on the spectrum, and now they think the fourth one is also. I was always a grandma who was very involved since my son had problems with drugs and alcohol.

My involvement increased as my daughter-in-law became ill and then died from breast cancer. A while after she died, I was over one weekend to check out how things were going. My son had started to drink heavily—he was a binger and probably was taking drugs too. He was not well at all. So, he got angry at something that I said, and he walked out the front door and down the eighty-five steps to get to the trolley. He didn't turn around and just walked out with the children screaming, "Daddy Daddy!"

So I comforted them all, put them to bed, and decided that I needed to pack things up so I could take them to my home. It was only a mile and a half away and they knew it very well, so they would feel safe and secure there. I said to them, "This will work out." And I took them to school in the morning. I believed they should have the schedule that they normally have, and I explained, "This is what Mommy and Daddy would want."

I have a big house, and they all moved in. I also have a forty-something-year-old son [not their father] at home. It was kind of chaotic in the beginning. We needed a routine, but the children weren't used to routine. Most recently, they were being parented by a mother going through chemo until she died, all within the span of ten months.

Then it started. The first thing was that they thought I was "a little too fancy." The oldest asked me why I was so "fancy," and I had to say, "Hmm…that's interesting; I don't know." I had to take my ego out of all of this. These children are brutally honest, and if they notice something, they will tell you. They don't worry about whether it's going to hurt your feelings. It just comes out of their mouths, and really they're very funny. It makes me laugh now just thinking about some of the things they have said to me.

I am trying to learn to do things to make it easier on all of us. It has not always come naturally, but I am learning. One morning, I had taken everyone to church, and they were awful in church. I brought them all back and said that I was going to make eggs and bacon and cinnamon rolls. My friend said, "Why don't you just buy some cereal and make your life easier?" She was a dietician and a person with very high standards, so I thought I better take that advice.

That was not the last time I was told I had to lower my standards. So, I started to think about my standards and the fact that they were just rules that were in my head. I had rules in my head just the same way that my grandchildren with Asperger's and PDD-NOS have rules. Adults don't see their rules as logical. But, they're logical in their own thinking. They can defend their rules beautifully—sometimes better than I defend my rules.

So, I started to look at who I thought I was and who I needed to become to make everybody's life a little bit easier, especially mine. So, fancy or not, I found out that I didn't have to have everything picked up all around the house. That wasn't as important as I had thought it was. I found that I wanted one room (my living room) to be the room where we could sit and talk and have functions and people could come over and not look at a million toys and all the stuff.

You need to understand how much stuff you have to bring into your house for four children. The three boys all play football and soccer and baseball, so they need all that equipment. Oh! And then there is tennis and hockey. And so I'll go outside and I'll catch baseball with the kids or kick a soccer ball or do something like that. They think that it's cool that someone as old as me can do all that. I can be much younger with them and it's wonderful.

Living alone for twelve years, I really liked my silence, and I didn't have it anymore. And so I needed to have time where I could just chill out or do some things I needed to do to keep me happy. I wasn't willing to give that up because it wasn't going to be healthy for any of us. I like my privacy, and sometimes there is no place to go, so I'd find myself going to the library for some quiet time. I did not want to become that woman that people would talk about: "Look! She just gave up her whole life for those children and became bitter and resentful."

Then there is the little grandson who is a sweet child with a terrible temper. It took a very long time to get his curse words to stop flowing. It was kind of funny because I grew up in a house where you never swore, and my own kids didn't either. So, this little one would get angry and spout all these words. Once he called me an idiot. Another time, he said, "You old lady!" I laugh about it now because it was so funny. I said, "You can call me everything, but don't you call me an old lady." His mouth is a lot better now.

I have a nightly ritual with the children because I think it helps them to go to sleep better. Sometimes we do baths and we try to read a bit and then we say prayers. I tickle their backs and their legs and do this thing on their head that they like and then we sing songs. And if they want to sing, they can. Some of them like to sing with me and some of them don't want anybody to sing. Of course, if you get one word wrong, you have to go back and do it all over again because they know each and every word.

I take turns with everybody sleeping in the bed with me. I have a big bedroom and there's a couch. If they have a nightmare, they'll come in. I don't wake up as easily when another one climbs in my bed. They know they can come to me for comfort. And so sometimes when I wake up in the morning, there are three kids in my bed. I have found that I don't need as much space as I used to and I don't get tired. I think of this as marathon runner training.

They're still grieving, and I find that some people (not that many) want them to just get on with their lives. They don't all get it. The oldest told his therapist that he worried about being an orphan, and he worries about taking care of all these children, and he worries about me dying. For a long time, he was very angry that his uncle lived in the house and his daddy didn't always live in the house. His uncle was there; his daddy was not. Because of that, he would lash out at his uncle. It was very difficult. Now, two years later, they all see their uncle as that person who goes to their ball games, who kicks the ball with them, who is there for them.

But all the anger has not gone away. The other day, the oldest, Michael, was so angry about all that has happened. He was talking about baseball with his uncle and watching the baseball game on TV. His uncle mentioned that he was looking for houses in Florida so he could be near his daughter. So Michael (he's very good with computers) said, "Why don't I help you look for houses in Pittsburgh to live instead? You don't have to go all the way to Florida, you can just live right here in Pittsburgh!" And he started showing him all these houses in Pittsburgh that were listed online. So, Michael went from wanting his uncle out of the house in the beginning to this. It did not end there. It ended with his throwing his uncle's really good phone out the third-floor window. It landed in the snow.

The boys let me comfort them more than my grand-daughter Amelia will. She will sit in my lap and let me comfort her, but she doesn't do that as well as the boys do. I somewhat think it's just her personality, but I also suspect that it's part of her grieving issue. Grieving is something that they're going to do for the rest of their lives. It is sad but true, and I have told them this.

We did meet with a psychologist who specialized in grieving children. In fact, we worked on grief with people when their mother went into hospice. This psychologist said that the studies have confirmed that they will always have this ache that will come up at times in their heart. But, they will be stronger because they've had to learn ways to cope. And most of them do okay.

Amelia was only two when her mother was diagnosed. So, to tell you the truth, nobody said "no" to her until she came to my house. And Amelia didn't like it. And she would scream and kick and have meltdowns, and I'd have black and blue marks all over me. She was so hard. She would go into her room and destroy anything that was on the walls. She was destructive! I had to say that I couldn't talk to her when she was like that and that if she destroyed her room, I would need to take her toys away for a while. She was tough. You could be in the middle of the grocery store, and she'd start screaming, "Let go of me, don't do that to me, you're hurting me!' Amelia's really smart. I've just learned that I need to go shopping by myself.

When you take any of them out, one on one, they are like angels. They're so sweet, and they don't have melt-downs; they don't need to. Somebody's listening to them and giving them some attention. I realize that a lot of times when I get meltdowns from them, maybe they just don't feel heard because I look too busy since everyone's running around following their schedules and stuff. And they are really sensitive to getting their needs met. If they don't, they will let me know, and it doesn't always make me happy. A lot of times it's in church.

I do ask them to go to church every Sunday because it is part of our religion. The third one is about to have his first holy communion. So the rule is you go to church every Saturday or Sunday. And the rule is that they should behave, although they don't always. They know when they can get to me and I can't do very much about it because I'm supposed to be behaving in church too. And they don't respond well to dirty looks, because they don't understand the looks.

I've been trying to teach them a little more about behavior. Sometimes they think I'm just goofy and old fashioned. The kids say to me, "Oh, you are goofy...you are so goofy," and then they laugh. And then I laugh. I try to have a sense of humor about it. Because when I get too serious, everyone gets serious. And I do think that being lighthearted has helped me an awful lot.

I know I'll make many more mistakes with them, and I don't like to make mistakes. I used to credit myself with these wonderful characteristics. They've made me see myself in a new light. I thought I was patient, but I'm not that patient of a person. I'm patient if I'm getting my own way. But, it's another story if I'm not getting my own way.

When I'm tired or hungry, I can be really crabby! A lot of times, they'll say to me, "God, have you eaten lately?" It's nice that they can or will say that to me. Sometimes they'll say, "God, that's enough! You're really wearing that out," and they'll be right. Recently I heard someone say we should ask ourselves, "Are you somebody that you'd like to live with?" I've thought about that many times. Am I somebody that I'd like to live with?

Resentment is like a poisonous pill that we take, expecting the person we resent to die. Resentment is like poison accumulates in our lives. I spent some time with somebody really sarcastic the other day. I said, "It's very difficult for me to be around you because I don't surround myself with people like you anymore." It was the truth. I have to be very aware of who I am allowing into my life.

It has been a little more than two years now that the children have been living with me. Sometimes, you get little "gifts" along the way and suddenly they accumulate and you see them. This happens to me at night. Usually, after the children fall asleep, I like to stay in their rooms a bit and watch them sleep because that's when I really get that feeling of gratitude. Like, they're in my life, and I'm so lucky. What a wonderful responsibility this is for me.

I have heard Bea say that we have to "cooperate with life on life's terms." She has a soul-deep understanding of this. She has had to let go of her idea of how life is "supposed" to be in favor of finding a way to thrive with life as it actually is. As life changed, Bea changed herself to adapt rather than simply succumbing. This means she retained her focus on living a life with meaning and enjoyment—just radically different from how she thought it would play out. She allowed her preferences and routines to become pliable and amenable to change. For example, she can laugh at her desire to be "fancy" while understanding that many of her rules about daily life are as arbitrary as her grandchildren's. She doesn't try to use her power to insist on her way, but uses it to keep growing, enjoying life, and raising her grandchildren well and with great love. This flexibility to adapt to life as it changes is one of several attributes that enables resilience.

Bea has practiced gratitude in daily life, and it now flows very naturally in her thoughts. But don't think for a moment that she acts "righteous"—she has a wickedly funny sense of humor. Humor and gratitude are a powerful combination.

Post-Traumatic Growth

Richard Tedeschi and Lawrence Calhoun use the term *post-traumatic growth* to describe the positive psychological change that sometimes results from a person's struggle with exceptionally challenging, stressful, and traumatic events. Such growth can develop and exist alongside of loss and open up new ways of living. Post-traumatic growth may sometimes resemble resilience, but is more the product of being plunged into such extreme circumstances that the person emerges simply different. It reminds me of the saying about someone being "stronger in the broken places." This does not mean that the person does not still experience suffering sometimes. It is important to recognize that strength and heartache or fear can coexist.

The next life story, Olivia's, focuses less on her experiences parenting a child with bipolar disorder and more on making life work despite tremendous obstacles. As for many solo parents, many of these obstacles were unrelated to child-rearing. She has walked through the type of storm described by Haruki Murakami (2005) in his book *Kafka on the Shore*:

> "And once the storm is over, you won't remember how you made it through, how you managed to survive. You won't even be sure, whether the storm is really over. But one thing is certain. When you come out of the storm, you won't be the same person who walked in" (p. 5).

Olivia's story illustrates post-traumatic growth. She grew a strong backbone and became unwilling to let life (or any person) dominate her.

Resilience Personified

The Backstory: Olivia's story includes the suicide of a husband, an acting-out child with bipolar illness, an escape from an abusive relationship, and a struggle to complete her education while feeling pressured to raise out-of-control step-grandchildren. If we had not talked candidly, I would not have guessed at the backstory. As a minority woman, she also shared her beliefs on how cultural attitudes toward mental health disorders made the whole situation far worse.

"Sometimes, if it's only the little things that you can control, it can make a big difference."—Olivia

My son was fourteen when my husband killed himself; my daughter turned nine the day after the funeral. The suicide was unexpected, but my husband had threatened before when things didn't go his way. He would work just long enough to fake an "on the job" injury and collect. It was horrible. This was not how I was raised. We never had anything and were so poor that there often wasn't enough money to buy detergent. I was thirty-three when he died, and leading up to it, I was just so sick of it all.

He was a controlling man in a pitiful kind of way. He didn't want me to work or go to college, and there were certain people he didn't want me to associate with. As you can imagine, especially from meeting me now, it did not suit me in the least. But I also felt sorry for him, and I didn't want to give him anything extra to worry about.

The day that he died, we had been arguing back and forth about my right to go to a job interview alone. I was so tired of it all. He asked me what I would do if he killed himself. This was nothing new. He had tried three weeks before this by taking pills, and he threatened suicide a lot. He ran out of the room, and I thought he had left the house by a side door. So when I heard a bang, we thought it was just a door slamming. But it was from his gun in the basement. My son found him later—he had shot himself with a hunting rifle.

I hope readers of my story will see that ignoring a mental disability will not make it go away. Had this fact been emphasized, my husband would still be alive today—or at the least, he would not have died of suicide. When I went to my husband's family about his suicide threats, they laughed at me, made fun of me, and told me that black people do not commit suicide. It is my opinion that this is not an un-common attitude, and I hope readers learn something from my story. Even after he killed himself, they insisted to the po-lice that he had to have been murdered, and even went as far as to say that my son or I had to have killed him.

My son was only fourteen at the time. He was never the same after the police interrogation, which was emo-tionally brutal and traumatizing. Before that, he had been an honors student and then he changed. I think he also changed his views of me and said to himself, "She's just a woman and has no real control over me—I'm almost as big as her." So he started doing whatever he pleased. He and my out-of-control daughter, Ciera, were both acting like clowns in the community. My family was telling me that I should beat them. Their attitude was that if I was not going to take their advice, I shouldn't ask for their help. So I was on my own.

I got into a relationship six months after my husband died. This new guy was abusive to me after a while—but only me. We were living with him, and I could not meet the rental expenses without both of our finances. And I said to myself, "Well, the kids never see him hitting me...they don't even know he hits me." I also didn't want to be without a man. You are not subjected to the same things if you have a man around. People don't say it, but they make you feel like you're worthless if you don't have a man in your life. It's like you're incomplete, like you're nothing. So, I thought it was worth it back then.

But I got to the point that I was desperate to get out of the relationship. I decided to move several states away. It was a huge move, and I had to save up money to do it. So I signed up for work at one of those temp agencies and I started selling my things. By the time we moved, my kids and I and all our things fit into a nineteen-foot U-Haul. So eventually, I got to Ohio when I was thirty-six. I don't know if I would have had the guts to do this again—but I did it.

After we moved, Ciera, whose behavior had started to go out of control several years prior, was still giving me trouble. She was running around with older guys and then began running away for a few days at a time. In fact, she ran away the first day that I started college. This was the third time she had done this. To make a long story short, I had to file an "unruly" order. When child protection services came out, the woman was nice, but it took about six months for the agency to catch up with her. The woman from the agency told Ciera that I thought she was an unfit mother (she had a child by age seventeen). Ciera called me up and cursed me out and we didn't speak for two or three years.

For a while, I raised my step-grandchildren, but now I just live with my youngest daughter and we have peace in our lives. We enjoy ourselves together; this has included volunteering at a thrift store we liked for an entire summer. It was kind of odd because all the other volunteers they took in were people who were in trouble with the law. But the people that "hired" us obviously knew we weren't in trouble with the law; we were just Good Samaritans.

Actually, our favorite place to be in the world is in the thrift shop. My daughter won't buy things from regular stores because she likes the vintage look. And I can fix and alter the old clothes she buys. We leave the house with twenty dollars for each of us and literally spend six hours in thrift shops.

We also became friends with the people at our local Burger King, Arby's, and Starbucks. It takes hardly any money, and you can sit there forever. They don't like to see us leave. There are so many free things you can do. There's a whole world out there of things you can do to have fun.

Another thing that gets me through everything is my sense of humor. That's one thing I inherited from my father. A lot of times, I make people laugh, and my youngest daughter and I laugh all the time about everything.

*You asked me what advice I have for other parents
on their own. I think they need to know to use their own
mind in deciding what's best for their child. No one knows
that child better than the person taking care of him or her.
And, no one knows your situation, regardless of what they
think they know.*

*I used to cry at night sometimes because I thought it
was my fault that Ciera developed bipolar disorder. People
would say that it was my fault because I was a bad parent who
wouldn't spank her. And people would tell me, "Spare the rod
and spoil the child" and a whole bunch of other things.*

*I know it is not Ciera's fault that she has bipolar. I hate
to say that she can't be held accountable for much of it,
though, because everybody should have accountability. At
the same time, it's hard not to get mad at a person when
they're doing things that are sometimes so offensive. I worry
about her children, and her husband is just as bad off as she
is, but I love him too. Ciera was diagnosed with bipolar only
three years ago. Today, she is enrolled in college and earning
more than respectable grades.*

*I don't want to be a bitter woman. I fought for myself. I
stood up for myself, and that makes me feel good. Because
there's been a lot of times in my life when I didn't. I think
it's human nature to become bitter when things are out of
your control.*

*I refuse to give people the right or the power to change
me because I like who I am. That's what I always say: I like
who I am and I will fight to my death to keep from giving a
person the power to change who I am.*

Olivia's life reminds me of the words of the painter Georgia
O'Keefe: "I got half-a-dozen paintings from that shattered plate."
Speaking of resilience, when Georgia O'Keefe lost her vision in
her last decade of life, she found ways to create art without vision.
That is the spirit of creativity that contributes to resiliency and is
evident in how Olivia lives her life and prospers. When I met her, she

was dressed in an outfit that she had stitched and refashioned into something unique that she liked. She has taken a similar approach to daily life. After a life with harrowing experiences and some regrets, she primarily immerses herself in her daily life, which she has assembled from all that she finds valuable. In essence, she has worked to have "the best and get rid of the rest."

Olivia is an avid writer and has published her work. She is finishing her college degree so that she can work with troubled young people. She provides guidance and workshops to custodial grandparents and single parents. In addition, she has a booming laugh and embraces unadorned pleasures of daily life with her youngest daughter. Her story also exemplifies the importance of moving ahead—even with great fear—so that you can make it out of a storm. She moved ahead while paying attention to the lessons she learned along the way.

Taking Positive Action

The next story highlights resilience in the form of remaining steadfastly positive while juggling the demands of autism, child-rearing, and a hostile ex-spouse. Julia exemplifies another aspect of being resilient: a willingness to take action to shape life's outcomes as much as you can.

Taking Charge

The Backstory: Julia spent twenty-three years in the military working on an emergency medical unit—i.e., a MASH unit. At fifty, she is retired from the military but continues to serve vets through her service. She is the divorced mother of young twin boys. One is neurotypical and one is not.

> *"I think the greatest thing about my children is that they have forced me to become creative, and I didn't have a creative bone in my body."—Julia*

An excerpt from Julia's story follows:

> *I don't trust my children to be in my ex-husband's care. To this day, he refuses to let me talk to them on his week-*

ends (a problem that is going to be addressed in court soon). Let me give you an example of the type of conflict I have with him. A little boy in the neighborhood gave my sons a little Razor scooter that they just love to ride on. So, they wanted to take it to their father's house that weekend when he came to get them. He said, "I'm not taking that beat-up thing" and threw it in a yard. The kids were both crying, so I said, "You always put yourself first...and, by the way, that's not my yard—that's somebody else's."

He got in my face, and these three moms got out of their cars and surrounded us. The teenage boys in the yards also immediately came around—they are very protective. I live in a nice housing development with a lot of divorced moms. We have a nice support network going and are blessed to have such a great neighborhood.

I force myself to talk to the boys about positive things. When they come back from their dad's I ask, "How was your weekend?" I want them to have good memories of him. I have pictures of my ex in the house, in their bedrooms.

You have to get out of the past even though you're still dealing with issues. I enjoy doing silly things. My kids have forced me to become creative even though I did not have a creative bone in my body. My one son, Jack, gets really stressed when he can't play outside. One day, it was raining and I knew I had to figure something out, so I bought all this crazy duct tape and I made an obstacle course that went through my whole living room.

My other son, Jordan, is so disciplined. He's been saying ever since he was three years old, "Mommy, I'm going to grow up, go in the army, be a flight surgeon." When I heard that, I told him I had to show him something. I showed him an ultrasound picture where it looks like he's giving a salute.

I was an operating nurse and spent twenty-three years in the military. I loved it. To this day, I am a "service officer" and help a lot with the VA. We have a lot of younger vets. My kids are also very involved. I'm also an honor guard at a veteran cemetery, and the kids come out and help me put the flags on the graves. I keep them very involved.

We do a lot for kids and actually recently had a fund-raiser for my son Jack. I wanted him to have brain balance therapy because it was the first thing that made sense to me about how his brain worked and what could be done. I found this place where he could get treatment, but it was ridiculously expensive. I was telling some of the guys at the VFW about it, and they said, "Let's have a fundraiser." The neatest thing was that Jordan said, "Mommy, I have a great idea—I'll be the campaign manager." He kept track of all the money. Every VFW in the state of New Jersey helped out, and we raised the entire amount. When Jordan learned that, he was bouncing off the walls with joy; he is an amazing kid and he just loves his brother so much.

During autism awareness month, Jordan asked his first grade teacher, "Can I please say something about autism?" Forty-five minutes later, the teacher had to leave the room because she was bawling at how passionate he was. I really want him to know that he is the most important person to his brother, and he always will be.

I learned a lot in the military that really helps me with life and my kids—the need for structure, organizational skills, the ability to not sweat the small stuff. When I was in Korea, we were out in the field for like a month in the bitter cold and we had to walk a hundred meters to use a bathroom. We were lucky to get a shower once a week. I became a strong person, both physically and emotionally, and I'm just not intimated at all by anyone. My military training is also reflected in what I teach my children about being respectful and giving back.

Every Thursday is silly bath night. This was Jack's idea, and he calls it the Jersey Boy Show. I turn the lights down low and with a flashlight that flickers, I'll say, "Now announcing"...and the show will begin. We just laugh. They can wear their underwear in the tub. The water really calms

Jack. When he's upset I say, "Let's go take a bath." And then I play with him. I tell him it's raining and splash water on him—just little goofy stuff like that is so much fun.

Fortunately, I'm the mom in the neighborhood that everybody wants to play with. I love having a house full of kids, but it is also really good for Jack because he's a very social kid and loves to be around other kids.

You asked me what I find most stressful. It is when the boys want to do different things. Although it has gotten better, it has been hard for them to compromise. I tell one he can choose today and the other chooses tomorrow. Jack has this fixation where he has to do everything first, so sometimes he gets a little upset. But most of the time he just gives in.

I met an amazing guy recently. He was married to a woman whose child had a brain injury and a shunt, so he pretty much raised her. If I meet someone and they don't put their kids first, it's a big red flag for me. I'm always putting my kids first, and that's really important to me.

Other parents have been the best resource in helping me learn how to parent well. You can truly have so many people advising you. We share our stories and are receptive to criticism. Let me give you an example. My friend called me one day when Jack was crying in the background, so she asked me what was wrong with him. I replied, "He's upset because I don't have the kind of potato chips he likes." And she said, "Oh well, that's why I go to Sam's Club and I buy a carton of them for Jeff."

I said to her, "How are you ever going to teach him to deal with not getting what he wants?" And I thought at first she was really going to get upset, and this was the case at first. A half hour later, she called back and said, "Ya know what? You're right. When I'm not here to buy him a case of potato chips, who's going to do that for him?"

When it comes to parenting, my biggest role model is Temple Grandin's mother. I think she was just the most amazing mom because she said to her daughter, "I'm not *going to be here someday. You have to fit into the world be-cause it's either that or an institution."*

That's how I've raised Jack. We travel all over the place. We've been to fifteen zoos, and Jack's just always out there in social settings. If he has a tantrum, he has to work through it. I don't take him away. It's hard for Jordan, but we don't leave "just because."

I was a dyslexic kid who just got pushed through school. I did not find out about the dyslexia until I was in the military. Getting the diagnosis made a lot of things make better sense for me. It has made me realize how much I need to advocate for Jack in school. I took on a school district: I filed for due process and I got an advocate to help me with this. The advocate was so calm, but he laughed at me during the first meeting we went to. I had this big bag, and he asked if it was to carry all my notes. I told him he would see. When we got seated in the meeting, I took out this huge picture of Jack and set it in front of me. The advocate loved it, but the case manager didn't. She said, "We can't see Mrs. White's face." The answer they received was, "You don't need to. You need to look at that child—that child that you're denying!"

Now I volunteer my time as a special education advocate. I'm actually thinking about going back next year as a child advocate for the state, and I'm still working with military spouses. I think you have to give back.

The essence of Julia's resilience is envisioning what she wants for her family (and others including veterans) and taking action to try to make it happen. Learning to take action is a hallmark of resilient people. Julia described herself as not easily intimidated and credits this characteristic to her military training.

Maya Angelou wrote that courage is the preeminent virtue because, without it, we can't consistently practice other virtues. If you don't find yourself to be as courageous as Julia, consider what author Mary Anne Radmacher wrote about courage:

"Courage doesn't always roar.
Sometimes courage is the quiet voice
at the end of the day saying,
'I will try again tomorrow.'"

Moving though Fear

I value the author Marilyn Ferguson's words that remind us that freedom lies at "the other side of every fear." I believe that Tasha, our final solo parent in the chapter, understood this intuitively.

Making Space for Growth, Continued

The Backstory: Tasha is the mother of an adult daughter with a serious mental illness. You may have read her story in Chapter 10. It focused on helping her daughter grow into adulthood despite past traumas and several psychiatric hospitalizations.

"I spent so much time in the emergency room that they thought I was staff. We would be there for twelve to fourteen hours waiting for crisis to come and do an evaluation to determine whether or not my daughter would be hospitalized. And then I would leave there and go to work"—Tasha

I was not always a solo parent. My first husband was murdered when my daughter, Stephie, was just turning three. It was a case of mistaken identity, and he was shot and killed on his way home from work. He typically finshed work between three and four in the morning. Usually, I would put my daughter in the car, and we would go get him because we shared a single car. But that particular day, I had overslept and we were not with him when it happened. His death began my single parenting when I was twenty.

I got married to my second husband about five years later. Everything was going pretty good for a while, and we moved across the state and away from family. Things changed when my daughter was about fifteen, around the time when my terminally ill father came to live with us after being diagnosed as HIV positive (and later bipolar). My (now ex) husband Steven and I agreed that I would stop working to take care of my dad and that he would continue to work and support all of us.

I noticed that my daughter started to withdraw from her friends, and she always wanted to be in her room by herself. She was okay at school, but she started to give me a harder time in general. As a young mom, I hadn't really known much about parenting, so I had done the best I could. But Steven had a military-style kind of discipline and he would step in and give her these week-long punishments.

The incident happened on a day when Stephie was about to finish a week-long punishment. She and I had sat down and my father had just turned on the television. Steven walked in the door, saw the television on, and immediately added another week to her punishment. It was an extreme reaction, but I always made a point to never have a heated argument in front of my daughter. We would usually wait until she went to bed before we had conversations about this kind of thing.

Stephie stormed off to her room and closed the door, and he left the house. I was sitting quietly at the computer when she came up behind me and said, "I can't stop this from bleeding." I was thinking maybe she had a nosebleed or something. I casually turned to face her, and she showed me her wrist. She had taken a blade from a shaving razor and had cut her wrists. I went into panic mode, but wrapped the cut. I called my pastor and his wife, they met me at the house, and we got the bleeding to stop. The next morning, I scheduled an appointment with a child psychologist.

He missed how serious her disturbance was and recommended family therapy to find out how family dynamics and stress affected her. I said fine, but Steven said, "I don't have a problem and I'm not going." This didn't sit well with me. After a few days of barely speaking, I asked him again. I told him how important it was for the family and that our daughter needed help because something wasn't right.

He still refused to go, so I told him that I was going to do what I had to for my kid. She is my number-one priority and I needed to make sure she was going to be okay. My husband told me that marriage was overrated and that he refused to go, even for our own relationship. At that point, I felt like there was nothing I could do. So, I agreed to remain there until our lease was up in six months and then I'd look for someplace else to go. One night, he just decided he didn't want to do that. It was almost ten o'clock, and he said, "Go!" At first I thought he was joking. He said, "Go and go now!"

When I looked into his eyes, I knew that he was serious. He said, "If I had a gun, I would kill you." I looked around at my dad and said, "Let's go." My father and daughter were able to grab some of their belongings. I left with what I had on my back and was driving down the street with no idea where I was going or what I was going to do, especially since I didn't have a job.

The phone rang, and it was my pastor's wife, Ella, calling and asking me if I was okay. I told her about the situation and she said, "I'll call you right back." She did call and asked me if I could get to her house. She told me another minister had a big house that he said we were welcome to rent and he understood about the financial situation.

Ella asked us to stay with her that night. Then, she ended up packing dishes, groceries, blankets, pillows, and more and took it over to the house that I was going to rent. It had mattresses all laid out for us until we could get beds. In a week, that house was completely furnished with furniture. That's where we started our new life. I was a single parent again, for the second time.

We all struggled. I was taking my father to specialty clinics, and I started to homeschool my daughter because she would cry and say she couldn't go back to public *school. I had previously agreed to homeschool her for the first two years of high school. At the same time, I got really sick and was eventually diagnosed with fibromyalgia. For months, it was difficult to even get out of bed. But by then, my father was much better, so I moved him to a senior active living complex. My daughter and I moved in with my mother and stepfather.*

Then, a month after Stephie's sixteenth birthday, her reaction to something my mother did was so over-the-top that I didn't understand what was going on. I had to wrap my legs around her and hold her in my arms to contain her because she was in this place of rage. She looked at me and said, "Mom, I need you to get me some help. If you don't get me some help, I'm gonna die or someone else is gonna die." So, I called to schedule an appointment for her, and they told me to hang up and get to the emergency room. From there, she was hospitalized.

Even after that, she was suicidal a lot and she was always talking about not wanting to live. Hearing that from your child is difficult. I was always trying to convince her that she has everything to live for, even though she didn't see things that way.

Sending her back to high school was hard, but luckily I was not working yet and was still at home. Stephie would go to school and walk past groups of kids who would be having a conversation among themselves. But she would call me and say people were talking about her. She'd think they were laughing at her and teasing her.

It was such a fight to get her the help she needed in school. In fact, county mental health helped write a letter regarding her needs around an IEP. The school's response was that they saw no manifestations of any of these problems. So, there was no help until she went downhill fast. She ended up locking herself in the bathroom at school and tried to commit suicide. They had to call the police to get her out. She was seventeen and back in the hospital again.

*Around that time, the two of us moved into an apart-
ment and I got the job I have now, at an organization that
helps parents of kids with disabilities. I was often up all
night because she would keep me up. But I spent this time
researching all night long until I could finally get her to go
to sleep. You know, every time she was hospitalized, she
got a new diagnosis. I needed to figure out what she had
so we could get the right help. I knew it was more than
bipolar disorder.*

*I spent so much time in the emergency room that
they thought I was staff. We would be there for twelve to
fourteen hours waiting for a crisis team to come and do an
evaluation to determine whether or not she would be hospitalized. And then I would go to work, which for me became
my outlet. Sometimes, I don't know how I managed to drive
to work or help another family. But I did. Helping other families helped me cope, and I was able to be very good at my
job, even under these circumstances.*

*Unfortunately, we had family members who didn't
understand what Stephie was dealing with, and they didn't
understand why she had to keep going to the hospital. I
was a balled-up mess, but I got a good therapist who really
helped me.*

*During these years, her paternal grandmother said
there was absolutely nothing wrong with Stephie and that
all her problems were due to my parenting skills. This same
grandmother had fought me for custody of Stephie after my
first husband was murdered. Her request was that I would
not be able to remove her from the state of California and
make no medical or educational decisions without her ap-
proval and that we would split custody 50/50. So, for three
years, I had battled her. She saw me as a teen mom in high
school who drank a lot. But, her son had been physically
abusive. She was the adult that I'd confided in, and she had
taken all of that and presented it to a judge to say that I
was not fit to be a parent. As you know [see Chapter 10], it*

was on her watch that my daughter was sexually molested, and she kept it from me. This woman also discouraged my daughter from taking her medication.

But my daughter and I ended up working well together on what she needed to do to get better. I used to tell her, "I'm going to be your biggest cheerleader, but I need you to work with me, not against me, because I'm trying to help you." Although her grandmother still confronts her about her medication, she is now able to say, "I know it may look like a lot, but I need them all and that's okay." We are both doing well. Her mental illness is only one facet of her life—not all of her.

Now I am figuring out what I want to do with the next part of my life. Just when I was growing content with being single, I met a wonderful man who was single and parenting his eight-year-old son. His son had some speech delays, so we had crossed paths. To make a long story short, we were married on my birthday. Just the other night, he suggested I write my own book.

One factor that contributes to Tasha's resilience is her willingness to get help. This is as natural to her as her habitual giving of help. Tasha was not without fear. She simply felt her fear and did what she had to do regardless. As with Julia, taking action was a critical approach for Tasha—an approach she was able to take by not listening to the voice of fear telling her what *could* go wrong.

Conclusion

Before bringing this chapter to a close, I can't resist one last quote by an unknown but wise author. It reminds me of each of the solo parents who shared their stories of resilience and growth in this chapter:

The sturdiest tree is not found in the shelter of the forest but high upon some rocky crag, where its daily battle with the elements shapes it into a thing of beauty.

Chapter 13

Conclusion

To be a person is to have a story to tell.
—Isak Dinesen (also known as Karen Blixen)

THIS BOOK IS full of the stories of ordinary people going solo while raising children with disabilities. In the introduction, I mentioned that I included excerpts from the life story of each person who agreed to be interviewed. None of these stories were of lives lived perfectly or without a single regret. I don't think this is possible in life. All of the solo parents' stories contained some genius moments that were easy to spot as well as some that were more subtle.

The way that you live your life becomes your story. This is the story that becomes part of your identity and that you show your children, share with your friends, and sometimes reveal to the general public. The comedian Fred Allen expressed it well: "A human being is nothing but a story with skin around it." As demonstrated by the solo parents in this book, life stories can teach, comfort, inspire, and connect us.

Life stories don't begin with a blank page. Our initial story line is written and developed during our childhood. Daydreams of who we hope to be in adulthood are often woven into childhood stories. Many people want lives that include the typical spouse, typical children, typical daily life, and the option of a white picket fence. If you are reading this book, in all likelihood, you experienced plot changes similar to those of the solos who shared their stories—i.e., life events that did not go as planned.

Unexpected plot changes are illustrated in abundance by the solos in this book. Some never found the romantic love they expected, or they found it and their loved one died, or they knew they couldn't be part of a Barbie-and-Ken type of couple. Some of the solos' original story lines veered far off expected course when long-term marriages dissolved or when they gave birth to children who were totally different from the ones they imagined.

Although we live a while with many of the characters and plot elements in our lives already put in place, at some point we grow to a point where we can and need to assume some authorship. We have the option of developing new story lines, changing our role as the lead character, and illuminating new meanings. We can write characters out of our story and add ones we prefer. We can take stagnant stories of being a victim and add new chapters that lead to fulfillment. I would argue that the first draft of a story line should rarely be the final one.

The solo parents who shared their life stories in this book can serve as wonderful examples of personal authorship. Many changed the direction of the plots, one rewrote a drama and turned it into a comedy, and others decided to look at their personal stories from entirely new perspectives. Many changed the stories they told themselves about who they are. Some solos saw their characters reveal sides that really pleased them in terms of their capacities to enjoy life, demonstrate strength, heal from hurt, and be resilient in the face of life's unpredictability. Many also changed the story of what it meant for them to have a child with a disability or illness. The catalysts for such rewrites were in recognizing freedom to exercise some control over how they wanted to live. We saw some of them make large decisions (such as leaving a marriage) and small ones (such as joining a support group) that changed their life stories.

A human being is a deciding being.
—Viktor Frankl

Opportunities to make decisions and take hold of life are not easy to spot against the backdrop of life, especially when it is fast-paced, chaotic, or dark. By highlighting personal strategies in each story, I hope to point out some of the ways these solo parents exercised control over their role in their own life stories and how they experienced transformations.

The life stories in this book generally involve transformations related to solo parents changing their stance in life. Some achieved transformations by opening themselves up to the life events they were given, and others transformed by doing things differently than they had before.

You can find transformations in each chapter of the book. They began in the first chapter with several solo parents, including Whitney, initially regarding the birth of their children and their "plight" as unfair and a sign of God's displeasure. Later on, these feelings were transformed into viewing their children as blessings, sources of joy and contentment, and opportunities for unconditional love.

In the second chapter, Jasmine transformed from the youngest child in a pain-filled childhood home to the mother of two kids with autism and the queen of "Misfit Island"—a place where laughter and quirkiness are prized. Later on, she even transformed how she partnered with her ex-husband (and ex-nemesis), and he is now a platonic partner in the home for financial reasons.

The solo parents in the divorce chapter made decisions not to let anger and bitterness consume them even while raw feelings sometimes ran "soul deep." We met a mother whose husband left just before a big twenty-fifth wedding celebration and then dropped out of sight (and support) for a long time. She made the decision to accept her recently graduated daughter's plan to live with him in another state, and she decided to open up to the possibility that this could work with some help and cooperation. We met some women who flexed their muscles and made decisions to believe in their own strength rather than in the illusion that they could not manage on their own.

The fathers who shared their lives likewise had many deep transformations. These include Bruce, a career military man, who for years after his divorce had so little knowledge of his son that he did not even know he had autism. He changed and transformed into a parent who is now constantly searching out the best strategies for his son to thrive. In the same chapter, we met Bobby, who followed in his father's footsteps as both an alcoholic and workaholic, until he decided to change his labels and his life and to help others change theirs as well.

The book includes many solos who transformed their relationships with family members by deciding to try to change estrangements. We saw one military spouse do this successfully with a father whose alcoholism in her childhood was deeply damaging to her. In adulthood, she decided to set boundaries with him regarding drinking around her children and to reconnect on new terms. She now speaks of deep love for him.

Some solos transformed themselves through the help of a therapist, and many others, through linking arms with other parents of children with disabilities. In these ways, they discovered new sides to themselves and shared moments of undeniable pride in themselves. Many spoke of changed self-identities in other ways. Solos who saw themselves as victims or failures often saw their fortitude and best selves reflected in how their children and trusted others regarded them. As Mavis Staples, a gospel artist, sang:

I looked in the mirror
What did I see but a brand new image of the same old me
But now I wonder why I should be surprised
I like the things about me that I once despised.

Many of the solo parents were surprised by their own transformations. Some who decided they would have a solo life became married and once-marrieds, and others decided they were perfectly content as solos.

I met a few solos who were in the early process of transformation. They didn't know *how* they were going to achieve what they wanted, but they knew they were not going to succumb to a life that they dreaded. This brings me to one of the very last people who shared her story with me. She is a military wife and the mother of two children with a rare, life-threatening genetic disease that requires intensive medical care. She was born to drug-abusing parents; her childhood and adolescence were not happy stories either. She wanted a very different life in adulthood, and expected this would come as a result of her marriage and the birth of her first child. Reflecting on her children's genetic disease and the state of her marriage, she said:

> "Both parents have to have this gene, and it is really rare. What are the odds we meet and…boom…we have a special-needs kid?" Now we have another with the same devastating condition. I kept asking myself, 'What did I do wrong? What did I do to deserve this?' This is not fair, because I did everything right. I got married and I never did drugs in my entire life. I didn't have my first sip of alcohol until I was nineteen or twenty.
>
> "My husband also has a really hard time with a lot of this, but he handles it differently than me. He has really pulled away, keeps to himself, and he drinks. When I tell him he needs to do something, he says, 'Why would I give up the one thing that gives me joy?' I feel like I'm a train going full speed ahead, and there's my husband behind me sitting waiting for the next train to come back. I refuse to let history repeat itself."

Transformations begin with simply drawing a line in the sand for yourself, as this woman did when she said, "I refuse to let history repeat itself." This means you are embarking on a new story line. It may begin with saying "yes" to something that you want that scares you. Or it may begin when you decide to say "no" to doing the same old thing that hasn't worked. Change opens people up to new stories.

Helpful Strategies for All Solo Parents of Children with Disabilities

Throughout the book, I highlighted strategies that solos used to live well, and they can help guide readers to make desired changes in their own stories. I tried to take a bird's-eye view of these strategies to identify the most valued overall approaches. Here are the ones that I believe are the most helpful:

1. Celebrate your child without comparing.

Solo parents in this book often focused on enjoying their children and letting go of preconceptions regarding who the ideal child should be. For example, Lucinda celebrates the fact that her son is comfortable with all races and religions and is only prejudiced against "jerks." Parents also spoke of the need to avoid the trap of comparing their children with others with the same disability.

2. Live the Serenity Prayer.

Many solos in this book followed the wisdom of the Serenity Prayer, consciously or unconsciously. They changed the things they could in life, often by advocating for their children to get what they needed. But they also accepted what they could not control, such as the risks inherent in children being more independent, their ex-partners' actions, or the course of some medical condition.

3. Make space for joy and contentment to coexist with grief.

Contributors to this book spoke of enjoying life while they also mourned losses. We read of Joseph who was about to embark on an RV trip with his children to visit places he had thought he would go to with his wife before her death. Whitney shared her thoughts about grieving the perfect child she thought she would have but also delighting in the daughter she did have who was born with Down syndrome.

4. Realize that resentment is toxic and gratitude is an antidote.

As Bea, the solo grandmother raising four children on the autism spectrum, said, "Resentment is like taking poison and expecting others to die." Tips on managing resentment are in abundance in Chapter 11 and practiced by solos throughout the book. One of the most effective antidotes to healing resentment is the practice of gratitude. Many solos demonstrated deep gratitude for the things that were going well in their lives, even when everything else was falling apart.

5. Create helpful boundaries.

Many solo parents used boundaries to accomplish all kinds of good things. We saw Tasha set boundaries that limited how much she would visit her daughter during psychiatric hospitalizations. Others set boundaries to contain how much they would let disability consume them. Often, boundary-setting enables healing and growth.

6. Manage your moods and emotions.

Many solos included in this book tried hard to bring their "best selves" to the action in life. This means controlling anger even when provoked. For instance, Mark spoke of his strategy of "taking the high road" as often as possible. Parents offered strategies to keep from being paralyzed with fear or perpetually worried. Many also spoke of what they gained from good therapists.

7. Reach out and connect.

It is essential to connect with other parents of kids with disabilities. Many solos described how they would pick up the phone and call a friend to decompress when frustrated with family for "not getting it." They shared information and resources, found strength in numbers, and were able to engage in dark irony that only someone in their shoes could fully appreciate.

8. Live with faith and find meaning.

Many solos parents who participated in this book have great faith in a divine being and see their faith as essential to coping. They believe their efforts are part of a plan. Other parents have found meaning outside of a religious tradition, and this sense of purpose is equally essential to their well-being.

9. Empower yourself.

As illustrated in these pages, solo parents can use many strategies to develop and connect with their own capabilities. One spoke of "trusting her gut reactions" rather than assuming others knew what was best for her. It is important to learn to ask for what you need from others without seeing the need for help as a sign of weakness.

10. Connect with loved ones who are gone.

Many solos have found ways to connect with deceased loved ones as a way to continue to seek wisdom and strength and feel their love. We saw this with Alyssa and the grandmother who raised her and showed strength and compassion. And we saw this valuable strategy again with Paul and Joseph, who reported that they even wisecrack with their departed spouses.

11. Manage expectations and practice forgiveness.

Accepting "life on life's terms" is useful to many solo parents. This scaling down of expectations includes accepting the reality that sometimes tragic deaths do occur, sometimes loved ones are hurtful, sometimes bad things happen to great people, and sometimes we do things we regret. Acknowledging this more realistic picture of how the world actually is, rather than how we wish it was, was helpful to many solos I heard from. Some chose, for their own sake, to reconnect with family who had disappointed them or to forgive themselves when they didn't meet their own expectations.

12. Rethink success.

Parents often reframe for themselves what success actually is in life. Many of the solos in this book shared their view that success is not about acquiring advanced degrees, amassing money, owning showcase homes, or bragging about your "perfect kid." It is about loving your children well through thick and thin, delighting in who they become, and being proud of yourself in the process.

Freedom is man's capacity to take a hand in his own development. It is our capacity to mold ourselves.
—Rollo May

References

Introduction

Apter, T. (2012). *Difficult mothers: Understanding and overcoming their power.* New York: W. W. Norton.

Cargan, L. (2007). *Being single on Noah's ark.* London: Rowman & Littlefield.

Cohen, P. N., & Petrescu-Prahova, M. (2006). Gendered living arrangements among children with disabilities. *Journal of Marriage & Family, 68*(3), 630–38. doi:10.1111/j.1741-3737.2006.00279.x.

Duhigg, C. (2014). *The power of habit: Why we do what we do in life and business.* New York: Random House.

U.S. Census Bureau. (2013). *Custodial mothers and fathers and their child support: 2011.* Washington, DC: Government Printing Office. Retrieved from http://www.census.gov/prod/2013pubs/p60-246.pdf.

Chapter 1: Sorting Out the Big Picture

Boss, P. (2000). *Ambiguous loss: Learning to live with unresolved grief.* Boston: Harvard Press.

Frankl, V. (1959). *Man's search for meaning.* Boston: Beacon Press.

Gallagher, G., & Konjoian, P. (2000). *Shut up about your perfect kid: A survival guide for ordinary parents of special children.* New York: Harmony Books.

Green, L. (2007). *Parenting children with health issues: Essential tools, tips, and tactics for raising kids with chronic illness, medical conditions, and special healthcare needs.* Golden, CO: Love and Logic Press.

Klass, P. (October 14, 2013). Haunted by a child's illness. *The New York Times.* Retrieved from http://well.blogs.nytimes.com/2013/10/14/haunted-by-a-childs-illness.

Kübler-Ross, E., & Kessler, D. (2005). *On grief and grieving: Finding the meaning of grief through the five stages of loss.* New York: Scribner.

Naseef, R., (2009). Acceptance, if it doesn't mean giving up: what does it mean? *Spectrum Magazine, 72.*

Wright, B. (1983). "Value changes in acceptance of disability." *Physical disability: A psychosocial approach.* New York: HarperCollins.

Chapter 2: Coping Day to Day

Green, L. (2007). *Parenting children with health issues: Essential tools, tips and tactics for raising kids with chronic illness, medical conditions and special healthcare needs.* Golden, CO: Love and Logic Press.

Glasser, W. (1999). *Choice theory: A new psychology of personal freedom.* New York: HarperCollins.

Frankl, V. (1959). *Man's search for meaning.* Boston: Beacon Press.

Leahy, R. (2006). *The worry cure: Seven steps to stop worry from stopping you.* New York: Harmony Books.

McCullough, M., Tsand, J., & Emmons, R. (2004). Gratitude in intermediate affective terrain: Links of grateful moods to individual differences and daily emotional experience. *Journal of Personality and Social Psychology, 86,* 295–309.

McKinney, V. (2004). FASD: Adoption advice from the experts. North American Council on Adoptable Children. Retrieved from http://www.nacac.org/adoptalk/fasd.html.

Rifkin, J. (2004). *The healing power of anger: The unexpected path to love and fulfillment.* New York: Cosimo Publications.

Steindl-Rast, D. (2013). Want to be happy? Be grateful. TED talk. Retrieved from http://www.ted.com/talks/david_steindl_rast_want_to_be_happy_be_grateful.

Turnbull, A. (1993). *Cognitive coping, families, & disability.* Baltimore, MD: Brookes Publishing.

Wehrenberg, M. (2008). *The 10 best-ever anxiety management techniques.* New York: W.W. Norton & Company.

Chapter 3: Divorced Parents Making It Work

Philyaw, D., & Thomas, M. (2013). *Co-Parenting 101: Helping your kids thrive in two households after divorce.* Oakland, CA: New Harbinger Publications.

Ross, J., & Corcoran, J. (2011). *Joint custody with a jerk: Raising a child with an uncooperative ex.* New York: St. Martin's Press.

Sutherland, A. (2006). What Shamu taught me about a happy marriage. *The New York Times.* Retrieved from http://www.nytimes.com/2006/06/25/fashion/25love.html?_r=0.

Winnicott, D. (1992). *Babies and their mothers.* Boston: Da Capo Press.

Chapter 4: Finding Supports in All Kinds of Places

Alcoholics Anonymous (2014). *Local Meetings.* Retrieved from http://al-anon. alateen.org/local-meetings.

American Psychiatric Association. (2013). *Diagnostic and statistical manual of mental disorders* (5th ed.). Washington, DC

Autism Speaks (2011). A grandparent's guide to autism: Autism Speaks family support toolkit. Retrieved from http://www.autismspeaks.org/sites/default/ files/a_grandparents_guide_to_autism.pdf.

Baskin, A. & Fawcett, H. (2006). *More than a mom: Living a full and balanced life when your child has special needs.* Bethesda, MD: Woodbine House.

Baute, P. (1993). *Forgiveness: Why and how.* Retrieved from http://www.lexpages.com/SGN/paschal/FORGIVNS.67.html.

Bonior, A. (2013, May 18). Friendships in adulthood: Needing, making, and keeping them [web log]. Retrieved from https://www.psychologytoday. com/blog/friendship-20/201305/friendships-in-adulthood-needing-making-and-keeping-them

Bonior, A. (2011). *The friendship fix: The complete guide to choosing, losing, and keeping up with your friends.* New York: St. Martin's Press.

Findler, L. (2014). "The experience of stress and personal growth among grandparents of children with and without intellectual disability." *Intellectual and Developmental Disabilities, 52*: 32–48.

Gemelke, T. (2005). *Stay close: 40 clever ways to connect with kids when you're apart.* Chicago: Search Institute Press.

Katz, S., & Kessel, L. (2002). "Grandparents of children with developmental disabilities: Perceptions, beliefs, and involvement in their care." *Issues in Comprehensive Pediatric Nursing, 25*: 113–28.

Krumins, J. (2011). *Autism and the grandparent connection: Practical ways to help and understand your grandchild with autism spectrum disorder.* New York: Scribner.

Miller, E., & Woodbridge, S. (2011). "Impact of disability on families: Grandparents' perspective." *Journal of Intellectual Disability Research, 56*: 102–10.

National Organization on Disability (2014). *Home Page.* Retrieved from http:// www.nod.org/.

National Respite Network (2014). *Welcome.* Retrieved from http://archrespite.org/.

Solomon, A. (2013). *Far from the tree: Parents, children and the search for identity.* New York: Scribner.

Stepnowski, F. (2013). *Using the ADA for parents of children with disabilities.* Retrieved from http://www.stepnowskilaw.com/ADA-Parents.html.

United States Department of Labor (2014). *Wage and hour division.* Retrieved from http://www.dol.gov/whd/fmla/.

Chapter 5: Solo Fathers of Children with Disabilities

Anderson, C., & Bloom, B. Divorce: it can complicate children's special education issues. Retrieved from http://www.ldonline.org/article/12388.

Goldberg. E. (March 14, 2014). Single dad carries his son with disabilities 9 miles every day so that he can go to school. [Web log]. Retrieved from http://www.huffingtonpost.com/2014/03/14/dad-carries-son-9-miles_n_4965125.html.

Hook, J., & Chalasani, S. (2008). Gendered expectations? Reconsidering single fathers' child-care time. *Journal of Marriage and Family,* 70: 978–90.

Parker, K., & Wang, W. Modern parenthood. Retrieved from http://www.pewsocialtrends.org/2013/03/14/modern-parenthood-roles-of-moms-and-dads-converge-as-they-balance-work-and-family/.

Chapter 6: Bereavement: Solos and Their Grieving Children

Berns, N. (July 15, 2012). Beyond closure: Nancy Berns at TEDxDesMoines [Video file]. Retrieved from http://tedxtalks.ted.com/video/Beyond-Closure-Nancy-Berns-at-T.

Bowlby, J. (1980). *Loss: Sadness & depression.* Attachment and loss (vol. 3). London: Hogarth Press.

Holmes, T. (2012). Forgotten grief: Helping people with developmental disabilities manage personal loss. *The Alberta Counsellor,* 32: 3–26.

Hoover, J. H., Markell, M. A., & Wagner, P. (2005). Death and grief as experienced by adults with developmental disabilities: Initial explorations. *Omega-Detroit Then New York,* 50(3), 181–96.

Karst, P., & Stevenson, G. (2000). *The invisible string.* Los Angles: DeVorss & Company.

Kübler-Ross, E., & Kessler, D. (2000). *Life lessons: Two experts on death and dying teach us about the mysteries of life and living.* New York: First Scribner.

Kübler-Ross, E., & Kessler, D. (2007). *On grief and grieving: Finding the meaning of grief through the five stages of loss.* New York: Simon and Schuster.

Olin, R. (Nov. 1, 2014). A child's grief. Retrieved from http://www.brainchildmag.com/2014/11/a-childs-grief/.

Schwiebert, P., DeKlyen, C., & Bills, T. (2005). *Tear soup: A recipe for healing after loss.* Portland, OR: Grief Watch.

Sims, D. (n. d.). Anger and grief in children. Retrieved from http://www.touchstonesongrief.com/touchstones/articles/Anger%20and%20Grief%20in%20Children.pdf.

Stewart, T. (1977). Coping behavior and the moratorium following spinal cord injury. *Paraplegia,* 15, 338–42.

Chapter 7: Parents and Children Who Chose Each Other through Adoption

Baer, D. (2013). The neuroscience of trusting your gut. Retrieved from http:// www.fastcompany.com/3022954/leadership-now/the-neuroscience-of-trust-ing-your-gut.

Bond, J. (1995). Post adoption depression syndrome. Retrieved from http:// www.adopting.org/pads.html.

Finkel, E. (June 29, 2014). The trauma of parenthood. *The New York Times,* p. 12.

Greene, M. (2006). Post-adoption panic. In P. Kruger & J. Smolowe (Eds.), *A love like no other: Stories from adoptive parents* (59–69). New York: Penguin.

McCarthy, H. (Oct. 25, 2007). Post Adoption Depression. Retrieved from http://www.postadoptinfo.org/articles/07_05_depression.html.

Nazarov A. R. (April 3, 2013). My post-adoption depression. *Slate.com.* Retrieved from http://www.slate.com/articles/double_x/doublex/2013/ 04/ post_adoption_depression_it_s_as_crippling_as_postpartum_and_much_ less_recognized.html.

Chapter 8: Conceiving on Your Own

Baute, P. (1993). *Forgiveness: Why and how.* Retrieved from http://www.lexpages.com/SGN/paschal/FORGIVNS.67.html.

Beck, M. (2014). Anti-complain campaign. Retrieved from http://www.oprah.com/omagazine/Martha-Becks-Anti-Complain-Campaign.

Blincoe, N. (2013). Why men decide to become single dads. *The Guardian.* Retrieved from http://www.theguardian.com/lifeandstyle/2013/nov/02/ men-single-dad-father-surrogacy-adoption.

Brown, B. (2014). Why Brenee Brown says perfectionism is a 20 pound shield. Retrieved from http://www.oprah.com/search.html?q=perfectionism.

Burns, D. D. (2008). *Feeling good: The new mood therapy.* New York: Harper.

Dollar, E. P. (2012). *No easy choice: A story of disability, parenthood, and faith in an age of advanced reproduction.* Louisville, KY: Westminster John Knox Press.

Mittan, R. (2005). How to raise a child with epilepsy: Coping with guilt. *Exceptional Parenting Magazine,* Vol. 35 (12), 23–29.

Morrissette, M (2008). *Choosing single motherhood.* New York: Mariner Books.

Murray, C. & Golombok, S. (2005). Solo mothers and their donor insemination infants: Follow-up at age 2 years. *Human reproduction,* 20, 1655–60.

Siegel, J. (1998). Pathways to single motherhood: Sexual intercourse, adoption, and donor insemination. *Families in Society,* 79:75–82.

Chapter 9: Dating, and Sometimes "Happily-Ever-Afters"

Brown, H. (April 19, 2012). Devoted but dateless. *The New York Times.* Retrieved from http://www.nytimes.com/2012/04/22/fashion/devot-ed-but-dateless.html?pagewanted=all.

Ellis, A. (2007). Conquering the dire need for love. [Video Recording]. Retrieved from https://www.youtube.com/watch?v=aKby0E_U_F4.

Helfenbaum, W. (Feb. 1, 2013). Dating as a single parent of a child with special needs. Retrieved from http://www.dfwchild.com/Thrive/features/197/Dating-as-a-Single-Parent-of-a-Child-with-Special-Needs.

Hsu, D. T., Sanford, B. J., Meyers, K. K., Love, T. M., Hazlett, K. E., Wang, H...., Zubieta, J-K. (2013). Response of the μ-opioid system to social rejection and acceptance. *Molecular Psychiatry,* Vol. 18, 1211–17. doi:10.1038/mp.2013.96.

Komando, K. (2013, April 19). How to do a free online background check. Retrieved from http://www.usatoday.com/story/tech/columnist/komando/2013/04/19/online-background-check/2084917/.

Kübler-Ross, E. & Kessler, D. (2000). *Life lessons: Two experts on death and dying teach us about the mysteries of life and living.* New York: First Scribner.

Marshak, L., & Prezant, F. (2007). *Married with special-needs children: A couple's guide to keeping connected.* Bethesda, MD: Woodbine House.

Miller, W. (Oct. 11, 2011). 8 Things to think about when dating a parent of special needs children. Retrieved from http://www.examiner.com/article/8-things-to-think-about-when-dating-a-parent-of-special-needs-children.

Star, T. Why women pick the wrong men. Retrieved from http://www.daily-transformations.com/why-women-pick-the-wrong-men/.

Wetchler, J. (2005). Reflections from a single father of a teenage daughter with mental retardation. *Journal of Feminist Family Therapy,* 17(2): 65–78.

Chapter 10: Parents and Adult Sons and Daughters

Calabro, T. "Let me swim: The art of letting go of our transition-age sons and daughters." [Presentation, Working Order Disability Resource Breakfast, Pittsburgh, June 19, 2014].

Maslow, A. (1968). *Toward a psychology of being.* New York: Van Nostrand Company.

Michaud, D., & Temple, V. (2013). The complexities of caring for individuals with Fetal Alcohol Syndrome Disorder: The perspective of mothers. *Journal of Developmental Disabilities. 19:* 94–101.

Perske, R. (1972). The dignity of tisk and the mentally retarded. *Mental Retardation, 10* (1): 1–6.

Pincus, D. (2011). Adult children living at home? 9 rules to help you maintain sanity. *Cultivate Life, 46.* Retrieved from http://www.trans4mind.com/cultivate-life-magazine/issue-046/Debbie-Pincus.html.

Chapter 11: On Your Own for Long Stretches: Military Solos

The deployment diatribes. (June 17, 2013). Staying connected during deployment [Web log]. Retrieved from https://deploymentdiatribes.wordpress.com/2013/06/17/staying-connected-during-deployment/.

Gemelke, T. (2005). Stay close: 40 clever ways to connect with kids when you're apart. Chicago: Search Institute Press.

Marshak, L., & Prezant, F. (2007). *Married with special-needs children: A couple's guide to keeping connected*. Bethesda, MD: Woodbine House.

Chapter 12: Resilient Solos Creating New Life Stories

Murakami, H. (2005). *Kafka on the Shore*. New York: Alfred A. Knopf.

Tedeschi, R. G., & Calhoun, L. G. (1996). The Posttraumatic Growth Inventory: Measuring the positive legacy of trauma. *Journal Of Traumatic Stress, 9*(3), 455–72. doi:10.1002/jts.2490090305.

Index

About the Author

LAURA MARSHAK, Ph.D., has been involved for many years in different aspects of coping well with personal, family, and disability issues. She is a full professor in the Department of Counseling at Indiana University of Pennsylvania (Indiana, PA). Dr. Marshak is also a licensed psychologist and founding partner of North Hills Psychological Services, where she has a private practice. For more than 25 years, she has worked with people facing all kinds of life problems and issues. Many of them are parents of children with a wide range of developmental and physical disabilities as well as serious chronic illnesses. She also works with adults who have disabilities themselves. In addition, she is the professional advisor to the Friendship Circle (of Pittsburgh), which is a large social inclusion group that includes members with and without disabilities. Dr. Marshak previously co-authored six other books on disability-related topics for parents and professionals and one children's book. She speaks nationally and internationally on aspects of quality of life while raising children with disabilities. She has three sons and, naturally, has learned a lot along the way about coping.